FURNITURE

GREAT DESIGNS FROM FINE WOODWORKING
FURNITURE

The Editors of Fine Woodworking

The Taunton Press

The Taunton Press
Inspiration for hands-on living®

The Taunton Press, Inc., 63 South Main Street, PO Box 5506, Newtown, CT 06470-5506
e-mail: tp@taunton.com

EDITOR: MATTHEW TEAGUE
JACKET/COVER DESIGN: RENATO STANISIC
INTERIOR DESIGN: RENATO STANISIC
LAYOUT: LAURA LIND DESIGN
FRONT COVER PHOTOGRAPHER: JOHN SHELDON
BACK COVER PHOTOGRAPHERS: (TOP TO BOTTOM) JONATHAN BINZEN,
VINCENT LAURENCE, SETH JANOFSKY

Library of Congress Cataloging-in-Publication Data

Furniture / editors of Fine woodworking.
       p. cm. -- (Great designs from Fine woodworking)
    ISBN-13: 978-1-56158-828-2
    ISBN-10: 1-56158-828-8
    1. Furniture making. I. Fine woodworking. II. Series.
    TT197.F795 2006
    684'.08--dc22
                                2006011355

Printed in the United States of America
20 19 18 17 16 15 14 13 12 11

The following manufacturers/names appearing in *Furniture* are trademarks: Bessey K-Body®, Klockit℠,
Kmart®, Leigh®, Masonite®, Minwax®, Post-it® Note, Soss®, Tyvek®, Watco™, West System®

Working wood is inherently dangerous. Using hand or power tools improperly or ignoring safety practices can lead to
permanent injury or even death. Don't try to perform operations you learn about here (or elsewhere) unless you're certain
they are safe for you. If something about an operation doesn't feel right, don't do it. Look for another way. We want you to
enjoy the craft, so please keep safety foremost in your mind whenever you're in the shop.

ACKNOWLEDGMENTS

Special thanks to the authors, editors, art directors, copy editors, and other staff members of *Fine Woodworking* who contributed to the development of the articles in this book.

CONTENTS

INTRODUCTION

Whenever I walk through a furniture store, I find myself picking the pieces to death: Why didn't they tilt the seat a few degrees? Use a cabinet-grade plywood? Rout the edges instead of tacking stock molding sloppily into place? Furniture makers are like that. Many of us got into woodworking, after all, because it was the only way to get things that look and feel and work exactly like we think they should.

In the course of putting this book together, we've looked at numerous pieces that have appeared in *Fine Woodworking* magazine, then culled and compiled our favorites. They vary in style from gothic to contemporary and everything in between. Some are large, some small. Some were built in a day and others took months, but each was designed and built by woodworkers—evidence of careful eyes and hands are all over this book. The makers range from revered designers to humble builders working quietly in the corners of their garages and basements. But each piece, in its own way, succeeds.

The furniture found here is presented with full exploded drawings, which woodworkers can use to build or amend to their own tastes. For designers and decorators, this book will be a welcome resource when working with clients. For others, it will be like walking through a gallery. No matter which direction your tastes lean, whether you're a designer, maker, decorator, or simply someone who appreciates handcrafted work, I hope you'll find the same inspiration in this book that I have found in putting it together. I've spent many hours with these pieces, and I'm struck by how seldom I've said "why didn't they just …"

—MATTHEW TEAGUE
Former Managing Editor of *Fine Woodworking*

A CLASSIC CASE

by Gregory Paolini

This heirloom bookcase features shelves that are adjustable and removable. The shelves rest on shelf pins or the bottom stretchers and are notched to fit around the posts.

Anyone familiar with American furniture would immediately identify this bookcase as an Arts and Crafts design. However, it differs from traditional pieces in two important ways. Arts and Crafts furniture usually is made from quartersawn white oak, but I built this bookcase from curly cherry. Traditional Arts and Crafts pieces are joined with mortises and tenons, while I use a modern variation—the floating tenon.

In floating-tenon joinery, a wooden spline (the floating tenon) joins mortises routed in both pieces. I find floating-tenon joinery to be much faster than traditional mortise-and-tenon, and plenty strong.

I spent time choosing highly figured boards for the front rails and the side panels, which will be most visible. The back is made of shiplapped cherry, resawn (sliced in half to produce two thinner boards) from 4/4 stock. Shiplapping is a method of slightly overlapping boards by rabbetting the opposite edge of each side. Shiplapped boards rarely end up sitting exactly flush with each other. Those who don't like that look might substitute plywood or tongue-and-groove boards for the back.

Gregory Paolini is a Roycroft Renaissance Artisan who builds furniture part time in his Depew, New York, basement shop.

A CLASSIC CASE

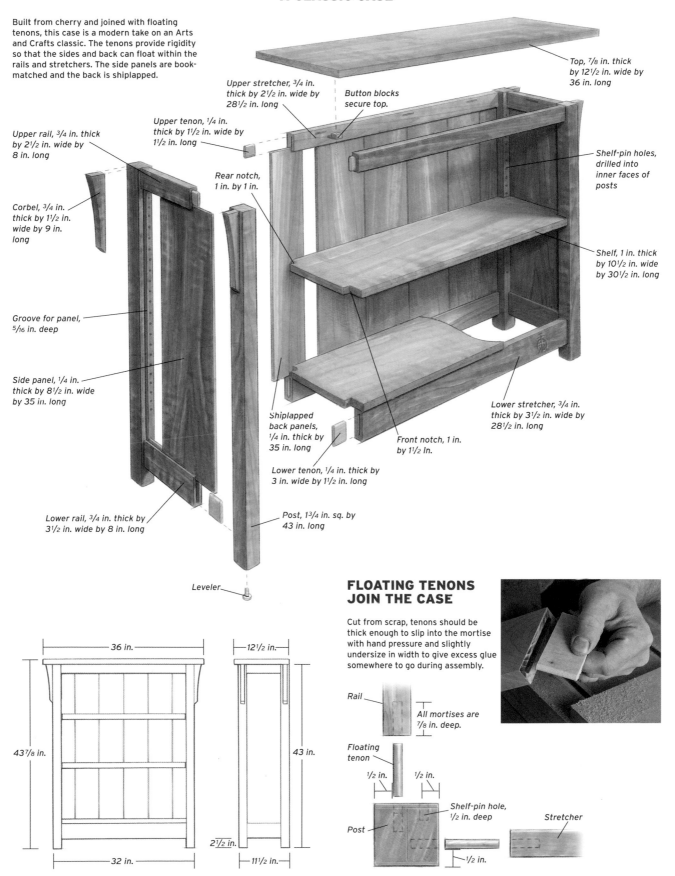

Built from cherry and joined with floating tenons, this case is a modern take on an Arts and Crafts classic. The tenons provide rigidity so that the sides and back can float within the rails and stretchers. The side panels are book-matched and the back is shiplapped.

Top, 7/8 in. thick by 12 1/2 in. wide by 36 in. long

Upper stretcher, 3/4 in. thick by 2 1/2 in. wide by 28 1/2 in. long

Button blocks secure top.

Upper tenon, 1/4 in. thick by 1 1/2 in. wide by 1 1/2 in. long

Upper rail, 3/4 in. thick by 2 1/2 in. wide by 8 in. long

Shelf-pin holes, drilled into inner faces of posts

Corbel, 3/4 in. thick by 1 1/2 in. wide by 9 in. long

Rear notch, 1 in. by 1 in.

Shelf, 1 in. thick by 10 1/2 in. wide by 30 1/2 in. long

Groove for panel, 5/16 in. deep

Side panel, 1/4 in. thick by 8 1/2 in. wide by 35 in. long

Shiplapped back panels, 1/4 in. thick by 35 in. long

Lower stretcher, 3/4 in. thick by 3 1/2 in. wide by 28 1/2 in. long

Front notch, 1 in. by 1 1/2 in.

Lower tenon, 1/4 in. thick by 3 in. wide by 1 1/2 in. long

Lower rail, 3/4 in. thick by 3 1/2 in. wide by 8 in. long

Post, 1 3/4 in. sq. by 43 in. long

Leveler

36 in.

12 1/2 in.

43 7/8 in.

43 in.

32 in.

2 1/2 in.

11 1/2 in.

FLOATING TENONS JOIN THE CASE

Cut from scrap, tenons should be thick enough to slip into the mortise with hand pressure and slightly undersize in width to give excess glue somewhere to go during assembly.

Rail

All mortises are 7/8 in. deep.

Floating tenon

1/2 in.   1/2 in.

Post

Shelf-pin hole, 1/2 in. deep

1/2 in.

Stretcher

TRADITIONAL BOOKCASE IN THE CRAFTSMAN STYLE

by Gary Rogowski

Of the many qualities that help define the Arts and Crafts style, perhaps the most apparent is straightforward and honest joinery. Wedged joints and through-tenons show the world how a piece was made. Open-grained woods like white oak give a piece a rustic unabashed look, that says, "Here's what I am—sturdy, well-made furniture." No abstractions get in the way, no conceptualizing need be done. This frank simplicity is just the style the progenitors of the Arts and Crafts movement in England hoped for—a direct counterpoint to the machines and machined look of the Industrial Age and its products—and it's just the style for the bookcase I made to fit in my bungalow.

The bookcase is just 50 in. high and 31 in. wide. Quartersawn white oak, the quintessential Arts and Crafts material, was clearly the wood of choice. For the sides and shelves, I glued two boards together, then scraped and sanded them. Wedges made of the same oak secure the through-tenons to the mortised sides and give the bookcase its strength and honest face.

Gary Rogowski is a contributing editor to Fine Woodworking. *He runs the Northwest Woodworking Studio, a woodworking school in Portland, Oregon.*

CRAFTSMAN-STYLE BOOKCASE

Wedged through tenons are key to both the visual design and structural integrity of the Arts-and-Crafts bookcase. All parts are made of 3/4-in.-thick quartersawn white oak.

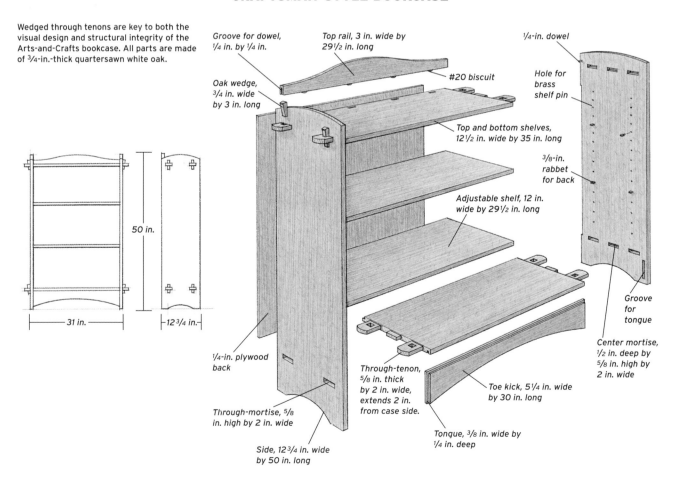

Groove for dowel, 1/4 in. by 1/4 in.

Top rail, 3 in. wide by 29 1/2 in. long

1/4-in. dowel

Oak wedge, 3/4 in. wide by 3 in. long

#20 biscuit

Hole for brass shelf pin

Top and bottom shelves, 12 1/2 in. wide by 35 in. long

3/8-in. rabbet for back

Adjustable shelf, 12 in. wide by 29 1/2 in. long

50 in.

31 in.

12 3/4 in.

Groove for tongue

Center mortise, 1/2 in. deep by 5/8 in. high by 2 in. wide

1/4-in. plywood back

Through-tenon, 5/8 in. thick by 2 in. wide, extends 2 in. from case side.

Toe kick, 5 1/4 in. wide by 30 in. long

Through-mortise, 5/8 in. high by 2 in. wide

Side, 12 3/4 in. wide by 50 in. long

Tongue, 3/8 in. wide by 1/4 in. deep

PROFILES

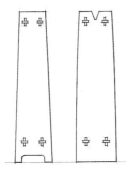

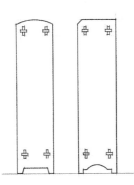

The way the bookcase is shaped on its sides and rails strongly influences the appearance of the piece. Try drawing out a few shapes on cardboard to see them full scale. Flat or beveled bottom edges, simple indents, shallow arcs, or other combinations of shapes all lend a certain feel to a piece. My advice is to keep the shaping details consistent throughout. So a negative shape cut out of the bottom of the sides can be nicely recalled at the top, in the toekick, or in the backsplash.

TOE KICKS

Don't overlook the toekick as a design element. It greatly influences how the bookcase "stands" and can also help tie all of the pieces in the case together. A toekick can be of a simple design, but you may find a complex pattern more suitable. The toekick on this case echoes the shallow arc of the top rail; arcs also appear in the sides, at both top and bottom. The motif is a unifying element.

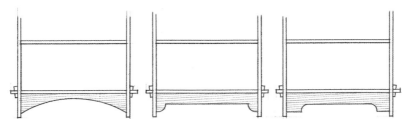

WEDGES

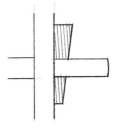

The material of the wedges and their shape and placement can really make a difference in the look and feel of the bookcase. Using a contrasting species, like darker rosewood, gives the wedges a visual punch. But be sure the wedge material is as tough as the white oak.

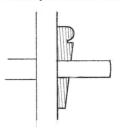

Oak wedges can be colored to provide contrast. An ebonizing solution of vinegar and rusty nails or steel wool will give oak a color anywhere from a dusky gray to black, depending on the solution and the amount of tannin in the oak. Wedges can be shaped any number of ways.

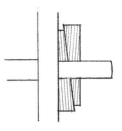

Double wedges allow you to mortise straight through the tenon at no angle. The angle of the wedges themselves creates the necessary force. The number of wedges can be varied to suit your taste; for instance, you can put three wedges at the bottom and two at the top.

CHERRY AND FIR BOOKCASE

by Peter Zuerner

The lamb's tongue. *A small bevel at each corner of the top is cut with a chisel to help soften the hard right angle of the edges.*

Several years ago, my sister Cicely was looking for a bookcase that would be attractive, functional, and reasonably easy to move. The piece I designed and built for her is now one of the stock pieces in my furniture shop. I call it, appropriately, Cicely's Bookshelf.

I wanted the bookcase to have a spare and elegant look, so I kept the frame parts to a minimum and elevated the piece off the floor by extending the corner posts to create four short legs. All four edges of the top, along with the front edge of each shelf, were given a generously sized cove to create the illusion of thinner stock. As a result, even when the piece is filled with books, it appears light and graceful.

Choose the Wood With Care

For me, the first and most important step in any furniture project is the process of selecting the wood. Consistent color and grain are important, and I'm always on the lookout for something interesting. I especially like to incorporate special grain or a natural defect. Not only does an odd grain or a small defect make each piece a bit more unique, it also provides a strong visual connection to the tree from which it evolved. For instance, the piece shown here has a small, sound knot near the front of the lower shelf, about midway across the span.

In this piece, I liked the idea of blending darker cherry with the strong grain of quartersawn Douglas fir. So I used cherry for the frame parts, the top, and the front edging on the shelves. The quartersawn fir is incorporated into the panels.

To add strength to the bookcase, the bottom shelf was fixed in place. It rests on two parts: the lower front rail and a cleat that's screwed to the inside face of the lower back rail. Six screws hold the shelf in place. The screws were driven up through counterbored holes in the lower front rail and the cleat.

I sanded all exposed surfaces, with 220-grit paper and applied four coats of hand-rubbed tung oil, sanding between each coat with 1,000-grit paper while the oil was still wet.

To allow the top to expand and contract in width as the humidity changes, I attached it to the frame using eight small wood buttons. A final rubdown with a soft, dust-free cloth completed the project.

Peter Zuerner, owner of Zuerner Design, builds furniture in Middletown, Rhode Island, just a silver-spoon's throw from the historic mansions of Newport.

CUT THE JOINERY FOR THE POSTS AND RAILS

POST DETAIL

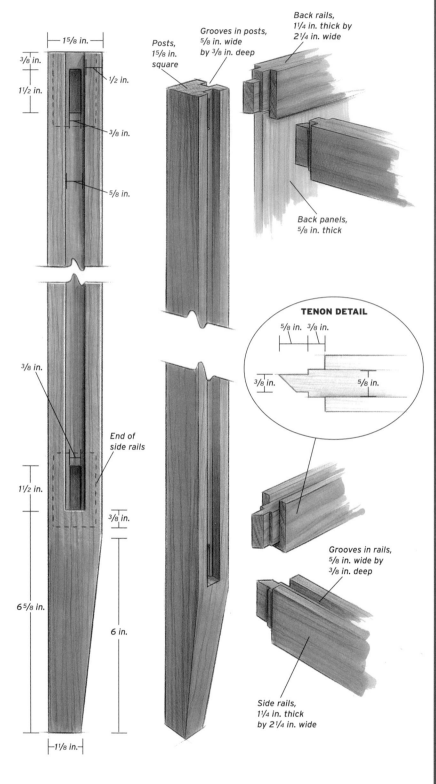

1⁵⁄₈ in.

³⁄₈ in.

1¹⁄₂ in.

¹⁄₂ in.

³⁄₈ in.

⁵⁄₈ in.

³⁄₈ in.

1¹⁄₂ in.

³⁄₈ in.

6⁵⁄₈ in.

6 in.

1¹⁄₈ in.

End of side rails

Posts, 1⁵⁄₈ in. square

Grooves in posts, ⁵⁄₈ in. wide by ³⁄₈ in. deep

Back rails, 1¹⁄₄ in. thick by 2¹⁄₄ in. wide

Back panels, ⁵⁄₈ in. thick

TENON DETAIL

⁵⁄₈ in. ³⁄₈ in.

³⁄₈ in.

⁵⁄₈ in.

Grooves in rails, ⁵⁄₈ in. wide by ³⁄₈ in. deep

Side rails, 1¹⁄₄ in. thick by 2¹⁄₄ in. wide

Cut the Coves in Two Steps

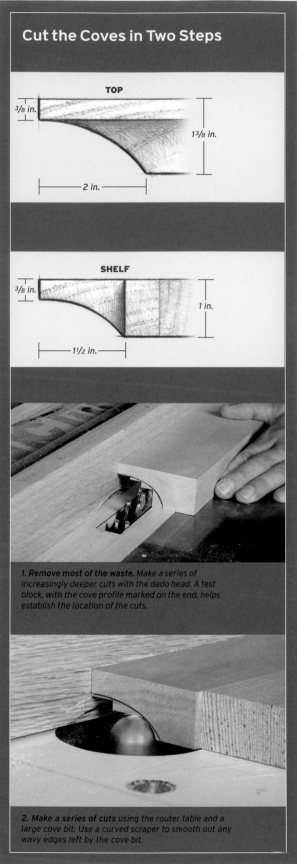

TOP

³⁄₈ in.

1³⁄₈ in.

2 in.

SHELF

³⁄₈ in.

1 in.

1¹⁄₂ in.

1. Remove most of the waste. *Make a series of increasingly deeper cuts with the dado head. A test block, with the cove profile marked on the end, helps establish the location of the cuts.*

2. Make a series of cuts *using the router table and a large cove bit. Use a curved scraper to smooth out any wavy edges left by the cove bit.*

FRAME-AND-PANEL BOOKCASE

Zuerner incorporated frame-and-panel construction in his bookcase, with the mortise and tenon accounting for most of the joinery.

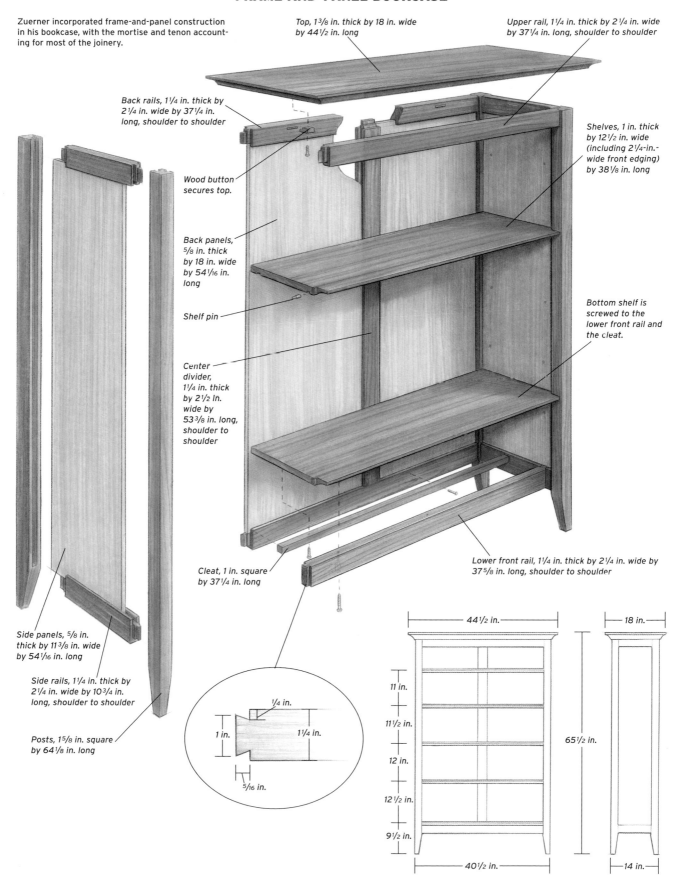

Top, 1³⁄₈ in. thick by 18 in. wide by 44¹⁄₂ in. long

Upper rail, 1¹⁄₄ in. thick by 2¹⁄₄ in. wide by 37¹⁄₄ in. long, shoulder to shoulder

Back rails, 1¹⁄₄ in. thick by 2¹⁄₄ in. wide by 37¹⁄₄ in. long, shoulder to shoulder

Shelves, 1 in. thick by 12¹⁄₂ in. wide (including 2¹⁄₄-in.-wide front edging) by 38¹⁄₈ in. long

Wood button secures top.

Back panels, ⁵⁄₈ in. thick by 18 in. wide by 54¹⁄₁₆ in. long

Bottom shelf is screwed to the lower front rail and the cleat.

Shelf pin

Center divider, 1¹⁄₄ in. thick by 2¹⁄₂ In. wide by 53³⁄₈ in. long, shoulder to shoulder

Side panels, ⁵⁄₈ in. thick by 11³⁄₈ in. wide by 54¹⁄₁₆ in. long

Side rails, 1¹⁄₄ in. thick by 2¹⁄₄ in. wide by 10³⁄₄ in. long, shoulder to shoulder

Posts, 1⁵⁄₈ in. square by 64¹⁄₈ in. long

Cleat, 1 in. square by 37¹⁄₄ in. long

Lower front rail, 1¹⁄₄ in. thick by 2¹⁄₄ in. wide by 37⁵⁄₈ in. long, shoulder to shoulder

¼ in.

1 in.

1¹⁄₄ in.

⁵⁄₁₆ in.

44¹⁄₂ in.

18 in.

11 in.

11¹⁄₂ in.

12 in.

12¹⁄₂ in.

9¹⁄₂ in.

65¹⁄₂ in.

40¹⁄₂ in.

14 in.

A BLANKET CHEST WITH LEGS

by John McAlevey

Ledger strips support a plywood bottom panel painted with odorless milk paint (above left). A liner of tongue-and-groove aromatic cedar (above right) is glued on top of the plywood and is notched to fit around the legs.

A filler strip holds the hinges. The strip is glued to the rear top rail and butts against the rear legs, whose inside back corners remain unchamfered.

I have always liked designing and making sideboards, chests of drawers and blanket chests. It is very satisfying to make a basic box that will contain and store the things that we use in our everyday lives. And when it works, the result can be as beautiful as it is useful. It's even more satisfying when you can transform a basic box into something with depth, dimension and visual power.

The blanket chest I designed and made for a family in New Hampshire is a piece of furniture that could have been just another unremarkable dovetailed box, but it is redeemed by frame-and-panel construction that allows for greater play with forms and materials. It pleases me to think that many years from now, someone will open this chest on a snowy December night, pull out a down comforter as proof against the cold, and think, "What a beautiful chest."

Legs Double as Stiles

A chest made of four solid slabs dovetailed together looks too heavy and traditional for my taste, and I can assemble frames and panels much more quickly than I can cut long rows of dovetails. But frame-and-panel construction has more going for it than lightness and economy of labor: It adds depth and shadow lines to the look of a piece, and it allows the use of contrasting wood—something you can't do with mitered or dovetailed chests made only from flat panels.

My client wanted a fresh design that incorporated elements of two of my previous frame-and-panel chests. In a departure from one

THE ACTION IS IN THE CORNERS

Because the legs serve as the stiles of the frame-and-panel sides, they are mortised for the rail tenons as well as grooved for the panel tongues. Both the mortises and grooves are centered on the inside faces of the leg, so layout is straightforward.

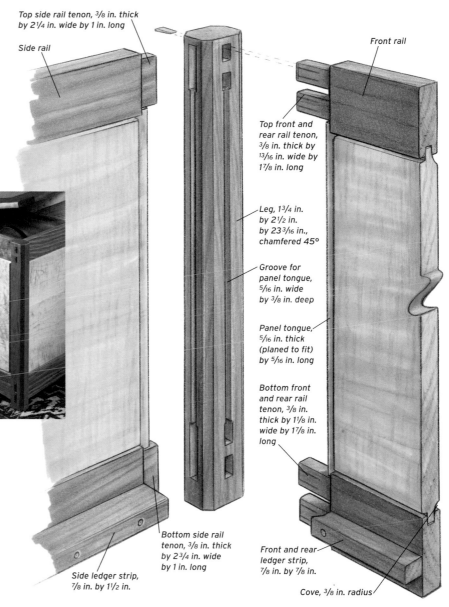

Top side rail tenon, 3/8 in. thick by 2 1/4 in. wide by 1 in. long

Side rail

Front rail

Top front and rear rail tenon, 3/8 in. thick by 13/16 in. wide by 1 7/8 in. long

Leg, 1 3/4 in. by 2 1/2 in. by 23 3/16 in., chamfered 45°

Groove for panel tongue, 5/16 in. wide by 3/8 in. deep

Panel tongue, 5/16 in. thick (planed to fit) by 5/16 in. long

Bottom front and rear rail tenon, 3/8 in. thick by 1 1/8 in. wide by 1 7/8 in. long

Bottom side rail tenon, 3/8 in. thick by 2 3/4 in. wide by 1 in. long

Side ledger strip, 7/8 in. by 1 1/2 in.

Front and rear ledger strip, 7/8 in. by 7/8 in.

Cove, 3/8 in. radius

PIN THE PANELS FROM THE INSIDE

Pin the center of each vertical tongue to the legs with a 1/8-in. dowel, so the panels will expand and contract evenly at the top and bottom rails. Angle the hole for the pin to prevent the drill from damaging the sides of the panels.

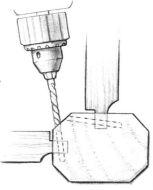

of the older designs, I decided to eliminate the stiles of the frame-and-panel sides and join the top and bottom rails directly to the legs so that the legs themselves serve as stiles (see the drawing at right and on p. 13). This legs-as-stiles approach, which I had first tried nine years ago on a cabinet, allows for simplified construction and a lighter look than full frame-and-panel sides attached to separate legs. (Squinting at the blanket chest, you can almost imagine away the light-colored panels, leaving behind an open frame of thin, table-like legs and rails.) A gentle curve in the bottom rail helps the legs visually lift the chest off the floor.

The frames are made of cherry and the panels are of curly maple. The legs are made from 8/4 lumber, lightened and made more interesting by chamfering on all four sides. To add even more visual character and a form of decorative detail, I brought the double tenons of the front and rear rails through and let them stand ⅛ in. proud of the legs. And to transform the top from a typical rectangular shape into a more pleasing and interesting form, I decided to curve the ends of the lid, carrying through the motif of the curved bottom rails.

Mortise-and-Tenon Joints Hold the Panels Together

Mortise-and-tenon joints, in one form or another, are the basis for all good furniture construction, and this blanket chest is no exception. As in a post-and-beam house or a post-and-rail fence, mortise-and-tenon joints draw horizontal and vertical pieces of furniture together simply and rigidly. Used with frame-and-panel construction, these joints make furniture that

FRAME-AND-PANEL BLANKET CHEST

The frame-and-panel sides of this chest are a departure from the solid sides and dovetailed corners of a traditional chest. Unlike solid box construction, frame-and-panel construction creates interesting shadow lines and allows for the use of contrasting woods.

Floating panels, ¹³⁄₁₆-in.-thick curly maple

Rails, ¹³⁄₁₆-in.-thick cherry

17 in.

23³⁄₁₆ in.

2³⁄₄ in.

43½ in.

42½ in.

22⁷⁄₈ in.

50½ in.

24 in.

47 in.

22 in.

Overhang at front, ⅞ in.

accommodates seasonal changes in the wood better than any other method.

The architect Louis Kahn said that the joint was the beginning of all ornament, and this holds true for the wedged, double through-tenons on my blanket chest. I worried that through-tenons would detract from the lines of the legs, but now that I've done them, I'd do them again. Details like these through-tenons add mystery because people at first

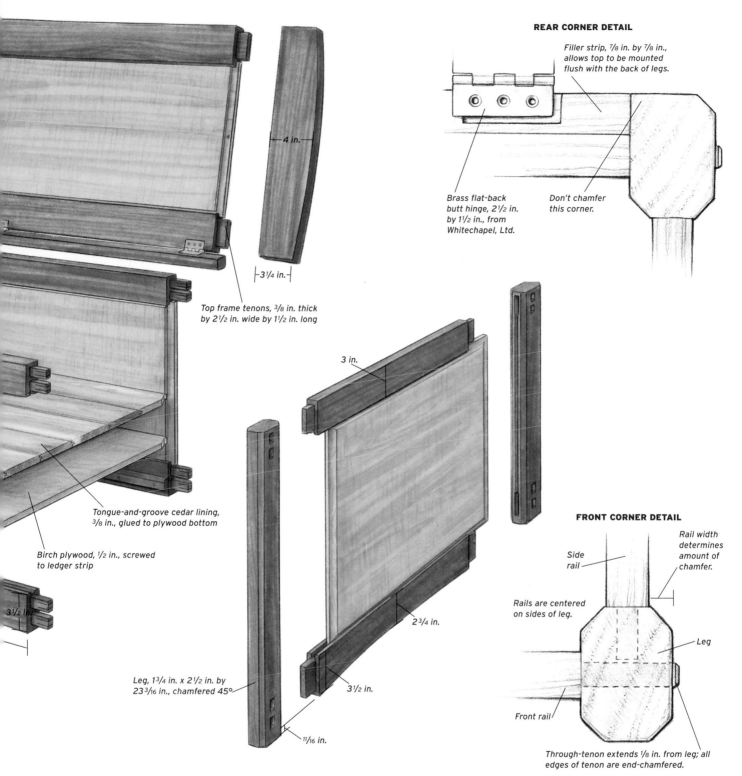

Filler strip, 7/8 in. by 7/8 in., allows top to be mounted flush with the back of legs.

Brass flat-back butt hinge, 2½ in. by 1½ in., from Whitechapel, Ltd.

Don't chamfer this corner.

—4 in.—

—3¼ in.—

Top frame tenons, 3/8 in. thick by 2½ in. wide by 1½ in. long

3 in.

Tongue-and-groove cedar lining, 3/8 in., glued to plywood bottom

Birch plywood, ½ in., screwed to ledger strip

3½ in.

2¾ in.

Leg, 1¾ in. x 2½ in. by 23 3/16 in., chamfered 45°

3½ in.

11/16 in.

FRONT CORNER DETAIL

Rail width determines amount of chamfer.

Side rail

Rails are centered on sides of leg.

Leg

Front rail

Through-tenon extends 1/8 in. from leg; all edges of tenon are end-chamfered.

wonder why they're there, and yet they take away mystery because they ultimately reveal the nature of the construction. I've noticed at shows that people make a beeline to just such details.

John McAlevey teaches at the Center for Furniture Craftsmanship in Rockport, Maine, and builds one-of-a-kind furniture in a shop next to his home in Tenants Harbor, Maine.

FRAME-AND-PANEL BED

by David Fay

My favorite designs have come to me unexpectedly, in a flash of an idea, far away from the drafting table. The ensuing challenge to develop that vision into a finished product requires a lot of time spent refining what may seem like small details.

I begin with a sketch, nothing fancy or beautiful. The back of an envelope or a napkin will do. Drawing this way frees me from the constraints of trying to perfect the piece; all I'm after is getting the inspiration down on paper.

If the piece is a commission, the next step is listening to the customer. That often influences the dimensions of a project. For this bed, the customer wanted a queen-size frame that could accommodate a futon mattress or a standard box-spring-and-mattress set. As a result, I had to make the bed rails wide enough to accommodate an adjustable inner rail.

A dimensioned drawing comes next. Although an accurate drawing can help me visualize a piece, this two-dimensional tool has limitations. That's why I build a full-scale model of any tricky parts to work out design and construction needs and to perfect technical skills.

The model allows me to evaluate how the details relate to the rest of the design. For example, I used a model to determine the proportions of the posts and rails. I experimented with the reveal at various widths. A 7/8-in. reveal looked chunky, and a 5/8-in. reveal looked skinny. But when I tried a 3/4-in. reveal, it looked right. I also used the model to determine the size of the granadillo reveal as it related to the panel and posts and rails. Using the model, I was able to refine subtle details and their proportions. There's nothing scientific here, no golden rules. It's a matter of trial and error and trusting your instincts.

David Fay builds custom furniture in Oakland, California.

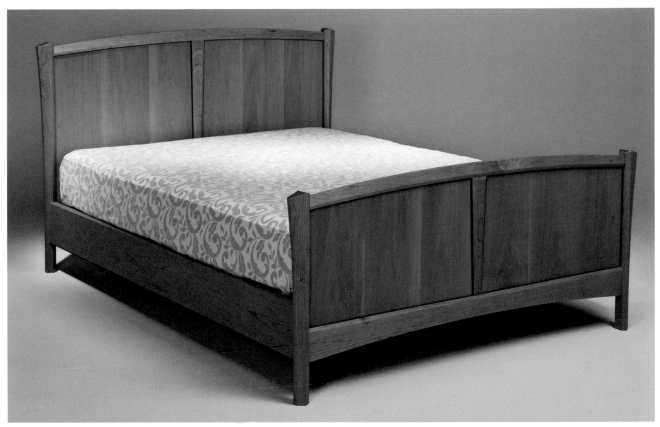

A bed made in three types of wood. The framework, including the posts, is made of cherry. The panels are resawn, slipmatched pear wood. Accent strips along the inside of the frames and along the bottoms of the bed rails are granadillo.

Inlay Adds Contrast

Degree of separation. Granadillo provides contrast and separation between the similarly toned cherry and pear wood.

Before the joint is assembled. The granadillo strips are glued into the grooves for the panels using a battery of small spring clamps.

FRAME-AND-PANEL BED

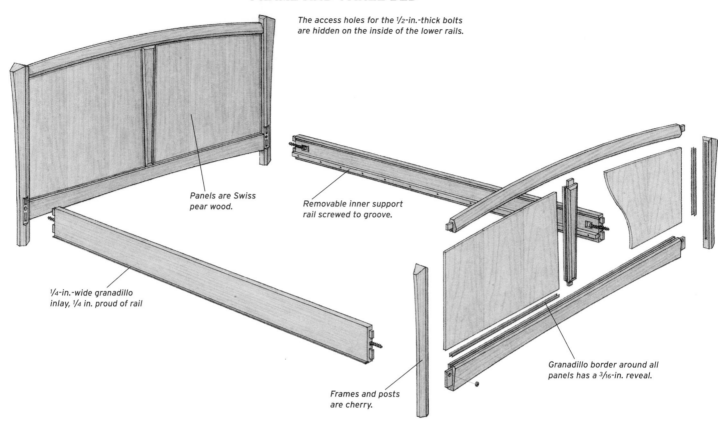

The access holes for the 1/2-in.-thick bolts are hidden on the inside of the lower rails.

Panels are Swiss pear wood.

Removable inner support rail screwed to groove.

1/4-in.-wide granadillo inlay, 1/4 in. proud of rail

Frames and posts are cherry.

Granadillo border around all panels has a 3/16-in. reveal.

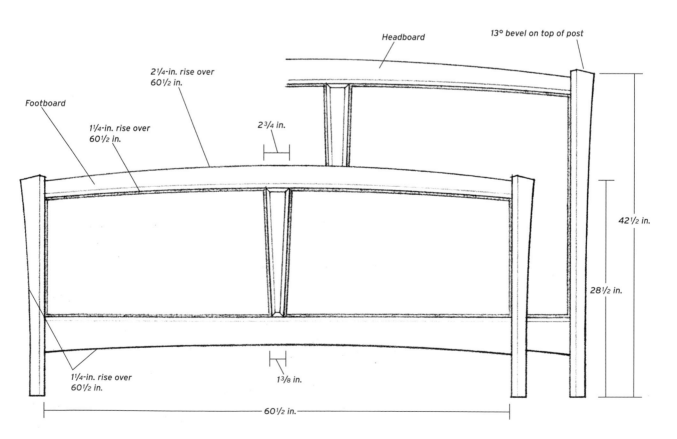

Headboard

13° bevel on top of post

2 1/4-in. rise over 60 1/2 in.

Footboard

1 1/4-in. rise over 60 1/2 in.

2 3/4 in.

42 1/2 in.

28 1/2 in.

1 1/4-in. rise over 60 1/2 in.

1 3/8 in.

60 1/2 in.

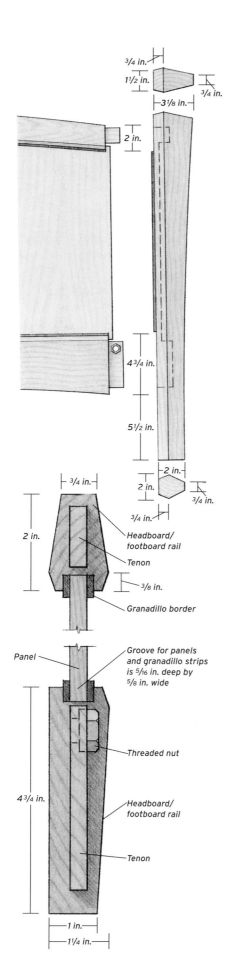

¾ in.

1½ in.

¾ in.

3⅛ in.

2 in.

4¾ in.

5½ in.

2 in.

2 in.

¾ in.

¾ in.

¾ in.

2 in.

¾ in.

Headboard/
footboard rail

Tenon

⅜ in.

Granadillo border

Panel

Groove for panels
and granadillo strips
is ⁵⁄₁₆ in. deep by
⅝ in. wide

Threaded nut

Headboard/
footboard rail

4¾ in.

Tenon

1 in.

1¼ in.

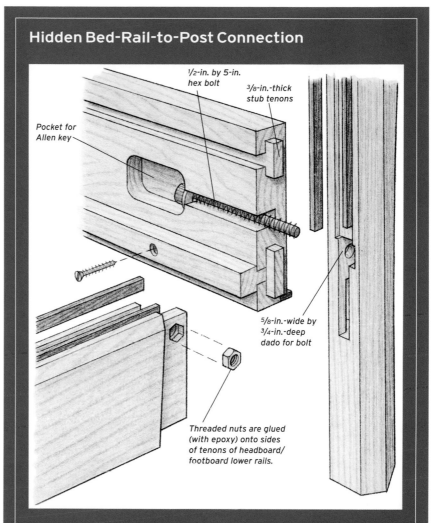

Hidden Bed-Rail-to-Post Connection

½-in. by 5-in.
hex bolt

⅜-in.-thick
stub tenons

Pocket for
Allen key

⅝-in.-wide by
¾-in.-deep
dado for bolt

Threaded nuts are glued
(with epoxy) onto sides
of tenons of headboard/
footboard lower rails.

Decorative caps made to cover bolt holes in bedposts work fine, especially when used on traditional-looking furniture. But I didn't want a cap to detract from the fluid shape of the posts of this bed. A friend, Mike Laine, showed me how to get a strong joint using mortise and tenons coupled with captured nuts and bolts. The joint is secure and leaves no trace of its mechanics once the bed has been assembled and a mattress or futon installed.

Refer to the drawing on the facing page for the size and location of the joinery, which is cut while the stock is still square. Clamp and dry-fit the posts to the lower rails of the headboard and footboard, one at a time. Then, on the drill press, align a drill bit with the already drilled bolt hole in the post and drill through the tenon of the rail, being careful not to drill too deeply.

Remove the lower rail and thread the bolt through the hole and into the nut. Scribe the outline of the nut onto the tenon. The mortise for the nut captures only half its thickness; any more would weaken the tenon. To make room for the protruding half of the nut, enlarge the mortise in the bedpost around the nut with a small router and finish up with a chisel.

The bolt is housed in a dado cut into the lower rails, centered between the two tenons. Mortise around the head to give you enough clearance to reach in with a hex wrench and cinch everything down. Check the joints for fit, then epoxy the nuts in place, being careful not to get any glue on the threads. —D.F.

ARTS AND CRAFTS BED

by Gary Rogowski

Certain design elements seem to fit quite naturally into the Arts and Crafts style of this bed, such as the gently curved and tapered posts that meet the floor with a solid presence, and the cloud lift, an element of Chinese furniture that Greene and Greene appropriated in the early 20th century. The cloud lift—a small S-curve, combined with a long, sweeping curve—appears in a few ways in this piece.

Texture in a piece is always important. I decided that inlaying raised strips of ebony in the post tops would give a stopping point for the eye and hand. The carved square plugs would do the same where I had pinned the joints. By stepping down the thicknesses of each adjacent part toward the center of the bed, I created shadow lines, another form of texture.

I finalized the design in a set of full-size drawings. A full-size drawing not only gives even better information about proportion, form, balance, and negative space, but it also lets you plan out the details, seeing how they will work in the piece. I also use full-size drawings to find graceful curves—bending a thin stick of oak, using a few weights to hold it in place, and tracing against it.

Because the headboard and footboard are symmetrical around their centerlines, I only had to make half views of each. Likewise, most of the template has to cover only half of the full profile.

You'll need to remember one important fact: Once you build a bed, you must be able to get it out of your shop and into the bedroom. Therefore, it needs to be a knockdown design.

I use a wedging, locking style of hardware that is pounded together. The more weight you place on it,

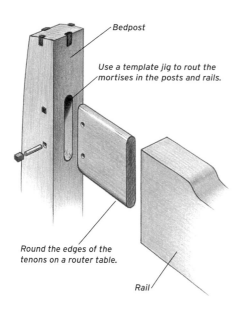

Bedpost

Use a template jig to rout the mortises in the posts and rails.

Round the edges of the tenons on a router table.

Rail

Pin the Joints in Two Steps

Use a dowel to pin the joint, with a square ebony peg on top. Before assembly, drill a shallow hole for the peg using the drill press. After glue-up, square the hole, then drill into the bottom of that hole and through the tenon to receive the dowel.

Leave the peg slightly proud and break the edges. Use a piece of laminate under the chisel to protect the surrounding wood. Finish with sandpaper to gently dome the peg.

the more it locks into position. Also, this knockdown hardware is invisible when the parts are joined, better suiting the style of the bed.

Many people believe the combination of box spring and mattress is the only way to rest easy. But consider that the purpose of the box spring is to provide spring, support, and ventilation for the mattress. All of this can be accomplished—at a fraction of the cost—by a row of slats laid on ledger strips (which are glued and screwed to the side rails). The slats are spaced out by means of dowels set into the ledger strips.

This bed is designed for a mattress or a futon alone. With this setup, most of the headboard will be seen, even if some well-meaning soul throws a gaggle of pillows across it.

If you're using a box spring and need more depth inside the rails, use an angle-iron ledger strip placed at the bottom of the rail to buy yourself a couple of inches.

Gary Rogowski is a contributing editor. He runs the Northwest Woodworking Studio, a woodworking school in Portland, Oregon.

The verticals are scribed and half-lapped into the rails. *The author uses a shallow gouge to complete the recess.*

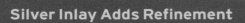

To take this Arts and Crafts bed to the next level, add a traditional silver inlay to the center columns.

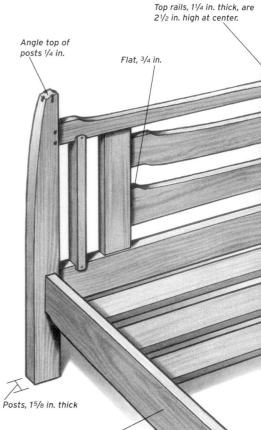

Top rails, 1¼ in. thick, are 2½ in. high at center.

Angle top of posts ¼ in.

Flat, ¾ in.

Posts, 1⅝ in. thick

Side rails, 1¼ in. thick by 82 in. long by 6¾ in. high at center

Silver Inlay Adds Refinement

When is a piece of furniture more than a piece of furniture? The answer is when it sings, when it shows the handwork and detailing of a careful craftsman. The details of a piece can make or break it, separating fine furniture from run-of-the-mill work.

This project can be further refined with silver inlay. The stylized floral inlay fits the Arts and Crafts idiom, but it also just looks good. A bed headboard, with its wide spaces, provides a broad canvas for embellishment.

I'm a sucker for the Scotch. Not the 16-year-old kind, although that is nice, but the 100-year-old work of Charles Rennie Mackintosh. His design work in furniture architecture and fabrics is a fascinating mixture of geometric shapes and naturalism. Strong tapering shapes are accented with stylized flowers, stalks, seed heads, and willowy waving-in-the-wind shapes. The floral patterns that occur regularly in his very masculine work gave me the inspiration to combine the heft of the bed with a series of waving stalks in the headboard and footboard. The ⅛-in.-sq. wire cost about $1 an inch, or about $100 total for the four columns on this bed.

Rough sketches, with an emphasis on creativity and freedom, coalesce into a series of variations on a theme.

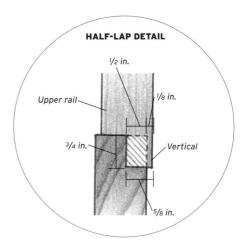

HALF-LAP DETAIL

½ in.

Upper rail

⅛ in.

¾ in.

Vertical

⅝ in.

MAHOGANY BED COMBINES GRACEFUL CURVES AND CLEVER JOINERY

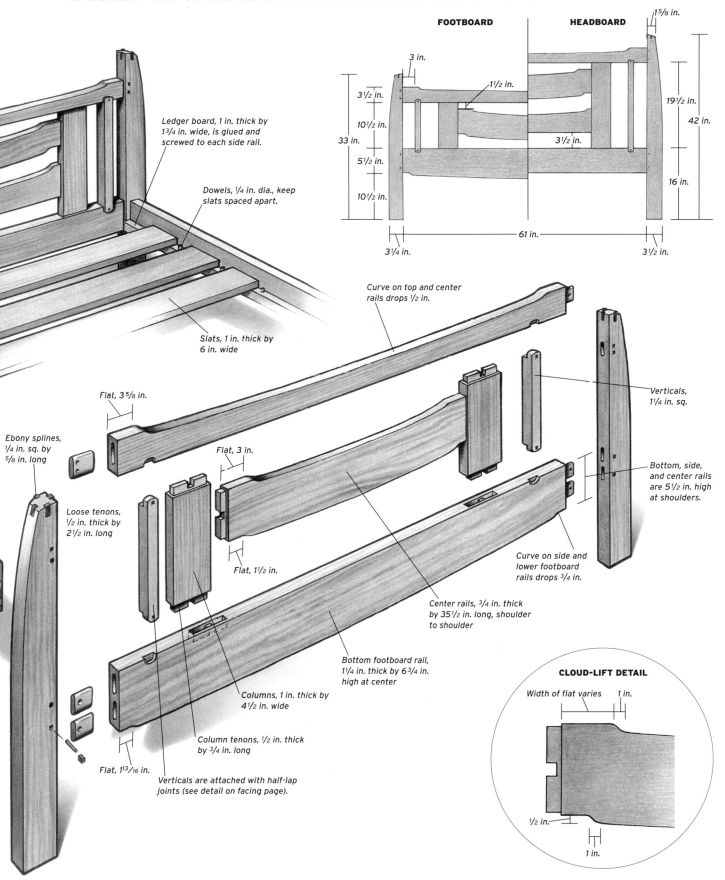

Ledger board, 1 in. thick by 1³/₄ in. wide, is glued and screwed to each side rail.

Dowels, ¹/₄ in. dia., keep slats spaced apart.

Slats, 1 in. thick by 6 in. wide

FOOTBOARD

HEADBOARD

1⁵/₈ in.

3 in.

1¹/₂ in.

3¹/₂ in.

10¹/₂ in.

33 in.

3¹/₂ in.

5¹/₂ in.

10¹/₂ in.

19¹/₂ in.

42 in.

16 in.

61 in.

3¹/₄ in.

3¹/₂ in.

Curve on top and center rails drops ¹/₂ in.

Verticals, 1¹/₄ in. sq.

Flat, 3⁵/₈ in.

Ebony splines, ¹/₄ in. sq. by ⁵/₈ in. long

Flat, 3 in.

Bottom, side, and center rails are 5¹/₂ in. high at shoulders.

Loose tenons, ¹/₂ in. thick by 2¹/₂ in. long

Flat, 1¹/₂ in.

Curve on side and lower footboard rails drops ³/₄ in.

Center rails, ³/₄ in. thick by 35¹/₂ in. long, shoulder to shoulder

Bottom footboard rail, 1¹/₄ in. thick by 6³/₄ in. high at center

Columns, 1 in. thick by 4¹/₂ in. wide

Column tenons, ¹/₂ in. thick by ³/₄ in. long

Flat, 1¹³/₁₆ in.

Verticals are attached with half-lap joints (see detail on facing page).

CLOUD-LIFT DETAIL

Width of flat varies

1 in.

¹/₂ in.

1 in.

BEDSTAND

by Roger Holmes

Most woodworkers that I know spend three-quarters of their time making boxes. Boxes for books, clothing, blankets, dishes, keepsakes, and odds and ends. We even spend a great deal of time making boxes for boxes, i.e., drawers for a chest or other case piece.

Designing with boxes is quite simple. First you figure out the size and configuration of box or boxes to store or display the desired items. Then you try to make the boxes attractive. A recent request to build a pair of cabinets for friends allowed me to explore methods of enhancing the basic box.

Wedged between the bed and a wall in many bedrooms, most bedside cabinets don't benefit from exposed joinery or lovely wood—you don't get much of a view of either. I started sketching various curvy alternatives, deciding on the simplest of them all—curving the front plane of the cabinet along a gentle arc. For centuries, simple curves have been used to break the four-square rigidity of a box without sacrificing the advantages of rectilinear construction.

I wanted to add some visual weight to the top and bottom, something more substantial than the 7/8-in.-thick edges of the box. The solutions—a 5-in.-tall plinth and 2-in.-high cornice—are traditional, even classical. Architects have historically used the plinth to raise a box off the ground and, in a sense, put it on display. They added a cornice on top, like a crown, terminating the structure with a flourish. Furniture makers have used both elements extensively. My plinth is slightly larger than the box it supports, and simple moldings make the transition between the two elements.

A bead molding announces the beginning of the cornice. The body of the cornice is the same size as the box, but the grain runs horizontally on the sides, setting it off subtly from the vertical grain of the box below. Set in slightly from the cornice body, the cove-molded top panel finishes the job.

Roger Holmes is a former associate editor of Fine Woodworking.

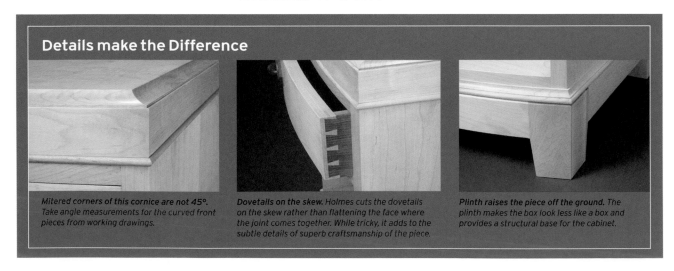

Details make the Difference

Mitered corners of this cornice are not 45°. Take angle measurements for the curved front pieces from working drawings.

Dovetails on the skew. Holmes cuts the dovetails on the skew rather than flattening the face where the joint comes together. While tricky, it adds to the subtle details of superb craftsmanship of the piece.

Plinth raises the piece off the ground. The plinth makes the box look less like a box and provides a structural base for the cabinet.

BEDSTAND

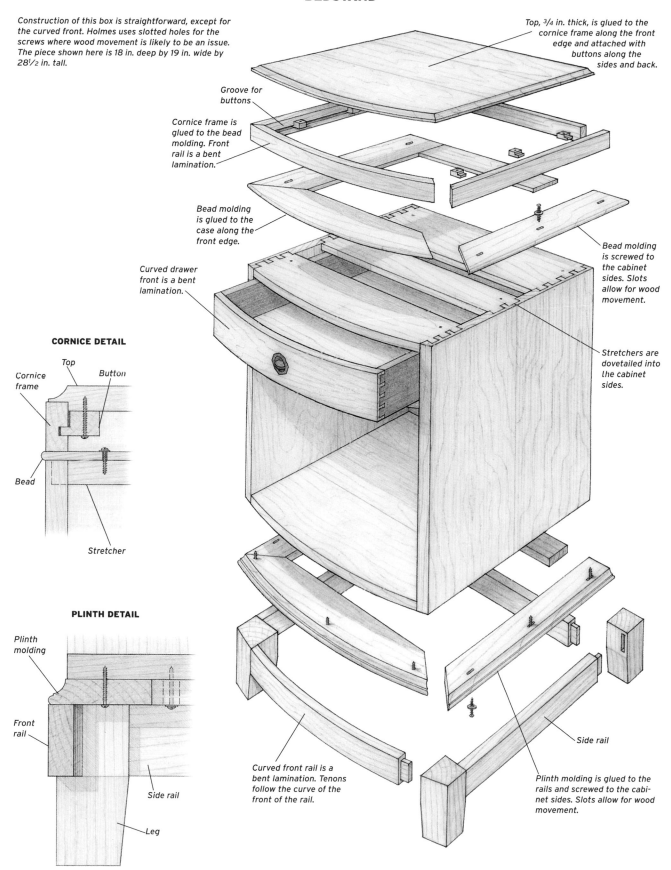

Construction of this box is straightforward, except for the curved front. Holmes uses slotted holes for the screws where wood movement is likely to be an issue. The piece shown here is 18 in. deep by 19 in. wide by 28½ in. tall.

Top, ¾ in. thick, is glued to the cornice frame along the front edge and attached with buttons along the sides and back.

Groove for buttons

Cornice frame is glued to the bead molding. Front rail is a bent lamination.

Bead molding is glued to the case along the front edge.

Curved drawer front is a bent lamination.

Bead molding is screwed to the cabinet sides. Slots allow for wood movement.

Stretchers are dovetailed into the cabinet sides.

CORNICE DETAIL

Top

Button

Cornice frame

Bead

Stretcher

PLINTH DETAIL

Plinth molding

Front rail

Side rail

Leg

Curved front rail is a bent lamination. Tenons follow the curve of the front of the rail.

Side rail

Plinth molding is glued to the rails and screwed to the cabinet sides. Slots allow for wood movement.

INSPIRATION FOR A BEDSIDE CABINET

by Michael Fortune

When designing a piece of furniture, I never know where an idea is going to come from. Indeed, it sometimes evolves quietly from an unlikely place. That certainly was the case when I designed this bedside cabinet.

During my college days, my apartment had virtually no furniture. One day, however, I had the good fortune to find an old pine chest of drawers in a ditch by the side of the road. I hauled the piece back to my apartment, all the while anticipating the luxury of getting my clothes off the floor.

I figured the chest to be about 200 years old. It was apparent that the builder was both clever and expeditious, as evidenced by back legs that simply were cut out of solid-wood side panels. I ended up living with that chest for 35 years. During that time, I came to appreciate the brilliance of the simple back-leg design. And when I began to design this bedside cabinet, I included the leg curve from that wonderful old chest.

The bedside cabinet also includes a wide cove that runs top to bottom along the back. Initially, it was to serve as a channel for cords from a lamp and an alarm clock. But some rough sketches I made, followed by more detailed drawings, revealed that the cove also introduced an interesting rhythm to the back surfaces of the form.

I included the semicircular cutout detail on the bottom of the doors to draw attention to the space under the cabinet. The door cutout also complements the cove at the back of the cabinet.

I wanted to avoid using

European-style concealed hinges for the door. Although you can't see these hinges when the doors are closed, European hinges become very visible once a door is opened. I thought the mechanism would look too big on a somewhat smallish piece. I solved the problem by incorporating a bead detail on both sides of the front legs. Then I put two butt hinges within each bead. As a result, the barrel of the hinge simply becomes part of the bead detail. First, though, I had to find a hinge with the appropriate thickness, and then I sized the bead to match the barrel of the hinge.

I've used this bead-and-hinge detail before, with an ebony bead and brass hinges acid-etched to make them black in color.

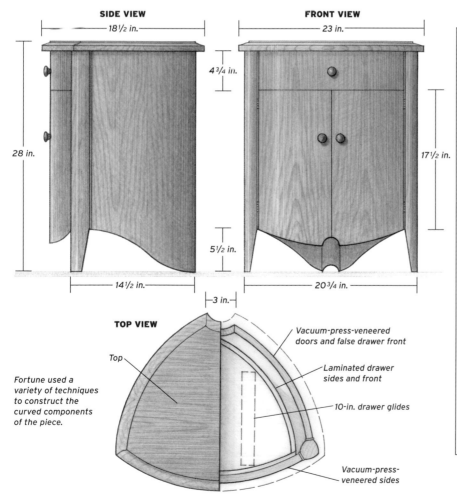

When installed, the hinges all but disappear into the bead, especially after coating them with the same clear lacquer used on the cabinet.

The drawer was planned as a simple curved-front box that would be hung on drawer glides mounted to the underside of the top. But then I realized that once the drawer was opened, the rectangular shape would be out of character with the curved lines of the cabinet. So, using bent-lamination techniques, I curved the drawer sides to match the curve of the cabinet.

Designing furniture can be a wonderful challenge. The process of waiting to see if the completed piece matches the one envisioned can sustain you through the long hours spent in the workshop. And when the finished piece matches perfectly with your design vision, the joy of making furniture goes up tenfold.

Michael Fortune is a furniture maker in Lakefield, Ontario, Canada.

A CABINET WITH CURVES

SIDE VIEW
18½ in.

4¾ in.

28 in.

5½ in.

14½ in.

FRONT VIEW
23 in.

17½ in.

20¾ in.

3 in.

TOP VIEW

Fortune used a variety of techniques to construct the curved components of the piece.

Top

Vacuum-press-veneered doors and false drawer front

Laminated drawer sides and front

10-in. drawer glides

Vacuum-press-veneered sides

BEAD MIMICS HINGE BARREL

To camouflage the hinges, the long beads in the legs are the same diameter as the hinge barrel.

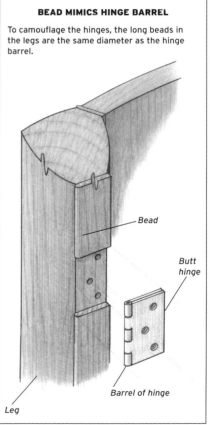

Bead

Butt hinge

Barrel of hinge

Leg

ONE-DRAWER LAMP STAND

by Mike Dunbar

This small table is a typical example of a furniture form that became popular in the 1790s and remained in favor through the first half of the 1800s. It is generally referred to by antique collectors as a lamp stand. That name distinguishes it from the tripod tables that had been popular during much of the 1700s. The name also explains this form's sudden development. Tripod stands are commonly called candle stands, from the practice of placing candlesticks on them to illuminate a room. Oil lamps became popular around 1790. But the lamps used highly combustible liquid fuel and so were more hazardous than a single candle flame.

To provide a more stable and safer resting place for oil lamps, the small, four-legged table was introduced. Outside the antique world, this form is called an end table, indicating the table's popular use at the ends of a sofa or on both sides of a bed. For this reason, many people prefer these tables in pairs. The pair I made are of woods native to New Hampshire—cherry with a curly maple veneer drawer front.

Mike Dunbar is a contributing editor to Fine Woodworking.

CHERRY LAMP STAND

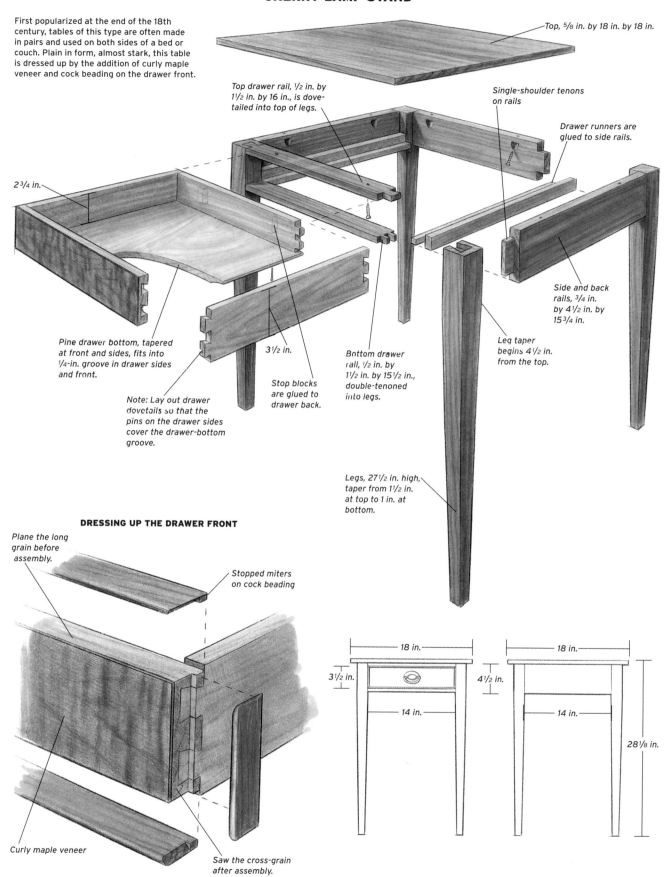

First popularized at the end of the 18th century, tables of this type are often made in pairs and used on both sides of a bed or couch. Plain in form, almost stark, this table is dressed up by the addition of curly maple veneer and cock beading on the drawer front.

Top, 5/8 in. by 18 in. by 18 in.

Top drawer rail, 1/2 in. by 1 1/2 in. by 16 in., is dove-tailed into top of legs.

Single-shoulder tenons on rails

Drawer runners are glued to side rails.

2 3/4 in.

Side and back rails, 3/4 in. by 4 1/2 in. by 15 3/4 in.

Pine drawer bottom, tapered at front and sides, fits into 1/4-in. groove in drawer sides and front.

3 1/2 in.

Stop blocks are glued to drawer back.

Bottom drawer rail, 1/2 in. by 1 1/2 in. by 15 1/2 in., double-tenoned into legs.

Leg taper begins 4 1/2 in. from the top.

Note: Lay out drawer dovetails so that the pins on the drawer sides cover the drawer-bottom groove.

Legs, 27 1/2 in. high, taper from 1 1/2 in. at top to 1 in. at bottom.

DRESSING UP THE DRAWER FRONT

Plane the long grain before assembly.

Stopped miters on cock beading

Curly maple veneer

Saw the cross-grain after assembly.

18 in.

18 in.

3 1/2 in.

4 1/2 in.

14 in.

14 in.

28 1/8 in.

SHERATON TABLE

by Steve Latta

Thomas Sheraton (1751–1806) is one of the more controversial furniture designers of the Anglo-tradition. He engaged in a wide variety of occupations ranging from cabinetmaking to preaching but could not stay at any one of his many endeavors long enough to make a solid living. He is most noted for his design book, *The Cabinet-Maker and Upholsterer's Drawing Book,* published in 1791, 1794 and then again in 1802. In it, Sheraton attempted to present a system for drawing a variety of furniture types based on the rules of perspective and, in this aspect, the work is exhaustive and merits study by any serious student of the history of furniture. In the latter sections of the book, Sheraton presented his own furniture designs, a wide variety of forms representing a level of sophistication not found in the simpler and more practical designs of George Hepplewhite. Sheraton, in the pages of the *Drawing Book,* criticized the quality of the work of both Hepplewhite and Chippendale. These attacks on his predecessors seem ironic in light of the fact that some contemporary scholars feel Sheraton "borrowed" many of his designs from the Gillows' Firm of furniture makers, a thriving enterprise founded in 1730 with shops and showrooms in both Lancaster and London. Certain design characteristics that are labeled today as "Sheraton" appear on Gillows' pieces, some dating back as early as 1767, more than two decades before the publication of the *Drawing Book.*

A good friend of mine, Dave Lunin, developed a nice end

table based on a Seymour sewing stand, complete with casters and a hanging bag for fabric scraps. I simplified his design and came up with the table you see here in order to offer my students a somewhat more sophisticated alternative to the stock Shaker table that is often used to teach joinery fundamentals. True to the Sheraton tradition, the legs are turned with a dynamic triple bead over an urn separating the pilaster from the slender tapered turning that terminates with a cuff and foot. Additionally, the design challenges a more energetic student to reed

the legs, a neoclassic characteristic with deep roots in antiquity. The drawer front, made from figured walnut, is framed with a scratch bead and features a Sheraton pull available from Horton Brasses. The bevel along the bottom edge of the top adds lightness to the overall feel of the piece. Finished with an aniline dye and shellac, the table fits within a wide range of decors.

Steve Latta teaches at the Thaddeus Stevens College of Technology in Lancaster, Pennsylvania.

SHERATON TABLE

The table derives its strength from mortise-and-tenon and dovetail joints. Much of the joinery may be completed on the tablesaw, making for straightforward construction.

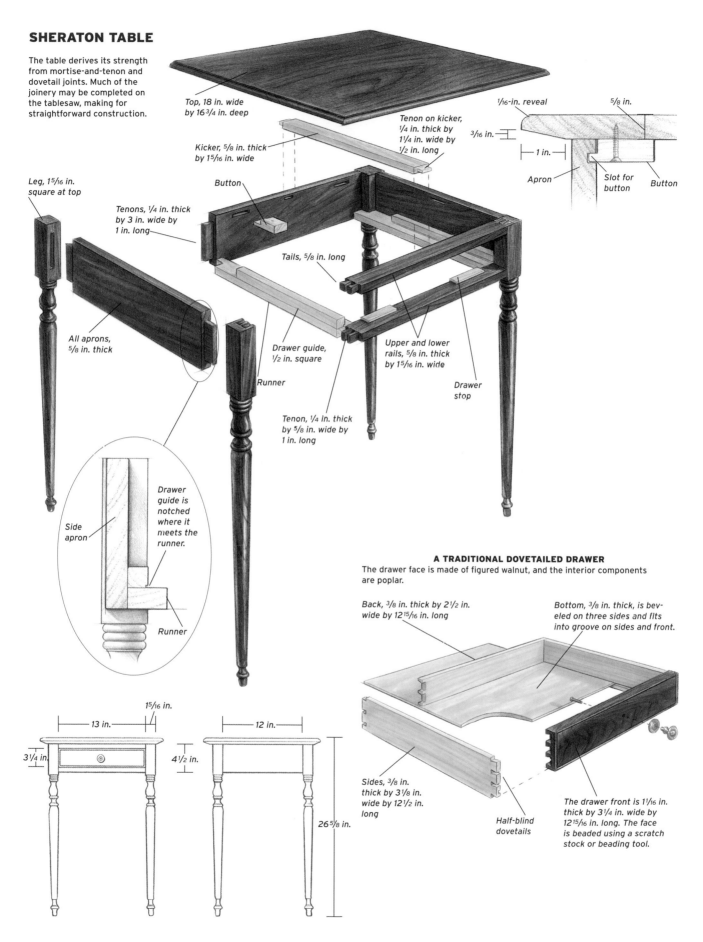

Top, 18 in. wide by 16 3/4 in. deep

Kicker, 5/8 in. thick by 1 5/16 in. wide

Tenon on kicker, 1/4 in. thick by 1 1/4 in. wide by 1/2 in. long

1/16-in. reveal

5/8 in.

3/16 in.

1 in.

Apron

Slot for button

Button

Button

Leg, 1 5/16 in. square at top

Tenons, 1/4 in. thick by 3 in. wide by 1 in. long

Tails, 5/8 in. long

All aprons, 5/8 in. thick

Drawer guide, 1/2 in. square

Runner

Upper and lower rails, 5/8 in. thick by 1 5/16 in. wide

Drawer stop

Tenon, 1/4 in. thick by 5/8 in. wide by 1 in. long

Side apron

Drawer guide is notched where it meets the runner.

Runner

13 in.

1 5/16 in.

3 1/4 in.

12 in.

4 1/2 in.

26 5/8 in.

A TRADITIONAL DOVETAILED DRAWER
The drawer face is made of figured walnut, and the interior components are poplar.

Back, 3/8 in. thick by 2 1/2 in. wide by 12 15/16 in. long

Bottom, 3/8 in. thick, is beveled on three sides and fits into groove on sides and front.

Sides, 3/8 in. thick by 3 1/8 in. wide by 12 1/2 in. long

Half-blind dovetails

The drawer front is 1 1/16 in. thick by 3 1/4 in. wide by 12 15/16 in. long. The face is beaded using a scratch stock or beading tool.

CHERRY CHEST OF DRAWERS

by Michael Pekovich

My daughter Anna, going on 3 years old, loves to dress up. But picking out her own clothes means she has to deal with the cumbersome drawers of the flea-market dresser in her room.

After she had an especially frustrating day wrestling with those drawers, I decided she needed a new place for her clothes. So I made her a simple dresser with seven drawers in four rows, with each row graduated in size and each drawer outlined with a thumbnail profile. The bracket base is decorated with dovetails at the corners, which echo the exposed dovetails at the top of the case. These small details, along with some carefully chosen lumber, complete the ornamentation.

There's a lot to consider when designing a chest of drawers, and the look you choose will affect your construction method. In this case, my decision to expose the dovetails at the top of the case required a molding applied around the edges of the top, which in turn required an extra drawer stretcher attached behind that top molding. When it comes to design decisions, this domino effect is common, and it's a big reason why I try to figure out the details on paper before I begin to build.

Like many woodworkers, I've made the mistake of trying to save money by choosing lesser-quality lumber, working around knots and sapwood and gluing up lots of narrow boards. I've come to realize that the investment in materials is small compared with the investment in labor.

For this piece, I purchased lumber from Irion Lumber Co. (570-724-1895; www.irionlumber. com), a mail-order dealer in Pennsylvania. The supplier found multiple boards from the same tree, saving me the trouble of dyeing or staining mismatched boards.

Michael Pekovich is Fine Woodworking *magazine's art director and an avid furniture maker.*

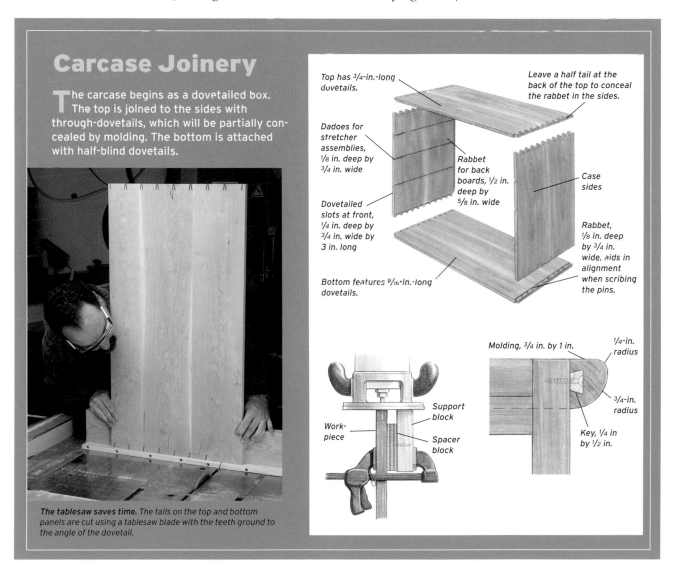

Carcase Joinery

The carcase begins as a dovetailed box. The top is joined to the sides with through-dovetails, which will be partially concealed by molding. The bottom is attached with half-blind dovetails.

The tablesaw saves time. The tails on the top and bottom panels are cut using a tablesaw blade with the teeth ground to the angle of the dovetail.

Top has 3/4-in.-long dovetails.

Leave a half tail at the back of the top to conceal the rabbet in the sides.

Dadoes for stretcher assemblies, 1/8 in. deep by 3/4 in. wide

Rabbet for back boards, 1/2 in. deep by 5/8 in. wide

Case sides

Dovetailed slots at front, 1/4 in. deep by 3/4 in. wide by 3 in. long

Rabbet, 1/8 in. deep by 3/4 in. wide, aids in alignment when scribing the pins.

Bottom features 9/16-in.-long dovetails.

Support block

Work-piece

Spacer block

Molding, 3/4 in. by 1 in.

1/4-in. radius

3/4-in. radius

Key, 1/4 in by 1/2 in.

DRESSER CONSTRUCTION

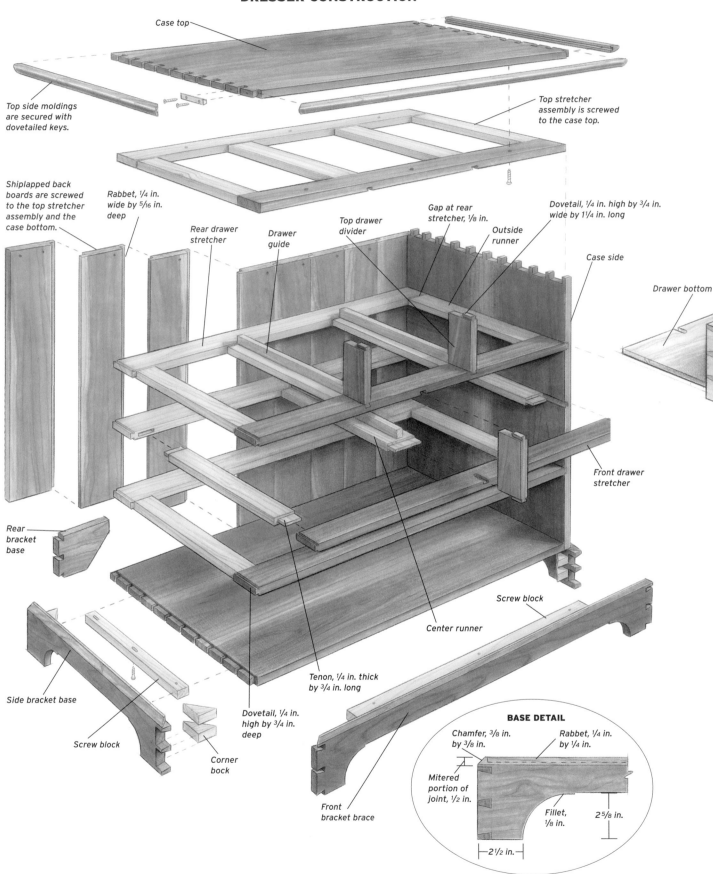

Case top

Top side moldings are secured with dovetailed keys.

Top stretcher assembly is screwed to the case top.

Shiplapped back boards are screwed to the top stretcher assembly and the case bottom.

Rabbet, 1/4 in. wide by 5/16 in. deep

Rear drawer stretcher

Drawer guide

Top drawer divider

Gap at rear stretcher, 1/8 in.

Outside runner

Dovetail, 1/4 in. high by 3/4 in. wide by 1 1/4 in. long

Case side

Drawer bottom

Front drawer stretcher

Rear bracket base

Center runner

Screw block

Side bracket base

Screw block

Corner bock

Dovetail, 1/4 in. high by 3/4 in. deep

Tenon, 1/4 in. thick by 3/4 in. long

Front bracket brace

BASE DETAIL

Chamfer, 3/8 in. by 3/8 in.

Rabbet, 1/4 in. by 1/4 in.

Mitered portion of joint, 1/2 in.

Fillet, 1/8 in.

2 5/8 in.

2 1/2 in.

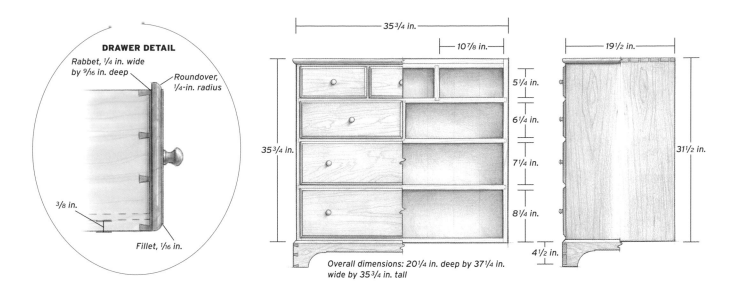

DRAWER DETAIL

Rabbet, 1/4 in. wide by 9/16 in. deep

Roundover, 1/4-in. radius

3/8 in.

Fillet, 1/16 in.

35 3/4 in.

10 7/8 in.

19 1/2 in.

35 3/4 in.

5 1/4 in.

6 1/4 in.

7 1/4 in.

8 1/4 in.

31 1/2 in.

4 1/2 in.

Overall dimensions: 20 1/4 in. deep by 37 1/4 in. wide by 35 3/4 in. tall

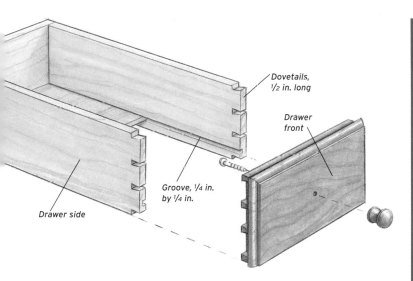

Dovetails, 1/2 in. long

Drawer front

Drawer side

Groove, 1/4 in. by 1/4 in.

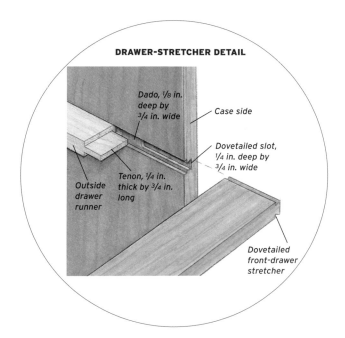

DRAWER-STRETCHER DETAIL

Dado, 1/8 in. deep by 3/4 in. wide

Case side

Dovetailed slot, 1/4 in. deep by 3/4 in. wide

Outside drawer runner

Tenon, 1/4 in. thick by 3/4 in. long

Dovetailed front-drawer stretcher

Cut List

WOOD	PART NAME	QUANTITY	DIMENSIONS
	Back boards	8	5/8 x 4 1/2 x 30 3/4
	Bracket base, front	1	3/4 x 4 1/2 x 36 3/4
	Bracket base, sides	2	3/4 x 4 1/2 x 20
	Case bottom	1	3/4 x 18 7/8 x 35 3/8
	Case sides	2	3/4 x 19 1/2 x 31 1/2
	Case top	1	3/4 x 19 1/2 x 35 3/4
	Drawer divider, second row	1	3/4 x 2 1/2 x 6 3/4
	Drawer dividers, top row	2	3/4 x 2 1/2 x 5 3/4
CHERRY	Drawer fronts, top row	3	7/8 x 5 3/8 x 11 3/8
	Drawer fronts, second row	2	7/8 x 6 3/8 x 17 1/4
	Drawer front, third row	1	7/8 x 7 3/8 x 34 3/4
	Drawer front, bottom row	1	7/8 x 8 3/8 x 34 3/4
	Drawer stretchers, front	3	3/4 x 2 1/2 x 35
	Molding, top front	1	3/4 x 1 x 37 1/4
	Moldings, top side	2	3/4 x 1 x 20 1/4
	Stretcher, top front	1	3/4 x 2 1/2 x 34 1/4
	Bracket base, rear	2	3/4 x 4 1/4 x 6
	Drawer backs, top row	3	1/2 x 4 1/2 x 10 7/8
	Drawer backs, second row	2	1/2 x 5 1/2 x 16 3/4
	Drawer back, third row	1	1/2 x 6 1/2 x 34 1/4
	Drawer back, bottom row	1	1/2 x 7 1/2 x 34 1/4
SOFT MAPLE	Drawer guides	3	3/4 x 1 x 13 3/4
	Drawer sides, top row	6	1/2 x 5 1/8 x 18
	Drawer sides, second row	4	1/2 x 6 1/8 x 18
	Drawer sides, third row	2	1/2 x 7 1/8 x 18
	Drawer sides, bottom row	2	1/2 x 8 1/8 x 18
	Drawer stretchers, rear	3	3/4 x 2 1/2 x 35
	Runners, outside	8	3/4 x 2 x 15 1/4
	Runners, center	5	3/4 x 3 x 15 1/4
	Stretcher, top rear	1	3/4 x 2 1/2 x 34 1/4
	Drawer bottoms, top row	3	1/2 x 17 3/4 x 10 3/8
	Drawer bottoms, second row	2	1/2 x 17 3/4 x 16 1/4
PINE	Drawer bottom, third row	1	1/2 x 17 3/4 x 33 3/4
	Drawer bottom, bottom row	1	1/2 x 17 3/4 x 33 3/4
	Misc. screw and corner blocks		3/4 in. thick

A SMALL BUREAU BUILT TO LAST

by Robert Treanor

The dovetail joint's prevalence and persistence is due to its unsurpassed ability to hold pieces of wood together. The painted chest of drawers I made illustrates the strength and versatility of the dovetail in a variety of forms. Tapered sliding half-dovetails lock the top to the sides; half-blind dovetails join the sides to the bottom; sliding dovetails link the drawer dividers to the sides; and through- and half-blind dovetails join the drawers.

All this dovetailing makes the piece rock solid, but the strength is all hidden from view. The chest has an unimposing scale that suits it to a living room, where it could stand at the end of a sofa and serve as an end table as well as a bureau. The moldings that hide its joinery are clean and simple, particularly the single-arch molding on the front of the chest with its bird's-mouth joints at the drawer dividers and its tapers, top and bottom.

A painted finish is in keeping with the early 18th-century origins of this chest of drawers. I like the finish for the bold field of color it provides from afar and for the way it emphasizes the texture of the wood when seen up close. I used Fancy Chair Green, a latex finish that simulates milk paint. On the drawers, I put strips of painter's masking tape just behind the lap of the half-blind dovetails, creating the detail shown in the photo on the facing page.

Robert Treanor, a former teacher in the woodworking program at San Francisco State University, builds and writes about furniture in the Bay Area.

Dovetails hide behind moldings and paint. *This sofa-side chest of drawers packs a robust array of joinery in a small frame.*

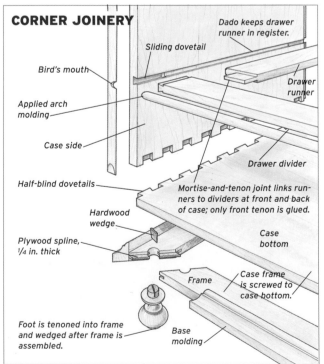

CORNER JOINERY

Dado keeps drawer runner in register.

Sliding dovetail

Bird's mouth

Applied arch molding

Case side

Drawer runner

Drawer divider

Half-blind dovetails

Mortise-and-tenon joint links runners to dividers at front and back of case; only front tenon is glued.

Hardwood wedge

Plywood spline, 1/4 in. thick

Case bottom

Case frame is screwed to case bottom.

Frame

Foot is tenoned into frame and wedged after frame is assembled.

Base molding

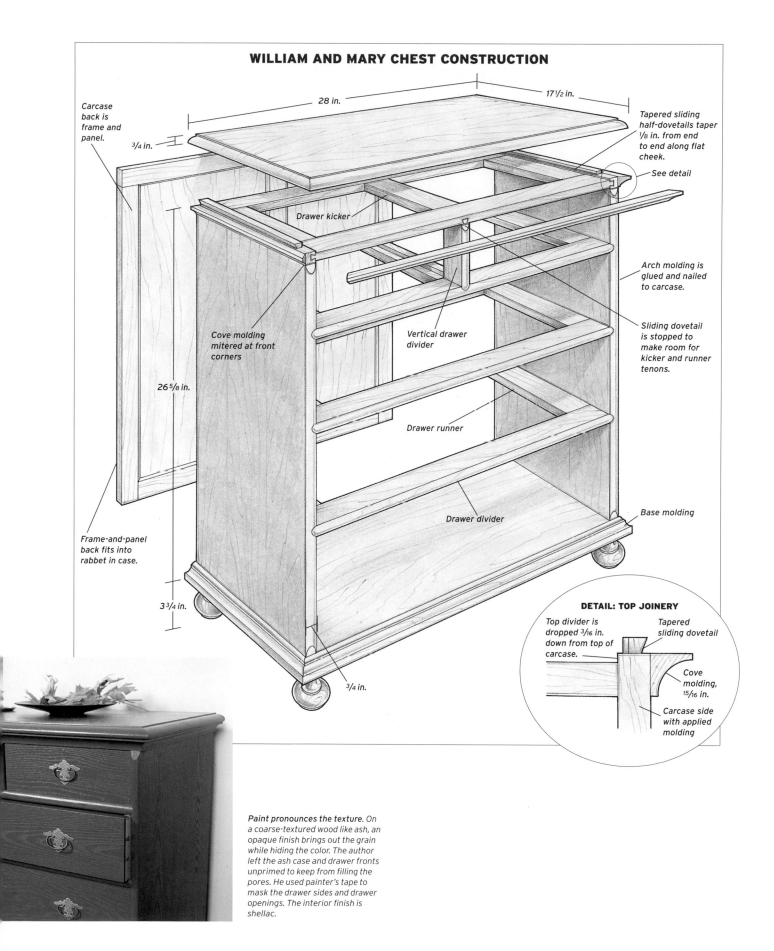

WILLIAM AND MARY CHEST CONSTRUCTION

28 in.

17½ in.

Carcase back is frame and panel.

¾ in.

Tapered sliding half-dovetails taper ⅛ in. from end to end along flat cheek.

See detail

Drawer kicker

Cove molding mitered at front corners

Vertical drawer divider

Arch molding is glued and nailed to carcase.

Sliding dovetail is stopped to make room for kicker and runner tenons.

26⅝ in.

Drawer runner

Drawer divider

Base molding

Frame-and-panel back fits into rabbet in case.

3¾ in.

¾ in.

DETAIL: TOP JOINERY

Top divider is dropped 3⁄16 in. down from top of carcase.

Tapered sliding dovetail

Cove molding, 15⁄16 in.

Carcase side with applied molding

Paint pronounces the texture. On a coarse-textured wood like ash, an opaque finish brings out the grain while hiding the color. The author left the ash case and drawer fronts unprimed to keep from filling the pores. He used painter's tape to mask the drawer sides and drawer openings. The interior finish is shellac.

A LITTLE MASTERPIECE

by Randall O'Donnell

Inside and outside come together. *After the carcase has been assembled, the dividers and valances are slid in from the back. The profiles of the drawer fronts match those of the drawer dividers and the base.*

As much as any known specimen, this 1750s document cabinet displays the creativity of the Rhode Island block-front style. Exquisitely crafted, this small piece possesses the features of the very best furniture made by the very best craftsmen. Most of the techniques are similar to those required to build any Newport block-front case piece. However, while you will save on materials, don't expect to save on time: The details and construction on such a small scale are very challenging (besides carving three fans, there are 271 hand-cut dovetails). This project will push your woodworking skills to a new level, but you will be rewarded with an exquisite piece of furniture.

Randall O'Donnell is a period furniture maker in Brown County, Indiana.

MAHOGANY DOCUMENT CABINET

The small size of this project allows you to spend money on some really good lumber. The author made the drawer sides from book-matched mahogany, but you can use a secondary wood (as shown here) and be faithful to the original.

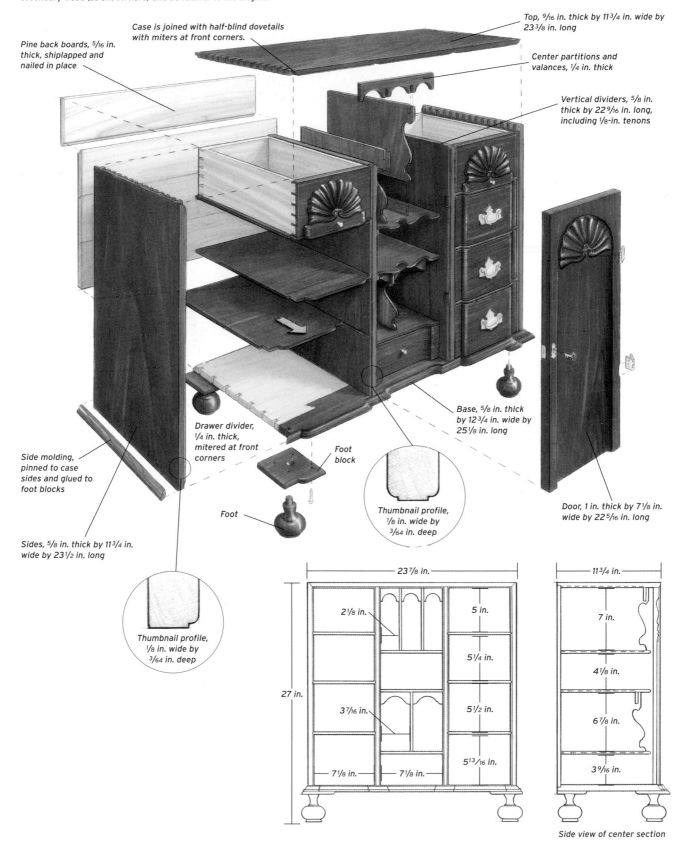

Top, 9/16 in. thick by 11 3/4 in. wide by 23 3/8 in. long

Case is joined with half-blind dovetails with miters at front corners.

Pine back boards, 5/16 in. thick, shiplapped and nailed in place

Center partitions and valances, 1/4 in. thick

Vertical dividers, 5/8 in. thick by 22 9/16 in. long, including 1/8-in. tenons

Side molding, pinned to case sides and glued to foot blocks

Drawer divider, 1/4 in. thick, mitered at front corners

Foot block

Foot

Thumbnail profile, 1/8 in. wide by 3/64 in. deep

Base, 5/8 in. thick by 12 3/4 in. wide by 25 1/8 in. long

Door, 1 in. thick by 7 1/8 in. wide by 22 5/16 in. long

Sides, 5/8 in. thick by 11 3/4 in. wide by 23 1/2 in. long

Thumbnail profile, 1/8 in. wide by 3/64 in. deep

23 7/8 in.

2 1/8 in.

5 in.

5 1/4 in.

5 1/2 in.

3 7/16 in.

5 13/16 in.

27 in.

7 1/8 in. 7 1/8 in.

11 3/4 in.

7 in.

4 1/8 in.

6 7/8 in.

3 9/16 in.

Side view of center section

Carving the Shells

The cabinet is graced by two convex shells, which are carved from wood resawn from the top drawer fronts and then reapplied. A third, concave shell is carved into the central door. While the concave and convex shells are similar, only the central fleurs-de-lis are identical.

Convex shells are applied to the drawer fronts.

The concave shell is carved into the door.

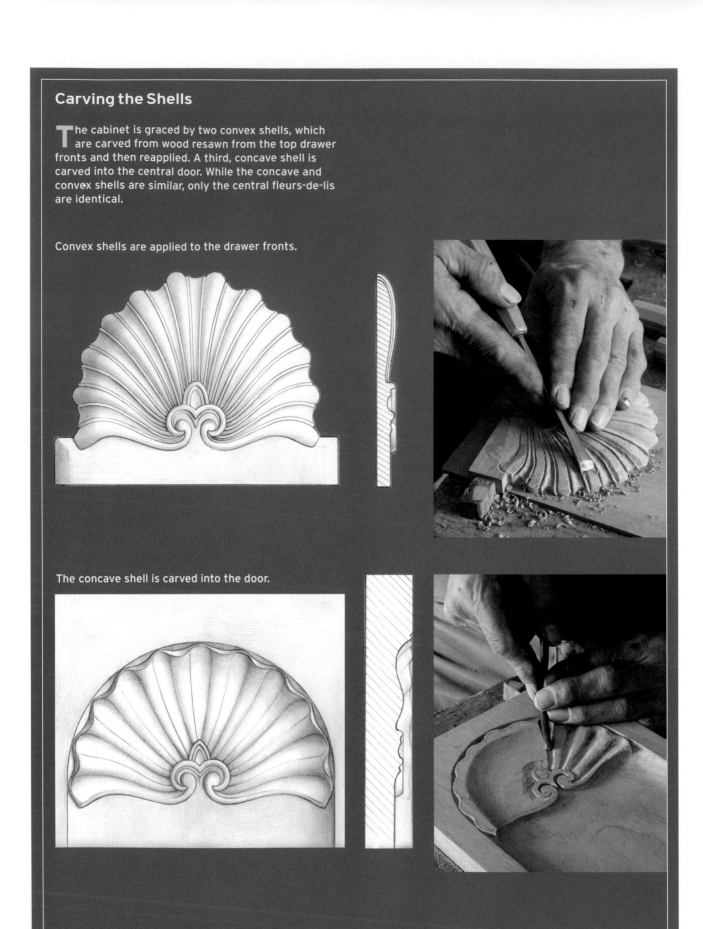

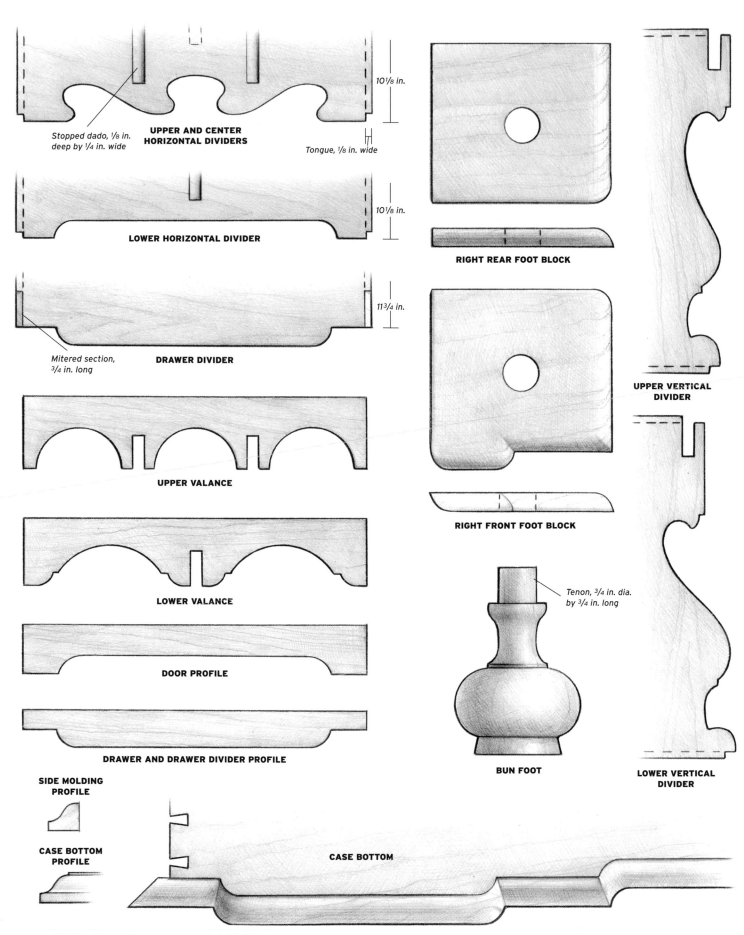

Stopped dado, 1/8 in. deep by 1/4 in. wide

UPPER AND CENTER HORIZONTAL DIVIDERS

Tongue, 1/8 in. wide

10 1/8 in.

LOWER HORIZONTAL DIVIDER

10 1/8 in.

Mitered section, 3/4 in. long

DRAWER DIVIDER

11 3/4 in.

UPPER VALANCE

LOWER VALANCE

DOOR PROFILE

DRAWER AND DRAWER DIVIDER PROFILE

SIDE MOLDING PROFILE

CASE BOTTOM PROFILE

CASE BOTTOM

RIGHT REAR FOOT BLOCK

RIGHT FRONT FOOT BLOCK

Tenon, 3/4 in. dia. by 3/4 in. long

BUN FOOT

UPPER VERTICAL DIVIDER

LOWER VERTICAL DIVIDER

Note: Drawings on this page are presented at half scale. Copy at 200% for full-size drawings.

COMPONENT-BUILT SIDEBOARD

by Seth Janofsky

As odd as it may sound at first, I think the finest furniture is the result of a lot of compromise. Not the kind of compromise that leads to cutting corners and doing less than the best possible work, but rather the compromise that's involved when you strive to balance three things: the aesthetic needs of a piece, the requirements of function, and construction that is sound and efficient. There should be a back-and-forth between aesthetics, function and construction during the design process; the craftsman has to see to it that all three purposes are well served and that none of the three dominates at the expense of the others. With skill and conscientious effort, and a little luck, the end result

will be a piece of furniture that sits, as it were, at the best possible balance point of these three demands.

When I set out to make this sideboard, I had a number of considerations in mind. In terms of function, I wanted a useful piece with a serving surface; compartments for dishes, probably with some adjustable shelves; and drawers for silverware. I didn't want a piece that was limited to use as a sideboard, however. I wanted one that could also function as a display cabinet for pottery or other decorative objects. Aesthetically, I had in mind something light and delicate looking, even as it was strong and durable. Nothing flamboyant but rather a quiet, refined kind

TWO CASES ON A BASE

For convenience of construction, the sideboard is built in stacking components. The upper case is indexed on the lower one by a pair of pins, and it can be lifted off; the base is screwed to the lower case. All parts are solid wood. To avoid wood-movement problems, the grain is run vertically on end panels and center partitions and end-to-end on horizontal panels.

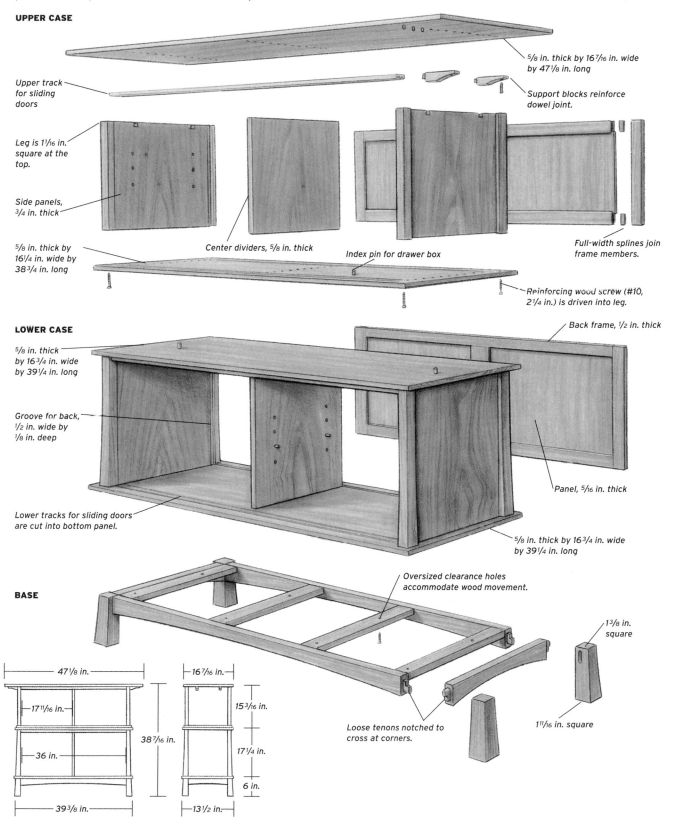

UPPER CASE

Upper track for sliding doors

5/8 in. thick by 16 7/16 in. wide by 47 1/8 in. long

Support blocks reinforce dowel joint.

Leg is 1 1/16 in. square at the top.

Side panels, 3/4 in. thick

5/8 in. thick by 16 1/4 in. wide by 38 3/4 in. long

Center dividers, 5/8 in. thick

Index pin for drawer box

Full-width splines join frame members.

Reinforcing wood screw (#10, 2 1/4 in.) is driven into leg.

LOWER CASE

5/8 in. thick by 16 3/4 in. wide by 39 1/4 in. long

Back frame, 1/2 in. thick

Groove for back, 1/2 in. wide by 1/8 in. deep

Panel, 5/16 in. thick

Lower tracks for sliding doors are cut into bottom panel.

5/8 in. thick by 16 3/4 in. wide by 39 1/4 in. long

BASE

Oversized clearance holes accommodate wood movement.

1 3/8 in. square

Loose tenons notched to cross at corners.

1 11/16 in. square

47 1/8 in.
17 11/16 in.
36 in.
39 3/8 in.
16 7/16 in.
15 3/16 in.
17 1/4 in.
6 in.
38 7/16 in.
13 1/2 in.

SLIDING DOORS AND THE DRAWER BOX

SLIDING DOORS

Providing closure without hardware, sliding doors are simple, functiona and elegant. Bridle-joined white oak frames surround cedar panels. Handles are scooped out on a router table against a high fence.

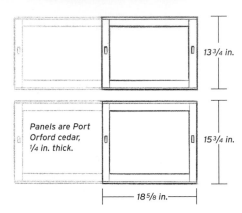

13 3/4 in.

Panels are Port Orford cedar, 1/4 in. thick.

15 3/4 in.

18 5/8 in.

1/4 in.

3/8 in.

1 3/8 in.

Rail

Rabbet cuts away the stile and glue line, revealing the rail.

1/8 in.

Stile

1 3/8 in.

1/2 in.

1 1/2 in.

Rail

Rabbet, 1/8 in. by 1/8 in.

1/4-in. space permits door to be lifted out of the lower track and swung forward for removal.

Chamfer eases insertion and removal of door.

Door rides on this ridge, not on the bottom of the groove.

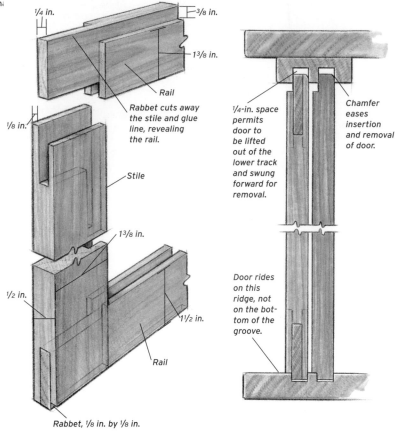

DRAWER BOX

The solid wood box is a separate component, which is indexed on a pin, and can be removed, if necessary. Inset sides facilitate fitting and create clearance on both sides of an opened drawer.

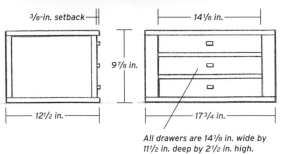

3/8-in. setback

14 1/8 in.

9 7/8 in.

12 1/2 in.

17 3/4 in.

All drawers are 14 1/8 in. wide by 11 1/2 in. deep by 2 1/2 in. high.

Top, bottom, and side panels, 5/8 in. thick

3/4 in.

Drawer dividers, 9/16 in. thick

Stopped groove mates with spline in the side of the box.

Drawers

Seth Janofsky doesn't argue the effectiveness of the dovetail joint, but for a change of pace he sometimes substitutes a handsome, half-blind, multiple through-tenon joint of his own devising.

Start with a square groove. The joint begins with blade-width grooves cut in the drawer sides. Blade height is set to half the thickness of the side. A flat-topped rip blade creates a clean, square-topped kerf.

Minimortises. Using a horizontal mortiser and a 1/8-in.-dia. end mill bit, the author cuts through-mortises in the drawer sides exactly aligned with the tablesawn groove.

Long tongue. In the first step toward making tenons, a tongue is made at each end of the drawer fronts and backs with two cuts on the tablesaw. The tongue is as long as the sides are thick.

File it away. A file is used to square up the round corners left by the mortiser. This takes time, so be sure to use a sharp file small enough to maneuver easily.

Mark through the mortises. To mark out the tenons, the author pushes the tongues into the grooves. Then he traces the mortises with a sharp pencil.

Quick saw. A thin saw makes quick work of cutting the tenons.

Chisel out the middle. Between the tenons where the handsaw won't reach, the author chops out the waste with a bench chisel. The waste can also be removed with the part held upright on a tablesaw crosscut sled.

Going home. The completed drawer, ready to be glued up and then veneered front and back.

A new face. Thick, shop-sawn veneers are glued to the front and back, tidying up and strengthening the joint.

Apt joinery. Squared-off tenons suit the author's largely rectilinear sideboard.

of thing. As for the specific style, I explored in the general direction of other cabinets I've made, which blend traditional Japanese and Scandinavian-modern influences. In terms of construction, I wanted solid, straightforward joinery—structurally sound, efficient to make, subjugated to the quiet design I envisioned.

Putting these factors together, I came up with a solid white oak sideboard that is, in its essence, simply two boxes on a base. To best use the beautiful wide boards I found, I opted for a solid wood structure, which is a hybrid of simple plank construction and post-and-panel construction. A top surface with long overhangs on both ends showcases the single-board top and establishes the visual tone of the piece. To give the separate boxes visual unity and to create a vertical sweep to balance the strong horizontal line of the top, I designed curved legs that extend up through the piece. The legs have a powerful impact both on the aesthetics of the sideboard and on the method of construction. They provide just one example among many of how an aesthetic decision dictates to the technical, and how the technical responds to the aesthetic and exerts its influence. Likewise with the functional requirements. Back and forth, as the design comes together.

Seth Janofsky is a furniture craftsman in Fort Bragg, California.

A STYLISH CREDENZA

by Patrick Warner

Symmetry and subtle shadow lines give Patrick Warner's maple and yellow satinwood office credenza a dynamic visual rhythm. The same piece could serve as a buffet or as a case for audio and video equipment.

redenza, the Italian word for sideboard, has come to mean a low, lateral piece of office furniture for storage. I designed this one for my office at home, and its dimensions and organization reflect that. It's fairly shallow because I couldn't afford to lose much floor space and because I don't like deep shelves—you can never get to the stuff at the back. Its top is counter height: I wanted to be able to work at it standing up sometimes. I chose sliding doors for the piece because of the tight quarters and because I like to roam around on my castered chair and

don't need more obstacles. But part of the piece's beauty is that all these elements are adaptable to your own situation and so is the overall function of the piece.

I decided early on that the whole thing would be solid maple with a top and accents of yellow satinwood. I planned a fairly simple box carcase lifted off the ground by a separate and removable base. I hoped the base would lend the piece an airy feeling and avoid the impression of immovable weight that such office furniture often gives.

Angled forms play off straight lines. Floating dovetail wedges, tapered muntins and recessed triangular handholds form a subtheme in Warner's rectilinear composition in lines and planes.

Patrick Warner manufactures the Warner router base and teaches woodworking at Palomar Community College in San Marcos, California.

CREDENZA

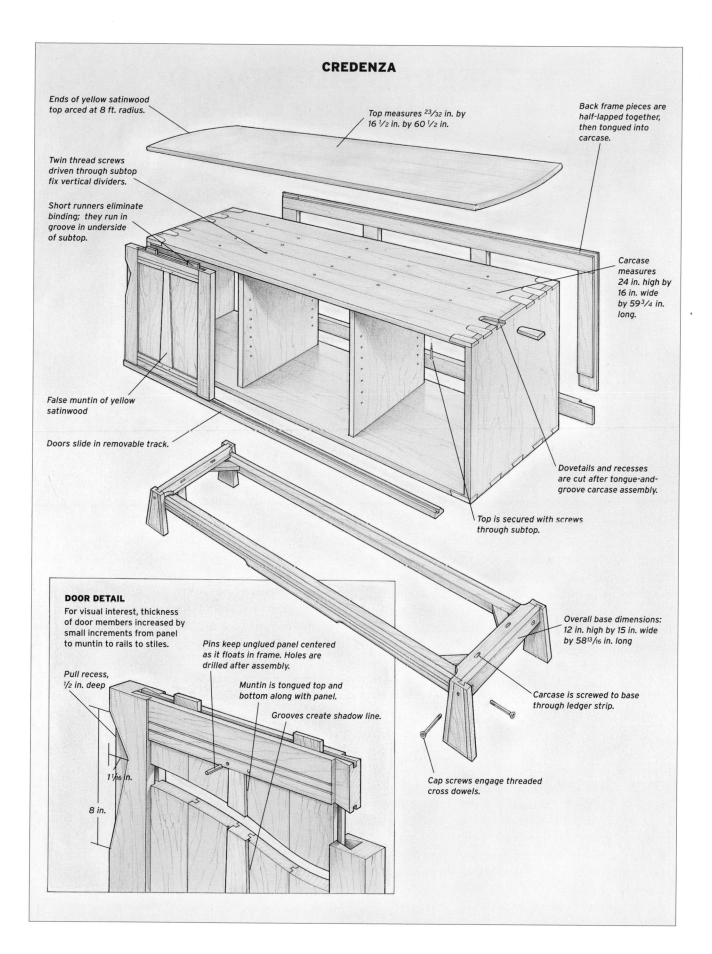

Ends of yellow satinwood top arced at 8 ft. radius.

Top measures ²³/₃₂ in. by 16 ¹/₂ in. by 60 ¹/₂ in.

Back frame pieces are half-lapped together, then tongued into carcase.

Twin thread screws driven through subtop fix vertical dividers.

Short runners eliminate binding; they run in groove in underside of subtop.

Carcase measures 24 in. high by 16 in. wide by 59³/₄ in. long.

False muntin of yellow satinwood

Doors slide in removable track.

Dovetails and recesses are cut after tongue-and-groove carcase assembly.

Top is secured with screws through subtop.

DOOR DETAIL

For visual interest, thickness of door members increased by small increments from panel to muntin to rails to stiles.

Pins keep unglued panel centered as it floats in frame. Holes are drilled after assembly.

Muntin is tongued top and bottom along with panel.

Grooves create shadow line.

Pull recess, ¹/₂ in. deep

1¹/₁₆ in.

8 in.

Overall base dimensions: 12 in. high by 15 in. wide by 58¹³/₁₆ in. long

Carcase is screwed to base through ledger strip.

Cap screws engage threaded cross dowels.

VENEERED SIDEBOARD

by Paul Harrell

Sideboard squeezed from a small plank. By doing his own sawing, the author coaxed the primary veneer and edging for this sideboard from a single plank of jarrah. The legs, stretchers and lighter veneer are mahogany.

I recently came upon a beautiful plank of jarrah—a hard, heavy Australian wood—that was exactly what I wanted for a piece of furniture I was planning. The plank was small, though, only 5 ft. long, 1¾ in. thick, and less than 6 in. wide. The only way I could get much use out of it was to saw it into veneer. With some careful planning, I squeezed out of it all the veneers and edge-bandings I needed to make the sideboard seen here. The same plank, just about 4 bd. ft., wouldn't have been enough to make even the top of the piece if I'd used it as solid.

I make my veneer on the bandsaw, cutting sheets 3/32 in. thick, which is thick enough to be worked much like solid wood with both hand and power tools. It's also stiff enough to be edge-joined with wedge-clamp pressure. The finished surface is more forgiving and durable than thinner commercial veneer (generally 1/28 in.). I also prefer shop-sawn veneer to the commercial variety because I can cut the solid-wood parts of a piece (legs, frame members, edge-bandings, pulls) from the same planks as the veneer. This means more control in matching grain and color patterns throughout the piece.

The plank of jarrah was straight-grained for most of its length but had an interesting pattern at one end. I decided to use the straight-grained veneer for the top, end panels, and drawer fronts, and the patterned veneer for the doors. I picked Honduras mahogany for the other parts of the sideboard because the color worked so well with the jarrah. I try to find straight-grained, rift-sawn stock for legs and stretchers so the grain will be calm and not distract from the veneered surfaces.

The legs taper and flare out slightly, which I think gives the piece a solid base. All the stretchers are curved on the bottom, but, like the legs, the curves are subtle—just enough to give the sideboard a little lift. The drawers are set back slightly from the doors, which helps to break up the plane of the front. I wasn't trying for drama in this piece, just using grain patterns, color, and gentle curves that all work together. The overall dimensions are 33 in. tall, 37½ in. wide, and 16 in. deep.

Paul Harrell is a furniture maker in Pittsboro, North Carolina.

A SIDEBOARD WITH SHOP-SAWN VENEER

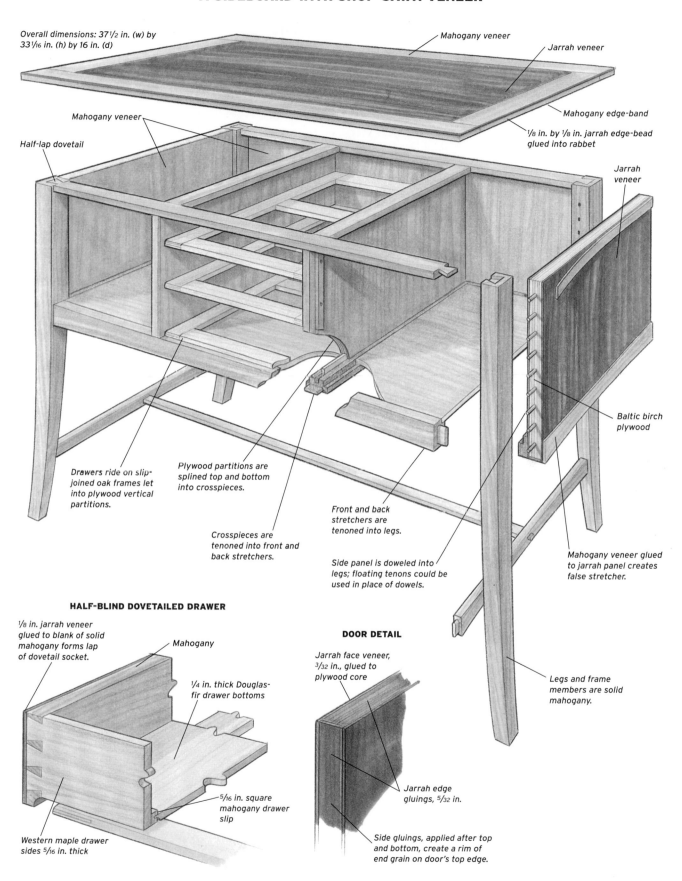

Overall dimensions: 37½ in. (w) by 33¹/₁₆ in. (h) by 16 in. (d)

Mahogany veneer

Jarrah veneer

Mahogany edge-band

⅛ in. by ⅛ in. jarrah edge-bead glued into rabbet

Mahogany veneer

Half-lap dovetail

Jarrah veneer

Baltic birch plywood

Drawers ride on slip-joined oak frames let into plywood vertical partitions.

Plywood partitions are splined top and bottom into crosspieces.

Crosspieces are tenoned into front and back stretchers.

Front and back stretchers are tenoned into legs.

Side panel is doweled into legs; floating tenons could be used in place of dowels.

Mahogany veneer glued to jarrah panel creates false stretcher.

Legs and frame members are solid mahogany.

HALF-BLIND DOVETAILED DRAWER

⅛ in. jarrah veneer glued to blank of solid mahogany forms lap of dovetail socket.

Mahogany

¼ in. thick Douglas-fir drawer bottoms

⁵/₁₆ in. square mahogany drawer slip

Western maple drawer sides ⁵/₁₆ in. thick

DOOR DETAIL

Jarrah face veneer, ³/₃₂ in., glued to plywood core

Jarrah edge gluings, ⁵/₃₂ in.

Side gluings, applied after top and bottom, create a rim of end grain on door's top edge.

HALL TABLE

by Garrett Hack

Designing and building smaller, more delicate pieces that still will stand up to the rigors of normal household life is a challenge of its own. Perhaps the most difficult situation is the table or desk with drawers.

Three pieces of wood joined to form a U-shape have virtually no structural integrity. Exert a little pressure on one side, and the corner joint will fail.

Furniture makers have come up with various ways of strengthening desks and tables whose fronts are mostly drawers, such as beefing up the frame internally and using heavy-duty front rails. Neither of these is ideal. An internal frame (basically, a shallow box around the internal perimeter of the carcase, sometimes with a crossbar) reduces usable drawer space, and thick, bulky front rails may fit the bill structurally, but they aren't the most aesthetic solution. My solution addresses both of these shortcomings.

Unless you use it to stand on while changing a lightbulb, most of the stress on a piece of furniture like this is from racking, not downward compression. What's needed, then, are not massive front rails, but deep rails—rails that tie the front of the piece to the three solid sides of the carcase and provide maximum resistance to racking. Together with the table's leg-and-apron construction, these thin, deep rails ensure a piece of furniture that is tough but still looks quite refined.

Garrett Hack is a furniture designer, furniture maker, and one-horse farmer in Thetford Center, Vermont.

Rosewood pegs strengthen the joint, and they add a distinctive touch to the author's table. The adjustable wrench keeps the pegs properly oriented, parallel to the case's top and sides, as they're driven home.

SHAKER SIDE TABLE

Simple lines, remarkable woods, and structural integrity combine with impeccable craftsmanship to make the author's Shaker-inspired hall table a jewel in wood. All drawer faces are from one pear board; the carcase is carefully grain- and figure-matched bird's-eye maple, and the pulls and pegs are rosewood.

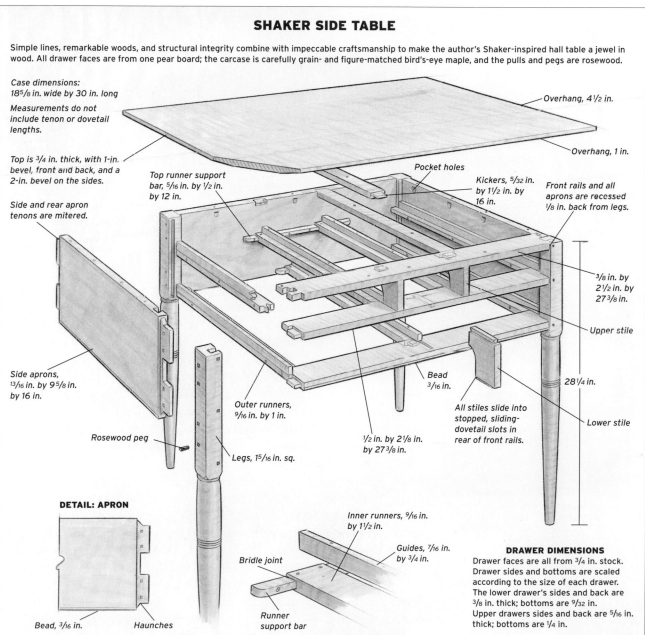

Case dimensions:
18⅝ in. wide by 30 in. long

Measurements do not include tenon or dovetail lengths.

Top is ¾ in. thick, with 1-in. bevel, front and back, and a 2-in. bevel on the sides.

Side and rear apron tenons are mitered.

Side aprons, ¹³/₁₆ in. by 9⅝ in. by 16 in.

Rosewood peg

Top runner support bar, ⁵/₁₆ in. by ½ in. by 12 in.

Outer runners, ⁹/₁₆ in. by 1 in.

Legs, 1⁵/₁₆ in. sq.

Pocket holes

Kickers, ⁵/₃₂ in. by 1½ in. by 16 in.

Overhang, 4½ in.

Overhang, 1 in.

Front rails and all aprons are recessed ⅛ in. back from legs.

⅜ in. by 2½ in. by 27⅜ in.

Upper stile

28¼ in.

Bead ³/₁₆ in.

All stiles slide into stopped, sliding-dovetail slots in rear of front rails.

Lower stile

½ in. by 2⅛ in. by 27⅜ in.

DETAIL: APRON

Bead, ³/₁₆ in.   Haunches

Bridle joint

Runner support bar

Inner runners, ⁹/₁₆ in. by 1½ in.

Guides, ⁷/₁₆ in. by ¾ in.

DRAWER DIMENSIONS
Drawer faces are all from ¾ in. stock. Drawer sides and bottoms are scaled according to the size of each drawer. The lower drawer's sides and back are ⅜ in. thick; bottoms are ⁹/₃₂ in. Upper drawers sides and back are ⁵/₁₆ in. thick; bottoms are ¼ in.

CONTEMPORARY CABINET

by Mark Edmundson

Dowel centers ensure matching holes. *Attach the legs to the bottom panel with two short dowels. Then drill a third hole through the bottom panel into the leg to accept a longer dowel that will extend up into the case side.*

One look at a stack of hardwood plywood and you know why there are fewer and fewer nice planks in a unit of lumber. The best logs are scooped up by veneer mills, ending up in kitchen cabinets and mass-produced entertainment centers. Wanting to rescue these attractive panels, I had to find a way to turn them into pieces my clients would accept as custom furniture. The freestanding cabinet featured here incorporates many of the techniques I've developed for overcoming the inherent drawbacks of using plywood.

By laminating ¼-in.-thick panels around a core of medium-density fiberboard (MDF), I create custom panels that are thicker than the standard ¾ in. This technique also allows me to contrast the exterior wood with a different interior species—in the cabinet shown here I used cherry and maple. I also locate the veneer seams carefully to create a solid-wood effect. The solid legs, corner posts, and door frames add to the furniture feel. Other custom touches include the raised-panel treatment on the plywood door panels and the mitered edge-banding on the top and bottom. The top also has a raised lip, or "pencil roll," applied at the back edge. An attractive drawer box, custom door pulls, and nice hinges complete the piece.

Mark Edmundson is a furniture maker in northern Idaho.

ASSEMBLY STRATEGIES FOR PLYWOOD FURNITURE

Edmundson uses biscuits and dowels for both strength and alignment. Custom panel thicknesses, innovative edge treatments, and a slide-in drawer assembly elevate a plywood case to custom furniture.

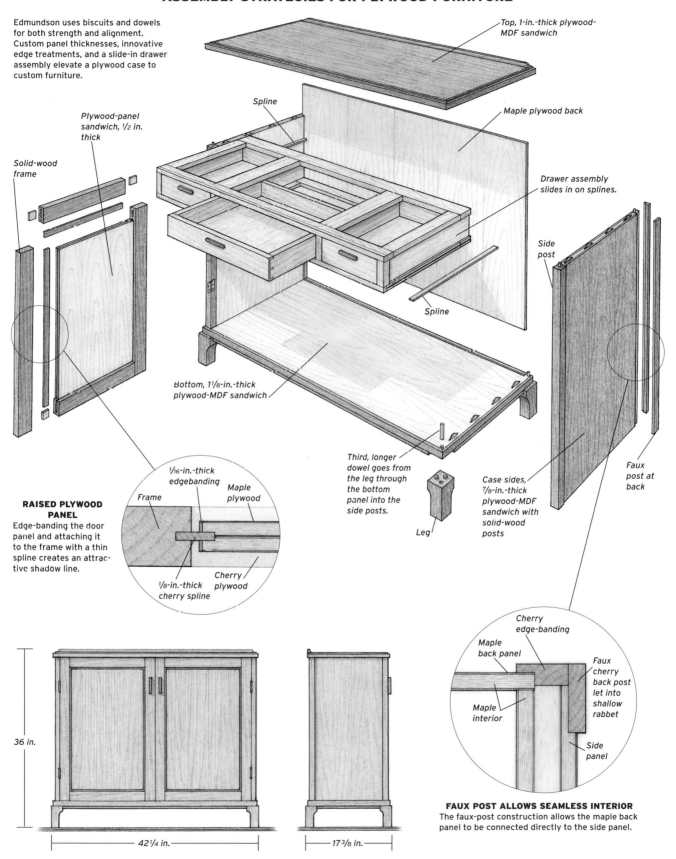

Top, 1-in.-thick plywood-MDF sandwich

Spline

Maple plywood back

Plywood-panel sandwich, 1/2 in. thick

Drawer assembly slides in on splines.

Solid-wood frame

Side post

Spline

Bottom, 1⅛-in.-thick plywood-MDF sandwich

Third, longer dowel goes from the leg through the bottom panel into the side posts.

Leg

Case sides, ⅞-in.-thick plywood-MDF sandwich with solid-wood posts

Faux post at back

RAISED PLYWOOD PANEL

Edge-banding the door panel and attaching it to the frame with a thin spline creates an attractive shadow line.

Frame

1/16-in.-thick edgebanding

Maple plywood

1/8-in.-thick cherry spline

Cherry plywood

FAUX POST ALLOWS SEAMLESS INTERIOR

The faux-post construction allows the maple back panel to be connected directly to the side panel.

Cherry edge-banding

Maple back panel

Faux cherry back post let into shallow rabbet

Maple interior

Side panel

36 in.

42¼ in.

17⅜ in.

Apply edgebanding. Edmundson uses Bessey K-Body® clamps to hold everything square, and MDF cauls to distribute the pressure over the 3/8-in.-thick banding.

CASE TOP: A LESSON IN EDGEBANDING

The edgebandings on the top and bottom are mitered at their front edges for a better-looking corner. But they're not mitered at the back edges, which makes it much easier to apply the side edgebandings.

PENCIL-ROLL DETAIL

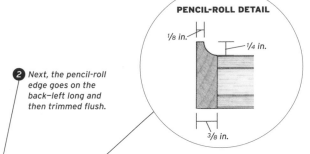

1/8 in.   1/4 in.

3/8 in.

2 *Next, the pencil-roll edge goes on the back—left long and then trimmed flush.*

PENCIL-ROLL PROFILE

1/4 in.

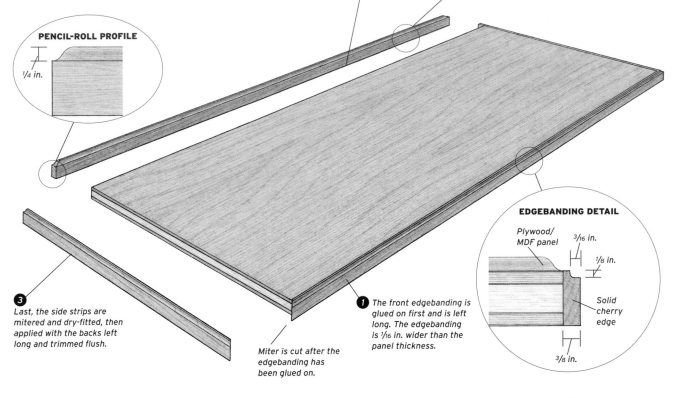

3 *Last, the side strips are mitered and dry-fitted, then applied with the backs left long and trimmed flush.*

Miter is cut after the edgebanding has been glued on.

1 *The front edgebanding is glued on first and is left long. The edgebanding is 1/16 in. wider than the panel thickness.*

EDGEBANDING DETAIL

Plywood/ MDF panel   3/16 in.

1/8 in.

Solid cherry edge

3/8 in.

Plane and scrape the edge-banding flush. *Don't go too far with the block plane before switching to a scraper. Use pencil squiggles to avoid the plywood.*

Miter the front edgebanding after it has been applied. *This sounds counterintuitive, but it's easier to glue a long strip on this large panel when you don't have to line up precut miters perfectly. Lay out the cuts, saw close to the line (left), then clamp on a guide block for the final paring (right). Miter the side edgebanding to fit.*

Detail the pencil roll. *The side edgebandings are butted against the pencil roll at the back. Edmundson carves a gentle S-curve on the ends of the roll lip.*

PEGGED POST-AND-BEAM ARMOIRE KNOCKS DOWN

by Chris Gochnour

Three skins, one skeleton. *The author's armoires in an array of styles all use a centuries-old cabinet structure originally borrowed from post-and-beam houses. The post-and-beam structure makes a cabinet that is strong and handsome and perfectly accommodates wood movement. If the major joints are pegged instead of glued, the cabinet can also be knocked down for transport or repair.*

The trouble with most armoires is that if they're big enough to fit all your clothes—or electronic gear, board games, or books— they're too big to fit through the door. This was brought home to me forcefully on several occasions when I received distress calls from people who, knowing I was a furniture maker, thought I might have a trick for shrinking the armoire they just bought to get it through their doorway. I soon found myself amputating a foot here, prying off a glued-on crown molding there.... When I decided to build an armoire myself, I discovered that a fine solution to this doorway dilemma has been around for centuries: the post-and-beam cabinet with pegged mortise-and-tenon joints.

Dutch and German *kasts*, Spanish *trasteros*, French *armoires*, and Chinese *gui* all were large storage cabinets designed around a straightforward post-and-beam structure, a system sturdy enough to have been employed as well to construct the very houses these cabinets resided in. Post-and-beam cabinet construction—vertical posts and horizontal beams connected by large mortise-and-tenon joints—creates a framework that, once secured with drawbore pegs, is very rigid and durable. Yet it can be easily disassembled into small, maneuverable components.

I particularly admire the beauty and grand scale of antique French armoires, and I've made several of them. But I've also built armoires in the Southwest style and the Arts and Crafts style, and I have found that the post-and-beam structure is adaptable to a range of styles.

Designing a post-and-beam cabinet begins with its primary skeletal structure: four corner posts connected by wide rails top and bottom. The strength of the

The skeleton of a French armoire in knotty alder stands dry-assembled with all its parts and panels leaning against it.

cabinet is derived mainly from these members and the joinery that connects them. For maximum stability in my large country French armoire, I used posts a beefy $2^{5}/_{8}$ in. sq. with rails ranging from 4 in. to 8 in. wide. Posts this big can accommodate large mortises without being unduly weakened; rails this wide have room for substantial shoulders along with wide tenons. On the widest rails, I used two tenons and left a bridge between them.

After the basic skeleton is designed, I subdivide the cabinet sides and back using rails and muntins. The subdivision creates smaller, more manageable panel sizes, has a strong visual effect, and contributes to the overall strength of the cabinet.

Embellishing the framework is the final step in the design process. Because the primary skeletal structure doesn't differ much from piece to piece, it is largely the details that distinguish one post-and-beam cabinet from another. These can include decorative panels, doors, crown and other moldings, turnings, and carvings.

Chris Gochnour builds furniture in Salt Lake City, Utah.

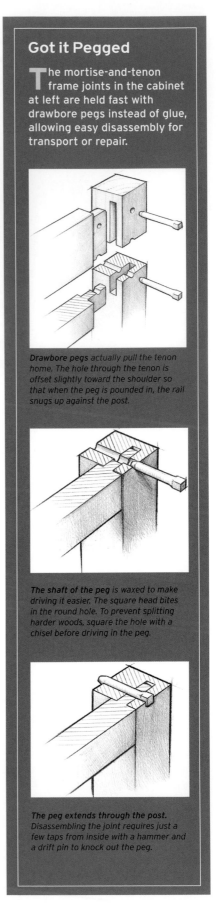

Got it Pegged

The mortise-and-tenon frame joints in the cabinet at left are held fast with drawbore pegs instead of glue, allowing easy disassembly for transport or repair.

Drawbore pegs actually pull the tenon home. The hole through the tenon is offset slightly toward the shoulder so that when the peg is pounded in, the rail snugs up against the post.

The shaft of the peg is waxed to make driving it easier. The square head bites in the round hole. To prevent splitting harder woods, square the hole with a chisel before driving in the peg.

The peg extends through the post. Disassembling the joint requires just a few taps from inside with a hammer and a drift pin to knock out the peg.

POST-AND-BEAM ARMOIRE

Main carcase joints are knockdown, secured with drawbore pegs. This country French piece is 57½ in. wide and 24 in. deep.

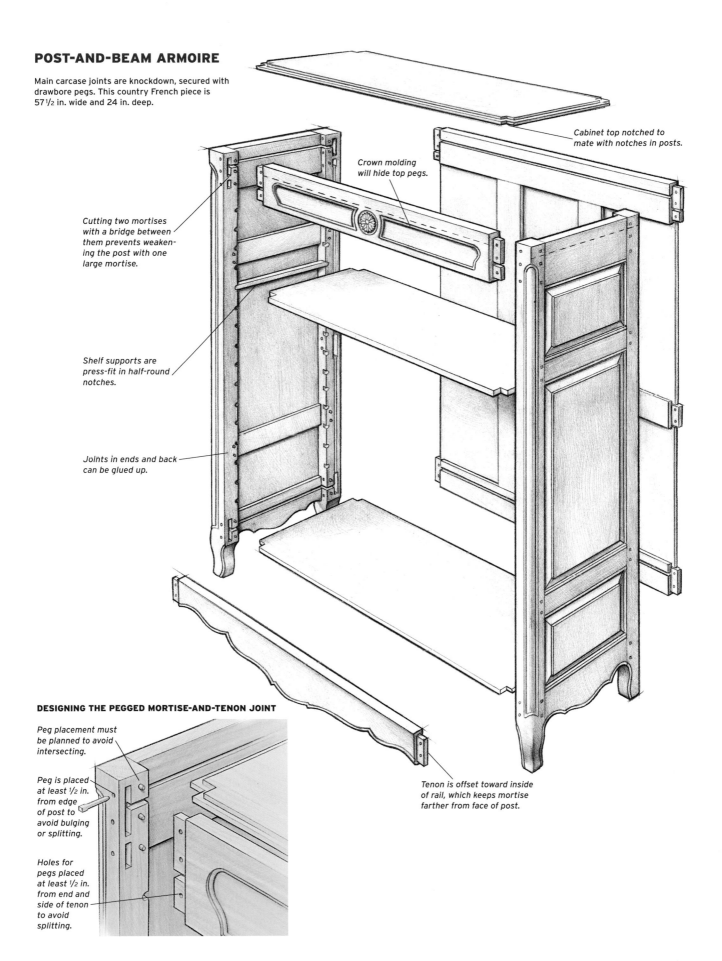

Cabinet top notched to mate with notches in posts.

Crown molding will hide top pegs.

Cutting two mortises with a bridge between them prevents weakening the post with one large mortise.

Shelf supports are press-fit in half-round notches.

Joints in ends and back can be glued up.

DESIGNING THE PEGGED MORTISE-AND-TENON JOINT

Peg placement must be planned to avoid intersecting.

Peg is placed at least ½ in. from edge of post to avoid bulging or splitting.

Holes for pegs placed at least ½ in. from end and side of tenon to avoid splitting.

Tenon is offset toward inside of rail, which keeps mortise farther from face of post.

ENTERTAINMENT CENTER IN QUARTERSAWN MAPLE

by Peter Turner

As my 2-year-old daughter, Morrigan, grew and became more mobile and curious, so did the urgency to design and build an entertainment center. My aim was to keep the unit looking more like a piece of furniture than a refrigerator while efficiently housing the television, VCR, and other audio components out of sight and temptation's way.

In an effort to move away from the large, heavy look of a typical entertainment center, my first design ended up as a horizontal case on a skinny, four-legged frame. I eventually scrapped this design because I realized the weight of components, especially a television, would overwhelm such a delicate piece. Instead, the cabinet evolved into a more conventional two-piece structure, with a lower section housing three drawers for storage of CDs and tapes and a slightly narrower but taller upper section enclosed by a pair of doors. I did what I could to keep the piece from getting bulky by maximizing the usable internal space and adding soft curves to the exterior, which help mask its rather hefty dimensions.

I chose cranked door hinges that allow a door to be opened a full 270 degrees instead of pocket door hardware, which would have added several inches to the width of the piece. The curved legs lift the case off the floor and help reduce its visual weight. And to blend the lower case with the upper, I applied cove moldings at the waist and at the crown. I really like the swoop of a cove, which lends vitality to a piece.

To ensure that components such as an amplifier, tuner, and CD player and a television would fit inside the upper cabinet, I took a tape measure to my electronic gear. I also checked the dimensions of stereo and TV components at an electronics store. New electronic components are fairly standardized, being about 17 in. wide or less and just a few inches tall. Older components vary more in size. I settled on four 18-in.-wide adjustable shelves that are shallower than the interior of the case, which allows room for routing wires and for air circulation. The cabinet will easily hold half a dozen components plus a 27-in. television. The back of the upper case has a panelless frame, which makes for easy access to wires and lets the heat produced by a television escape.

With the help of a friend, Sam Robinson, I built the cabinet within a narrow time frame—one month—because I wanted to exhibit the piece at the

FRAME-AND-PANEL BASE

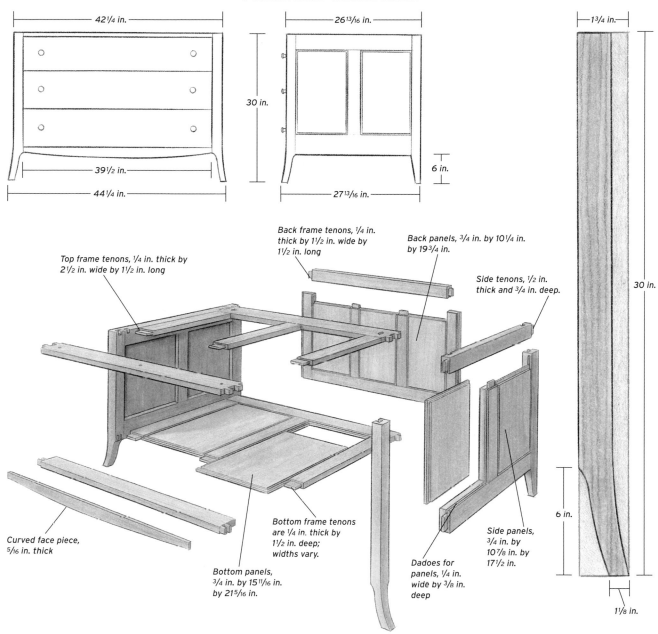

42¼ in.

26¹³/₁₆ in.

1¾ in.

30 in.

39½ in.

44¼ in.

27¹³/₁₆ in.

6 in.

30 in.

6 in.

1⅛ in.

Top frame tenons, ¼ in. thick by 2½ in. wide by 1½ in. long

Back frame tenons, ¼ in. thick by 1½ in. wide by 1½ in. long

Back panels, ¾ in. by 10¼ in. by 19¾ in.

Side tenons, ½ in. thick and ¾ in. deep.

Curved face piece, 5/₁₆ in. thick

Bottom frame tenons are ¼ in. thick by 1½ in. deep; widths vary.

Bottom panels, ¾ in. by 15¹¹/₁₆ in. by 21⁵/₁₆ in.

Dadoes for panels, ¼ in. wide by ⅜ in. deep

Side panels, ¾ in. by 10⅞ in. by 17½ in.

Philadelphia Furniture Show. Sam was assigned the upper case, and I took on the lower box. We kept our fingers crossed and hoped that the bridge would eventually meet in the middle.

Quartersawn maple is the predominant wood used in the piece. The wood was chosen for its light color and subtle grain. Soft maple was used for the drawer sides and one internal frame. The drawer bottoms are made of plywood.

My local hardwood supplier, Dennis Day of Day Hardwoods in Scarborough, Maine, has a knack for finding high-quality wood at fair prices. He supplied me with 200 bd. ft. of quartersawn maple with several pieces close to 8 in. wide, unusually wide for quartersawn stock. The widest planks were used for visible panels and drawer fronts. The narrower stock was used for frames, internal panels, and shelves.

We were unable to locate thicker quartersawn stock, so we used plainsawn 16/4 material when needed, sawing it to best show off the grain.

Peter Turner builds custom furniture in Portland, Maine.

DOVETAILED UPPER CASE

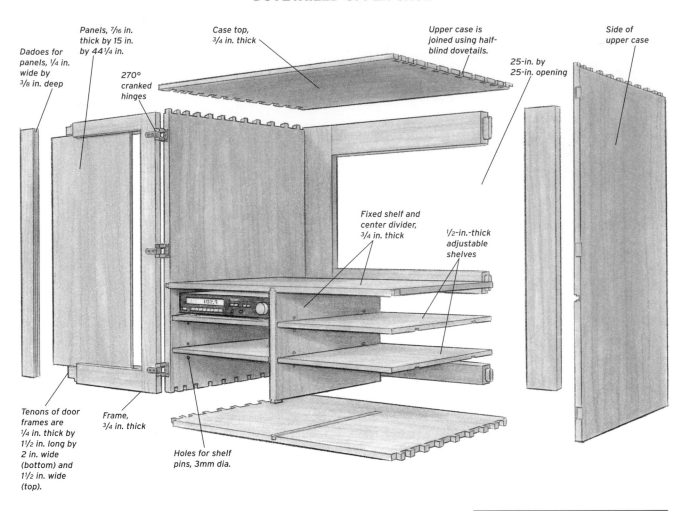

Dadoes for panels, 1/4 in. wide by 3/8 in. deep

Panels, 7/16 in. thick by 15 in. by 44 1/4 in.

270° cranked hinges

Case top, 3/4 in. thick

Upper case is joined using half-blind dovetails.

25-in. by 25-in. opening

Side of upper case

Fixed shelf and center divider, 3/4 in. thick

1/2-in.-thick adjustable shelves

Tenons of door frames are 1/4 in. thick by 1 1/2 in. long by 2 in. wide (bottom) and 1 1/2 in. wide (top).

Frame, 3/4 in. thick

Holes for shelf pins, 3mm dia.

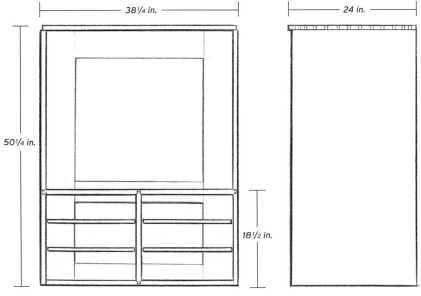

38 1/4 in.

24 in.

50 1/4 in.

18 1/2 in.

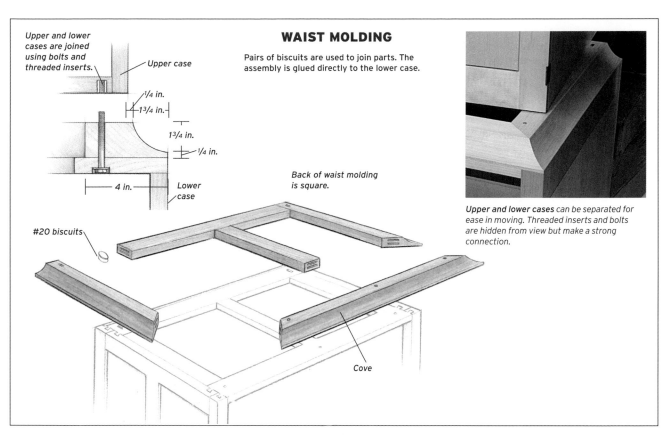

WAIST MOLDING

Pairs of biscuits are used to join parts. The assembly is glued directly to the lower case.

Upper and lower cases are joined using bolts and threaded inserts.

Upper case

¹/₄ in.

1³/₄ in.

1³/₄ in.

¹/₄ in.

4 in.

Lower case

#20 biscuits

Back of waist molding is square.

Cove

Upper and lower cases can be separated for ease in moving. Threaded inserts and bolts are hidden from view but make a strong connection.

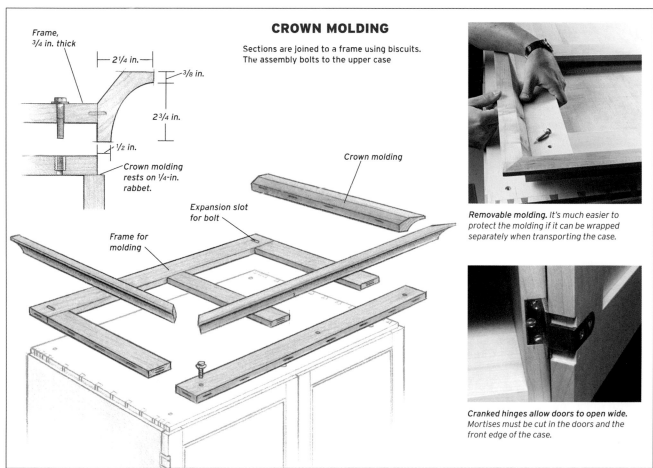

CROWN MOLDING

Sections are joined to a frame using biscuits. The assembly bolts to the upper case

Frame, ³/₄ in. thick

2¹/₄ in.

³/₈ in.

2³/₄ in.

¹/₂ in.

Crown molding rests on ¹/₄-in. rabbet.

Expansion slot for bolt

Frame for molding

Crown molding

Removable molding. It's much easier to protect the molding if it can be wrapped separately when transporting the case.

Cranked hinges allow doors to open wide. Mortises must be cut in the doors and the front edge of the case.

COLONIAL CUPBOARD

by Mike Dunbar

Options, options. At far left is the cabinet finished with Lexington Green milk paint, with a linseed-oil overcoat. The other version is finished with four washcoats of concentrated tea followed by a tinted shellac.

This little cabinet is based on a late-18th-century original owned by a friend of mine. It's a rare piece, and antique dealers regularly pester him about selling it. The dealers want his cabinet for the same reason you will want to make it. There is always demand for an attractive and handy storage space.

The cabinet is interesting for woodworkers for two reasons: First, it's a tutorial on hand-cut joinery. Although a small piece, this cabinet requires nine types of joints. You will get some practice on dovetails, dadoes, rabbets, shiplaps, coping, miters, panel-in-groove, and mortises and tenons (both blind and through-). While some of the work would be more straightforward if it were done on machines, there is value in sharpening your hand-tool skills (and certainly less dust and noise). The choice is yours, of course.

Second, this cabinet is a chameleon. It's a good example of how a piece of furniture can be dressed up or down. Another plus is that you can drastically change this cabinet's dimensions to make it fit a particular space or application: My cabinet was designed to house my 8-year-old's videocassette collection. You can even substitute a base molding for the bracket base and hang this cupboard on a wall.

Most of the stock is either 3/4-in.-thick or 1/2-in.-thick pine. The cornice is 5/4 stock. I went to a local home center and bought #2 common boards, 1x8x12. I was able to work around most of the large knots or place them in shelves or back boards. The dime-size knots that appear in the carcase and door give me just the look I had want—not too perfect but not knotty pine, either.

Two Finish Options

I wanted my cabinet to look as if it had some age. The color I had in mind was the pale tan that raw

A DOVETAILED BOX IS THE FOUNDATION

Shelves, back boards, face frame, cornice, and bracket base all attach to the dovetailed case. Then, all that's left is the, frame-and-panel door.

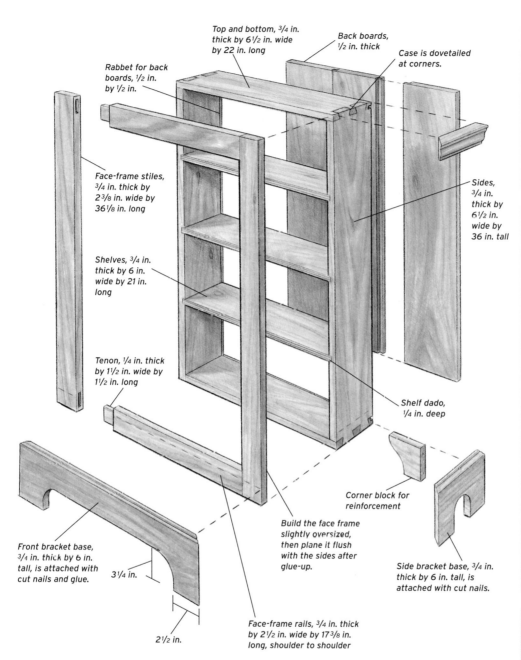

Top and bottom, 3/4 in. thick by 6 1/2 in. wide by 22 in. long

Back boards, 1/2 in. thick

Case is dovetailed at corners.

Rabbet for back boards, 1/2 in. by 1/2 in.

Face-frame stiles, 3/4 in. thick by 2 3/8 in. wide by 36 1/8 in. long

Shelves, 3/4 in. thick by 6 in. wide by 21 in. long

Sides, 3/4 in. thick by 6 1/2 in. wide by 36 in. tall

Tenon, 1/4 in. thick by 1 1/2 in. wide by 1 1/2 in. long

Shelf dado, 1/4 in. deep

Corner block for reinforcement

Build the face frame slightly oversized, then plane it flush with the sides after glue-up.

Front bracket base, 3/4 in. thick by 6 in. tall, is attached with cut nails and glue.

3 1/4 in.

2 1/2 in.

Face-frame rails, 3/4 in. thick by 2 1/2 in. wide by 17 3/8 in. long, shoulder to shoulder

Side bracket base, 3/4 in. thick by 6 in. tall, is attached with cut nails.

CORNICE DETAIL

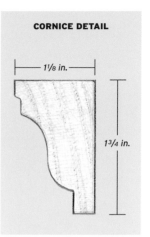

1 1/8 in.

1 3/4 in.

SHELF DETAIL

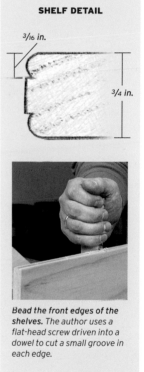

3/16 in.

3/4 in.

Bead the front edges of the shelves. The author uses a flat-head screw driven into a dowel to cut a small groove in each edge.

BRACKET-BASE DETAIL

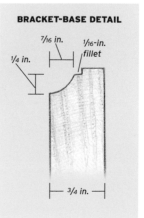

7/16 in.

1/16-in. fillet

1/4 in.

3/4 in.

FRAME-AND-PANEL DOOR

The door is the most challenging part: It has a floating raised panel and a thumbnail profile that is coped away at the mortise-and-tenon joints.

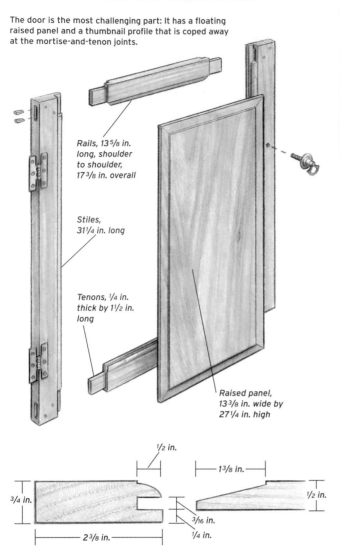

Rails, 13 5/8 in. long, shoulder to shoulder, 17 3/8 in. overall

Stiles, 31 1/4 in. long

Tenons, 1/4 in. thick by 1 1/2 in. long

Raised panel, 13 3/8 in. wide by 27 1/4 in. high

1/2 in.

1 3/8 in.

3/4 in.

1/2 in.

3/16 in.

1/4 in.

2 3/8 in.

Coping the Corners

Two edges of the mortise-and-tenon joint are relieved. Then a small amount of the thumbnail edge is coped so that the joint can close.

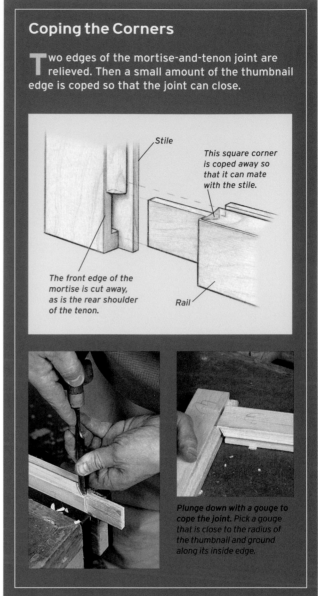

Stile

This square corner is coped away so that it can mate with the stile.

The front edge of the mortise is cut away, as is the rear shoulder of the tenon.

Rail

Plunge down with a gouge to cope the joint. Pick a gouge that is close to the radius of the thumbnail and ground along its inside edge.

Cut the thumbnail profile. Cut the small fillet with a rabbeting plane, and then round over the thumbnail profile with a block plane, working to a line.

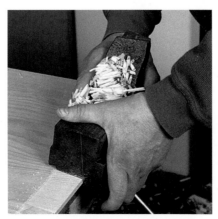

Sight down the spring lines of a panel-raising plane to maintain the proper angle. Cut the cross-grain sides first. Place a waste strip along the back edge to avoid tearout.

After glue-up, the joints are pinned and wedged. Drive the pins all the way through the door frame before cutting them flush. Then wedge the tenon ends to lock the joint.

pine turns to after about five years. However, I did not want to use a stain. Stains darken the softer latewood and leave the harder earlywood lighter in color, which is the opposite of the way pine darkens with age.

I achieved the look I wanted in one afternoon by using nothing more complicated than tea. I made a really strong mixture by steeping three bags in a cup of hot water. When it had cooled, I brushed the strong tea onto the wood, darkening the surface very slightly. I allowed this application to dry and sanded any raised grain. Each subsequent coat of tea darkened the pine further. It took four coats to give me the look I wanted. You can follow with varnish, or if you want to tweak the color slightly—to make it a bit less yellow, for example—use a topcoat of shellac tinted with aniline dye.

Milk paint is another attractive option, and it is probably the finish this cabinet would have received in the 1700s. The Old Fashioned Milk Paint Co. (978-448-6336; www.milkpaint.com) is an excellent source for powdered mixes and provides good instructions for their use. A key is to finish the painted surface with linseed oil, which evens out the color.

Hardware

I hung the door with solid brass H-hinges, which are appropriate for an 18th-century design, and I secured the door with a brass pendant latch. Both of these items came from Ball and Ball Hardware Reproductions (800-257-3711; www.ballandball-us.com). While more expensive than the brasses sold at hardware stores and home centers, the prices were not prohibitive. I have always thought it a shame that a woodworker would invest so much in a piece but then install cheap hardware.

Mike Dunbar is a contributing editor to Fine Woodworking.

BOW-FRONT STAND

by Stephen Hammer

One way to add interest to a case piece is to add a gentle curve to the front plane. I wanted to explore this element of furniture making while attending a 12-week class at the Center for Furniture Craftsmanship in Rockport, Maine, so I designed and built this cherry cabinet, finding ways to curve the door and drawers that did not require steam-bending or veneering. The drawer fronts and the door frame are sawn out of thicker stock, and the door panel is coopered to match that curve—methods well-suited to the average small shop.

The case consists of two solid sides joined to the legs, a solid bottom, and a frame-and-panel back. (The grain of the top, sides, and bottom runs in the same direction, so it will expand and contract together.) The front door is a curved frame and panel, and the two drawers are side-hung.

The final touch is to add carved ebony pulls. Getting the design right for these was a frustrating ordeal, but they are one of my favorite elements. I cut the facets on the bandsaw and formed the curves with a sanding drum. I left small tenons on the pulls so that I could mortise them into the door and drawers.

Stephen Hammer is a furniture maker in Brooklyn, New York.

CURVED DRAWER FRONTS

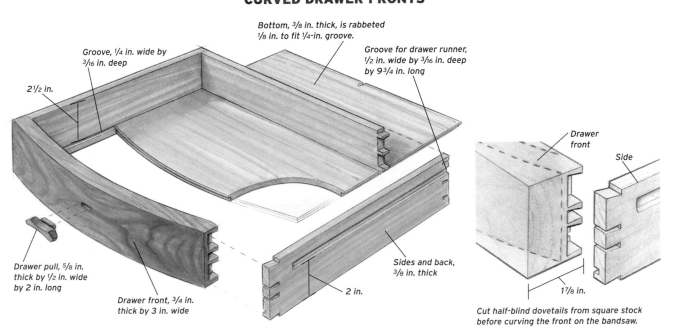

Groove, 1/4 in. wide by 3/16 in. deep

2 1/2 in.

Bottom, 3/8 in. thick, is rabbeted 1/8 in. to fit 1/4-in. groove.

Groove for drawer runner, 1/2 in. wide by 3/16 in. deep by 9 3/4 in. long

Drawer pull, 5/8 in. thick by 1/2 in. wide by 2 in. long

Drawer front, 3/4 in. thick by 3 in. wide

2 in.

Sides and back, 3/8 in. thick

Drawer front

Side

1 7/8 in.

Cut half-blind dovetails from square stock before curving the front on the bandsaw.

CURVED-FRONT STAND

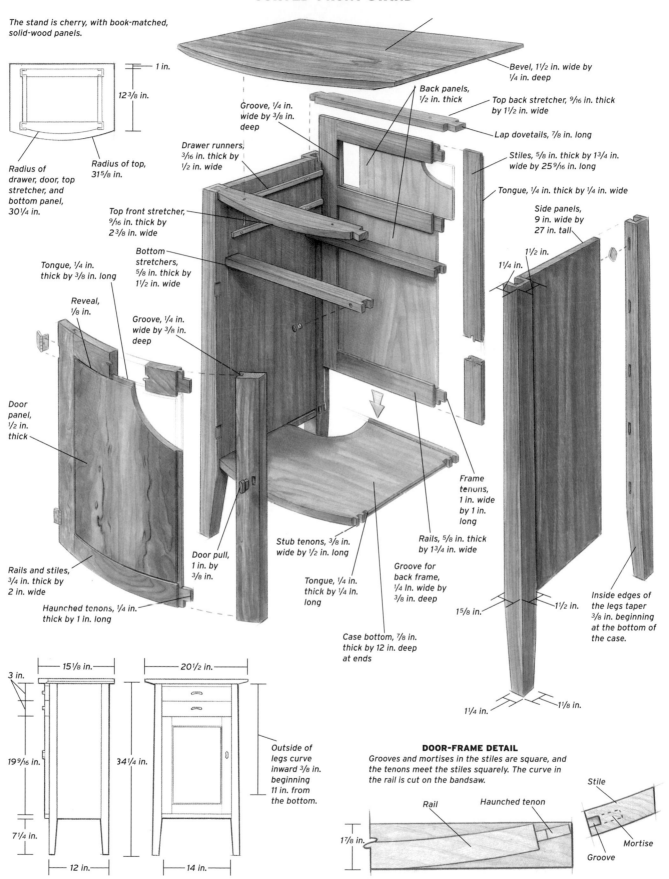

The stand is cherry, with book-matched, solid-wood panels.

1 in.

12 3/8 in.

Radius of drawer, door, top stretcher, and bottom panel, 30 1/4 in.

Radius of top, 31 5/8 in.

Bevel, 1 1/2 in. wide by 1/4 in. deep

Back panels, 1/2 in. thick

Top back stretcher, 9/16 in. thick by 1 1/2 in. wide

Lap dovetails, 7/8 in. long

Stiles, 5/8 in. thick by 1 3/4 in. wide by 25 9/16 in. long

Tongue, 1/4 in. thick by 1/4 in. wide

Side panels, 9 in. wide by 27 in. tall

1 1/2 in.

1 1/4 in.

Groove, 1/4 in. wide by 3/8 in. deep

Drawer runners, 3/16 in. thick by 1/2 in. wide

Top front stretcher, 9/16 in. thick by 2 3/8 in. wide

Bottom stretchers, 5/8 in. thick by 1 1/2 in. wide

Tongue, 1/4 in. thick by 3/8 in. long

Reveal, 1/8 in.

Groove, 1/4 in. wide by 3/8 in. deep

Door panel, 1/2 in. thick

Door pull, 1 in. by 3/8 in.

Stub tenons, 3/8 in. wide by 1/2 in. long

Tongue, 1/4 in. thick by 1/4 in. long

Rails, 5/8 in. thick by 1 3/4 in. wide

Frame tenons, 1 in. wide by 1 in. long

Groove for back frame, 1/4 in. wide by 3/8 in. deep

Inside edges of the legs taper 3/8 in. beginning at the bottom of the case.

Rails and stiles, 3/4 in. thick by 2 in. wide

Haunched tenons, 1/4 in. thick by 1 in. long

Case bottom, 7/8 in. thick by 12 in. deep at ends

1 5/8 in.

1 1/2 in.

1 1/4 in.

1 1/8 in.

3 in.

15 1/8 in.

20 1/2 in.

19 9/16 in.

34 1/4 in.

Outside of legs curve inward 3/8 in. beginning 11 in. from the bottom.

7 1/4 in.

12 in.

14 in.

DOOR-FRAME DETAIL

Grooves and mortises in the stiles are square, and the tenons meet the stiles squarely. The curve in the rail is cut on the bandsaw.

Rail

Haunched tenon

Stile

Mortise

Groove

1 7/8 in.

STEP-BACK CUPBOARD

by Mike Dunbar

Build this elegant 18th-century cupboard, and hone your hand-tool skills at the same time.

My wife had a narrow space in the kitchen where she wanted more storage. She had pestered me to make a piece of furniture to solve her problem, but I always had other things to do. One day I came home to discover she had bought a factory-made cupboard at a furniture store to fill the spot. One of the major reasons why I am a woodworker is that I want to be surrounded by furniture that is better than the mass-produced stuff. Factory furniture offends all of my sensibilities: It often lacks individuality, character, and craftsmanship; its designs are limited by the capabilities of machinery; and every surface is sanded to death.

I promised my wife that if she returned the piece, I would make something that we both liked better. She selected an antique cupboard on which this one is based. Besides the additional storage, she was happy to gain display space for some of her favorite items. The cupboard's small size also makes the piece versatile, and it can be used in any room if she redecorates or if we move.

The original piece that inspired this project was made in the late 18th century. The wood used in the original—eastern white pine—suggests that the piece was made in New England. While very handsome, the cupboard is not particularly complicated, especially if it is made using machines. However, the project presents a good opportunity to hone hand skills. So, even if you do use machines for most of the steps, I urge you to try at least some of the steps by hand.

The original cupboard's door was mounted with wrought-iron hinges and held shut with a wooden turn button. I spruced up mine with cast brass ornamental H-hinges and a matching catch. These

items cost about $80, but after all the work I put into the piece and the cost of the lumber, it seems only fitting.

Once the piece was complete, I finished it with milk paint. To match the color scheme of our home, I finished the outside surfaces of the cupboard with barn red. For the exposed inside walls and back boards, I used mustard.

Mike Dunbar is a contributing editor to Fine Woodworking.

Sources of Supply

MOLDING PLANES
Tod Herrli, 765-664-3325

HARDWARE
Horton Brasses, 800-754-9127
Ball and Ball, 800-257-3711

CUT NAILS
Tremont Nail, 800-842-0560

PAINTED PINE CUPBOARD

The 18th-century cupboard is made of 3/4-in.-thick white pine and finished with milk paint.

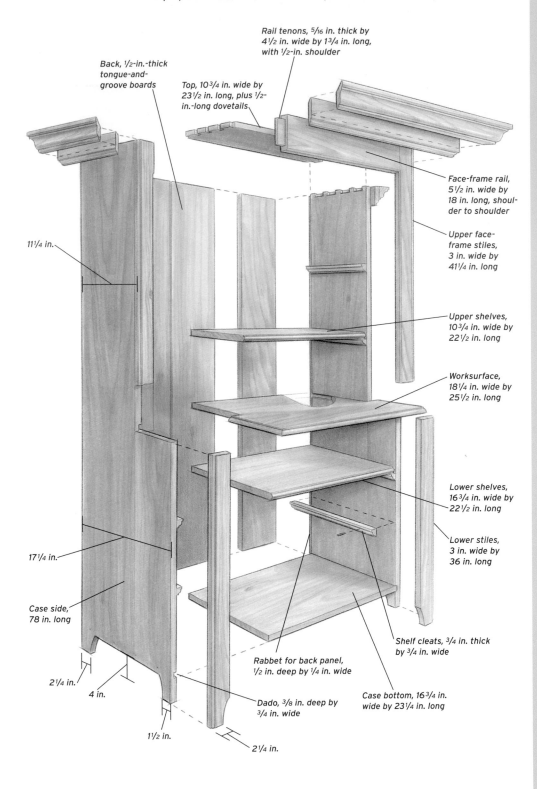

Back, 1/2-in.-thick tongue-and-groove boards

Rail tenons, 5/16 in. thick by 4 1/2 in. wide by 1 3/4 in. long, with 1/2-in. shoulder

Top, 10 3/4 in. wide by 23 1/2 in. long, plus 1/2-in.-long dovetails

Face-frame rail, 5 1/2 in. wide by 18 in. long, shoulder to shoulder

Upper face-frame stiles, 3 in. wide by 41 1/4 in. long

11 1/4 in.

Upper shelves, 10 3/4 in. wide by 22 1/2 in. long

Worksurface, 18 1/4 in. wide by 25 1/2 in. long

Lower shelves, 16 3/4 in. wide by 22 1/2 in. long

17 1/4 in.

Lower stiles, 3 in. wide by 36 in. long

Case side, 78 in. long

Shelf cleats, 3/4 in. thick by 3/4 in. wide

2 1/4 in.

4 in.

Rabbet for back panel, 1/2 in. deep by 1/4 in. wide

Dado, 3/8 in. deep by 3/4 in. wide

Case bottom, 16 3/4 in. wide by 23 1/4 in. long

1 1/2 in.

2 1/4 in.

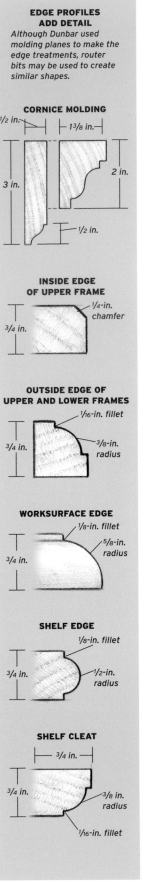

EDGE PROFILES ADD DETAIL

Although Dunbar used molding planes to make the edge treatments, router bits may be used to create similar shapes.

CORNICE MOLDING

1/2 in.
1 3/8 in.
3 in.
2 in.
1/2 in.

INSIDE EDGE OF UPPER FRAME

1/4-in. chamfer
3/4 in.

OUTSIDE EDGE OF UPPER AND LOWER FRAMES

1/16-in. fillet
3/4 in.
3/8-in. radius

WORKSURFACE EDGE

1/8-in. fillet
5/8-in. radius
3/4 in.

SHELF EDGE

1/8-in. fillet
1/2-in. radius
3/4 in.

SHELF CLEAT

3/4 in.
3/4 in.
3/8 in. radius
1/16-in. fillet

A jig for perfect miters. When cutting the miters on the door stiles and rails, Dunbar uses a jig with a 45-degree slope to guide his chisel.

Adding the panel: A solid door panel, raised using a panel-raising plane, slides into grooves cut in the rails and stiles.

Wedged tenons. Wedges driven into the tenons to secure them tightly in the offset mortises. Typical 18th-century tenoned doors were left unglued. Pinning the tenons will add even more strength.

HAND-CUT FRAME-AND-PANEL DOOR

Raise the door panel with a molding plane. Wedge, not glue, secure the tenons in the mortises.

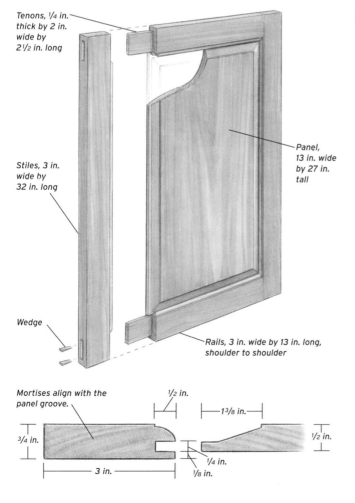

Tenons, 1/4 in. thick by 2 in. wide by 2 1/2 in. long

Stiles, 3 in. wide by 32 in. long

Wedge

Panel, 13 in. wide by 27 in. tall

Rails, 3 in. wide by 13 in. long, shoulder to shoulder

Mortises align with the panel groove.

3/4 in.

3 in.

1/2 in.

1 3/8 in.

1/4 in.

1/8 in.

1/2 in.

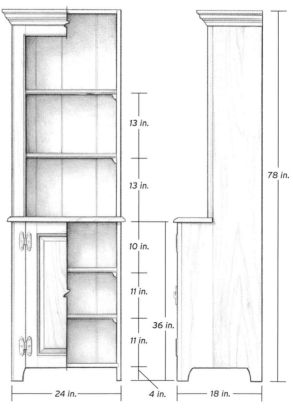

13 in.

13 in.

10 in.

11 in.

11 in.

36 in.

78 in.

24 in.

4 in.

18 in.

AN EVERYDAY CABINET

by Scott Gibson

When I set up an office and began working at home, I vowed to be careful with what little space I had. But before long I was awash in all of the junk any office accumulates—pencils, notebooks, phone books—and not enough storage room. Part of the solution was this small, shallow cabinet, which tucks beneath a window without blocking the view. Its two drawers offer useful storage, and the lower compartment is unobstructed by a center door divider.

I wanted to build the cabinet quickly and with a minimum of materials. The sides and back are frame and panel with frame stiles biscuited to the legs, making for a sturdy carcase that is easy to put together. With the exception of the drawers, the rest of the joinery is mortise and tenon.

The bottom of a table or cabinet leg can be hard to get right. This cabinet is boxy to start with, and I thought a straight leg would be too plain. In Wallace Nutting's *Furniture Treasury* (Macmillan Publishing Co., 1933), I found drawings of several legs that meet the floor in a graceful curve. The one I liked the most was a tall clock foot with Hepplewhite origins.

The cabinet's design is adaptable. It would be easy to alter the height of the drawers or even the overall dimensions of the cabinet without changing its look very much. Figured veneer door panels or drawer fronts would give the piece a much more formal feel. In the end, I kept the design simple.

Scott Gibson, a former editor at The Taunton Press, is a freelance writer.

SIDE-PANEL CONSTRUCTION

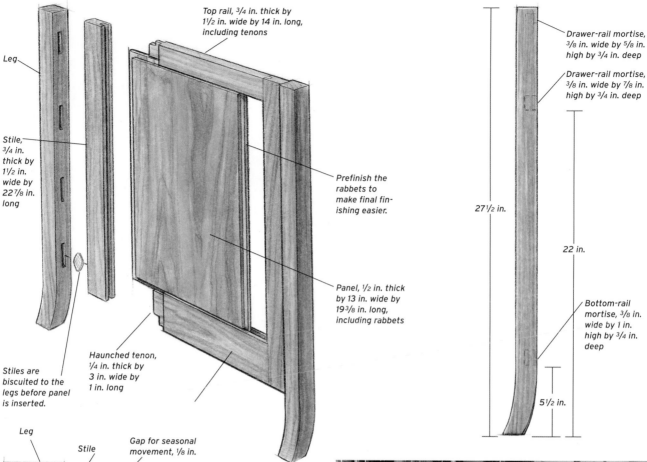

Leg

Stile, ³/₄ in. thick by 1¹/₂ in. wide by 22⁷/₈ in. long

Top rail, ³/₄ in. thick by 1¹/₂ in. wide by 14 in. long, including tenons

Prefinish the rabbets to make final finishing easier.

Panel, ¹/₂ in. thick by 13 in. wide by 19³/₈ in. long, including rabbets

Stiles are biscuited to the legs before panel is inserted.

Haunched tenon, ¹/₄ in. thick by 3 in. wide by 1 in. long

Leg

Stile

Gap for seasonal movement, ¹/₈ in.

Setback, ¹/₄ in.

Reveal, ¹/₈ in.

Panel

A LEG WITH FLARE

1 square = ¹/₂ in.

1¹/₄ in.

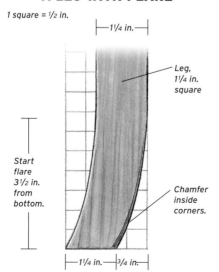

Leg, 1¹/₄ in. square

Start flare 3¹/₂ in. from bottom.

Chamfer inside corners.

1¹/₄ in.   ³/₄ in.

FRONT-LEG JOINERY

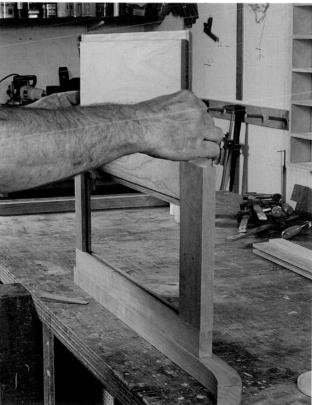

Drawer-rail mortise, ³/₈ in. wide by ⁵/₈ in. high by ³/₄ in. deep

Drawer-rail mortise, ³/₈ in. wide by ⁷/₈ in. high by ³/₄ in. deep

27¹/₂ in.

22 in.

Bottom-rail mortise, ³/₈ in. wide by 1 in. high by ³/₄ in. deep

5¹/₂ in.

Drop the panel in place. *Gibson prefinished the rabbets on the panel so that he wouldn't have to squeeze finish into the small gap between the frame and the panel.*

CASE CONSTRUCTION

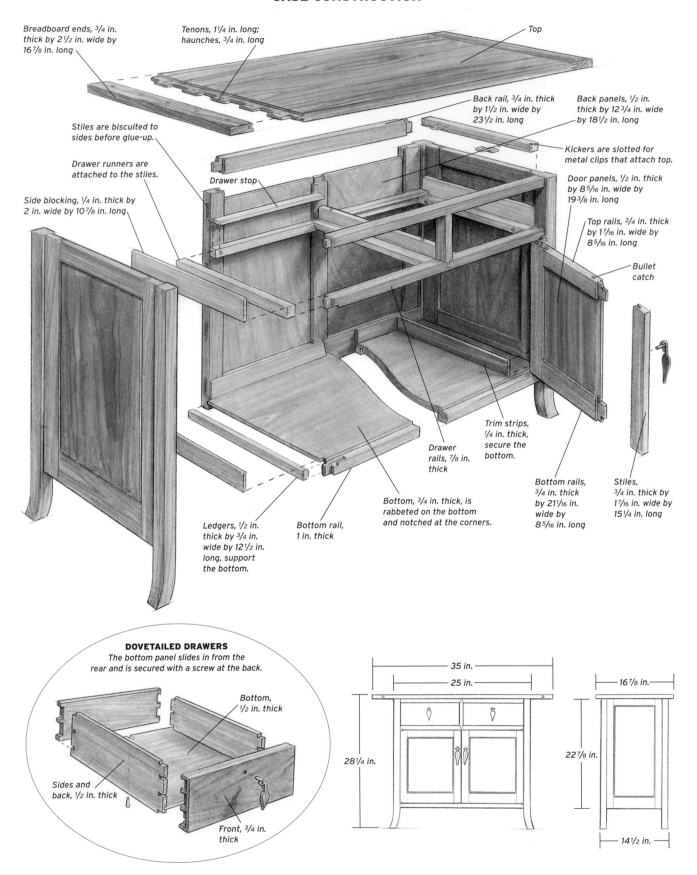

Breadboard ends, ³/₄ in. thick by 2¹/₂ in. wide by 16⁷/₈ in. long

Tenons, 1¹/₄ in. long; haunches, ³/₄ in. long

Top

Stiles are biscuited to sides before glue-up.

Drawer runners are attached to the stiles.

Side blocking, ¹/₄ in. thick by 2 in. wide by 10⁷/₈ in. long

Drawer stop

Back rail, ³/₄ in. thick by 1¹/₂ in. wide by 23¹/₂ in. long

Back panels, ¹/₂ in. thick by 12³/₄ in. wide by 18¹/₂ in. long

Kickers are slotted for metal clips that attach top.

Door panels, ¹/₂ in. thick by 8⁵/₁₆ in. wide by 19³/₈ in. long

Top rails, ³/₄ in. thick by 1⁷/₁₆ in. wide by 8⁵/₁₆ in. long

Bullet catch

Trim strips, ¹/₄ in. thick, secure the bottom.

Drawer rails, ⁷/₈ in. thick

Bottom, ³/₄ in. thick, is rabbeted on the bottom and notched at the corners.

Bottom rails, ³/₄ in. thick by 21¹/₁₆ in. wide by 8⁵/₁₆ in. long

Stiles, ³/₄ in. thick by 1⁷/₁₆ in. wide by 15¹/₄ in. long

Ledgers, ¹/₂ in. thick by ³/₄ in. wide by 12¹/₂ in. long, support the bottom.

Bottom rail, 1 in. thick

DOVETAILED DRAWERS
The bottom panel slides in from the rear and is secured with a screw at the back.

Bottom, ¹/₂ in. thick

Sides and back, ¹/₂ in. thick

Front, ³/₄ in. thick

35 in.

25 in.

16⁷/₈ in.

28¹/₄ in.

22⁷/₈ in.

14¹/₂ in.

CORNER CUPBOARD

by Garrett Hack

On every trip to the Shelburne Museum near Burlington, Vermont, I visit a favorite object— a small hanging corner cabinet. With a single curved door, nicely shaped cornice, and molded base, the cabinet beams from its corner. Shelburne's cabinet was on my mind as I set about designing one for my house. The result is a country-style piece with delicate details. But you can change the moldings or details to transform the basic design to anything from Shaker to Craftsman.

Because so much of the carcase is hidden, it's possible to build most of it from a less-expensive secondary wood, and the facade from some special figured wood. I decided on butternut, walnut's country cousin, for the entire piece because of its warm brown color, pleasing grain, and delightful workability with plane and chisel.

Garrett Hack is a furniture designer, furniture maker, and one-horse farmer in Thetford, Vermont.

Details Define a Style

Changing the style of the case moldings and panels can dramatically change the appearance of this cabinet. For instance, the Shaker-styled corner cupboard could have moldings of bullnose, and the Craftsman-styled one could be built with flat panels and large flat-angled cornice molding.

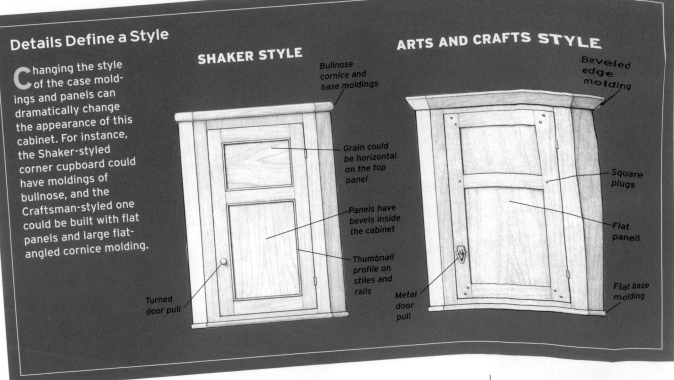

SHAKER STYLE

Bullnose cornice and base moldings

Grain could be horizontal on the top panel

Panels have bevels inside the cabinet

Thumbnail profile on stiles and rails

Turned door pull

ARTS AND CRAFTS STYLE

Beveled edge molding

Square plugs

Flat panels

Flat base molding

Metal door pull

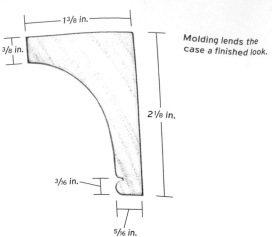

Molding lends the case a finished look.

1 3/8 in.

3/8 in.

2 1/8 in.

3/16 in.

5/16 in.

A perfect fit. When mitering the molding, fit the center section first, and then cut the side sections to fit. Use the quirk between the bead and the cove to hide the brads that help secure the crown molding to the face frame.

CORNER-CABINET CONSTRUCTION

Mill the sides, the back, the two shelves, and the door panels at the same time, as they are all the same ½-in. thickness. The shelves are planed later to fit snugly in the 7/16-in. dadoes. Then mill the door stiles and rails, the door frame, the wings, and the top and bottom to their ¾-in. thickness.

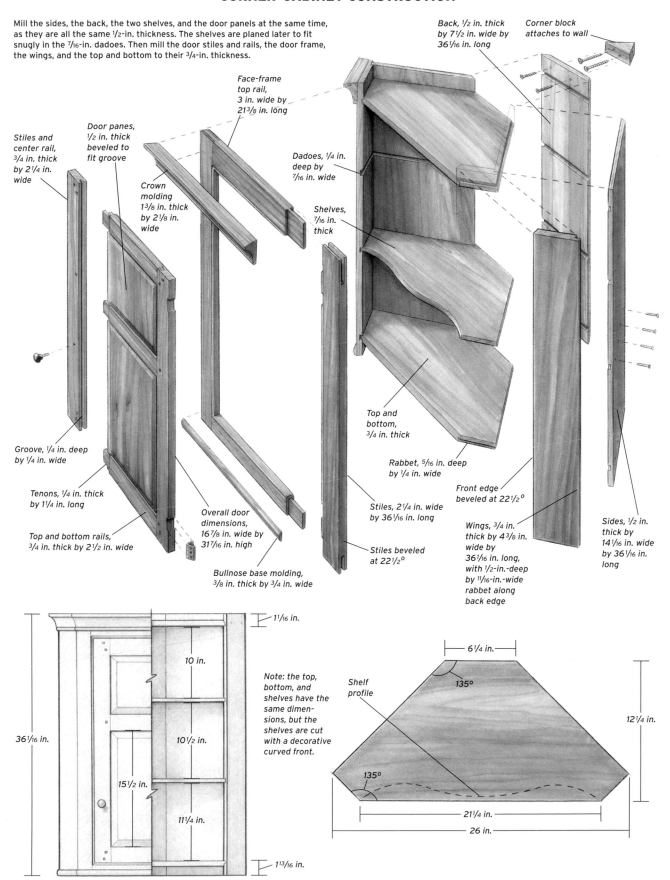

Stiles and center rail, ¾ in. thick by 2¼ in. wide

Door panes, ½ in. thick beveled to fit groove

Face-frame top rail, 3 in. wide by 21⅜ in. long

Back, ½ in. thick by 7½ in. wide by 36 1/16 in. long

Corner block attaches to wall

Crown molding 1⅜ in. thick by 2⅛ in. wide

Dadoes, ¼ in. deep by 7/16 in. wide

Shelves, 7/16 in. thick

Groove, ¼ in. deep by ¼ in. wide

Tenons, ¼ in. thick by 1¼ in. long

Top and bottom rails, ¾ in. thick by 2½ in. wide

Overall door dimensions, 16⅞ in. wide by 31⁷/16 in. high

Bullnose base molding, ⅜ in. thick by ¾ in. wide

Top and bottom, ¾ in. thick

Rabbet, 5/16 in. deep by ¼ in. wide

Stiles, 2¼ in. wide by 36 1/16 in. long

Stiles beveled at 22½°

Front edge beveled at 22½°

Wings, ¾ in. thick by 4⅜ in. wide by 36 1/16 in. long, with ½-in.-deep by 11/16-in.-wide rabbet along back edge

Sides, ½ in. thick by 14 1/16 in. wide by 36 1/16 in. long

1 1/16 in.

10 in.

10½ in.

15½ in.

11¼ in.

36 1/16 in.

1¹³/16 in.

Note: the top, bottom, and shelves have the same dimensions, but the shelves are cut with a decorative curved front.

Shelf profile

6¼ in.

135°

135°

21¼ in.

26 in.

12¼ in.

CRAFTSMAN WALL CABINET

by Ian Ingersoll

AN EASY AND ELEGANT DOOR

To lend a more elegant look to a simple door, muntins overlay a single piece of glass, giving the appearance that there are four separate panes.

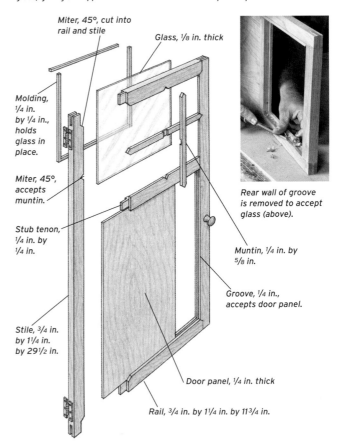

Miter, 45°, cut into rail and stile

Glass, 1/8 in. thick

Molding, 1/4 in. by 1/4 in., holds glass in place.

Miter, 45°, accepts muntin.

Stub tenon, 1/4 in. by 1/4 in.

Rear wall of groove is removed to accept glass (above).

Muntin, 1/4 in. by 5/8 in.

Groove, 1/4 in., accepts door panel.

Stile, 3/4 in. by 1 1/4 in. by 29 1/2 in.

Door panel, 1/4 in. thick

Rail, 3/4 in. by 1 1/4 in. by 11 3/4 in.

There is always a spot for a wall cabinet, especially a small one. This Craftsman-style piece is modeled after a clock, and at a little more than a foot wide, it fits well in almost any tight, vertical space. I made it out of butternut, an underused, medium-toned wood that works easily. Because this cabinet was destined for a kitchen, I outfitted the inside to accommodate spices, but the same-size cabinet could hold anything from pottery to small books. The shelves, in this case, are spaced to fit off-the-rack spice bottles, with the bottom shelf roomy enough for larger, bulk-size decanters. The tilting drawer at the bottom is made to fit large packages of tea.

When it comes to construction, the simplest answers are often best. On this small, vertical cabinet, I could have dovetailed the case, but I saw no need to spend the time when countersunk and plugged screws would do. And on such a simple piece, I didn't want anything to detract attention from the door, where I spent most of the design and construction energy. I used a flat panel at the bottom of the door to cover the drawer and bulk items, but at the top I installed glass to show off the nicer-looking spice bottles and

CABINET WITH GLAZED DOOR

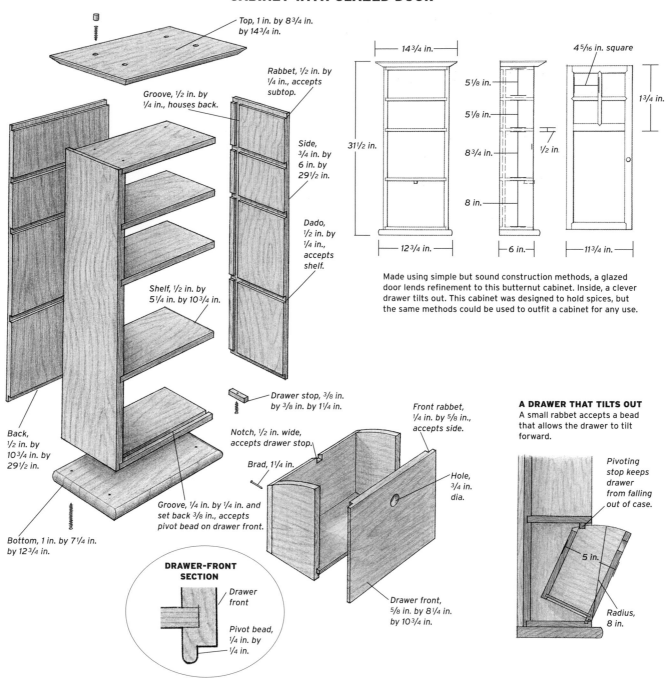

Top, 1 in. by 8 3/4 in. by 14 3/4 in.

Rabbet, 1/2 in. by 1/4 in., accepts subtop.

Groove, 1/2 in. by 1/4 in., houses back.

Side, 3/4 in. by 6 in. by 29 1/2 in.

Dado, 1/2 in. by 1/4 in., accepts shelf.

Shelf, 1/2 in. by 5 1/4 in. by 10 3/4 in.

Back, 1/2 in. by 10 3/4 in. by 29 1/2 in.

Bottom, 1 in. by 7 1/4 in. by 12 3/4 in.

Groove, 1/4 in. by 1/4 in. and set back 3/8 in., accepts pivot bead on drawer front.

Drawer stop, 3/8 in. by 3/8 in. by 1 1/4 in.

Notch, 1/2 in. wide, accepts drawer stop.

Brad, 1 1/4 in.

Front rabbet, 1/4 in. by 5/8 in., accepts side.

Hole, 3/4 in. dia.

Drawer front, 5/8 in. by 8 1/4 in. by 10 3/4 in.

14 3/4 in.

5 1/8 in.

5 1/8 in.

8 3/4 in.

8 in.

31 1/2 in.

12 3/4 in.

6 in.

1/2 in.

4 5/16 in. square

1 3/4 in.

11 3/4 in.

Made using simple but sound construction methods, a glazed door lends refinement to this butternut cabinet. Inside, a clever drawer tilts out. This cabinet was designed to hold spices, but the same methods could be used to outfit a cabinet for any use.

A DRAWER THAT TILTS OUT
A small rabbet accepts a bead that allows the drawer to tilt forward.

Pivoting stop keeps drawer from falling out of case.

5 in.

Radius, 8 in.

DRAWER-FRONT SECTION

Drawer front

Pivot bead, 1/4 in. by 1/4 in.

---

to make the piece a bit more interesting. Over the single piece of glass, I installed muntins, giving the appearance of two-over-two panes of glass.

When you open this case, the drawer at the bottom is a nice surprise. Instead of sliding as a normal drawer would, this tall drawer tilts forward and down so that you can reach in for tea or whatever you decide to store inside. The sides and back are rounded so that the drawer slides open easily with the pull—nothing more than a 3/4-in.-dia. hole in the front—but the stop keeps the drawer from falling out on the floor.

By twisting the stop, you can easily remove the whole drawer for easy cleaning or restocking.

I used an oil varnish from Waterlox (800-321-0377) to give this piece a natural look and to provide protection. The hinges I used are antiqued, solid brass H-hinges from Horton Brasses (860-635-4400), and the knob is a Shaker-style bronze knob from Colonial Bronze (860-489-9233).

Ian Ingersoll designs and builds furniture in West Cornwall, Connecticut.

WINEGLASS CABINET

by Scott Gibson

Wall cabinets are relatively small. It's one of their beauties. They can be used in many spaces that would be too cramped for larger pieces of furniture, and their scale makes them familiar and approachable. A wall cabinet also can be made from scraps and offcuts of prized lumber that would be unusable elsewhere.

This cabinet is made of quartersawn white ash and is less than 7 in. deep. It is designed for wineglasses and is intended for a dining room. It is less than 7 in. deep. With the exceptions of the cornice and the matching base, the cabinet is rectilinear. Door stiles are tapered slightly on the inside edge to help the cabinet appear lighter at the top. A coved cornice gives the top of the case some heft, and small windows at the tops of the doors give you a peek inside. There's minimal hardware, so the wood is really what's on display.

Size the Cabinet to Fit the Glasses

Unless the cabinet has no specific use, it makes sense to size it carefully for the things that are to be stored there. Wineglasses come in many sizes and shapes, but those in the mixed collection my wife and I own are about 3½ in. wide and about 7 in. tall. Those dimensions became the rough guide for laying out the cabinet. Although adjustable shelves allow some flexibility in height, there is no way to fudge a cabinet that is too shallow.

There are two other considerations: the thickness of the back, which is set into rabbets in the back of the case, and whether the doors will be inset or overlay. The back of this cabinet was made from four shiplapped boards. A frame-and-panel back was another good option, but shiplapping these boards was the best way to present the bands of browns and creams in the wood. Because the boards were set into the back of the case, the overall depth

of the cabinet had to be increased by at least that much. I added a safety margin of another ½ in. in case we ever get slightly larger glasses.

If you choose inset doors—those that fit inside the case—they also must be factored into the depth of the case. Doors should be a full ¾ in. thick, so the sides of the case must be that much wider if this

BASE MOLDING SUPPORTS THE CABINET

This simple box is accented by doors with tapered stiles, which give the illusion that the piece has a slight V-shape. The cornice and the matching base also provide some weight to the piece and reinforce the tapered appearance.

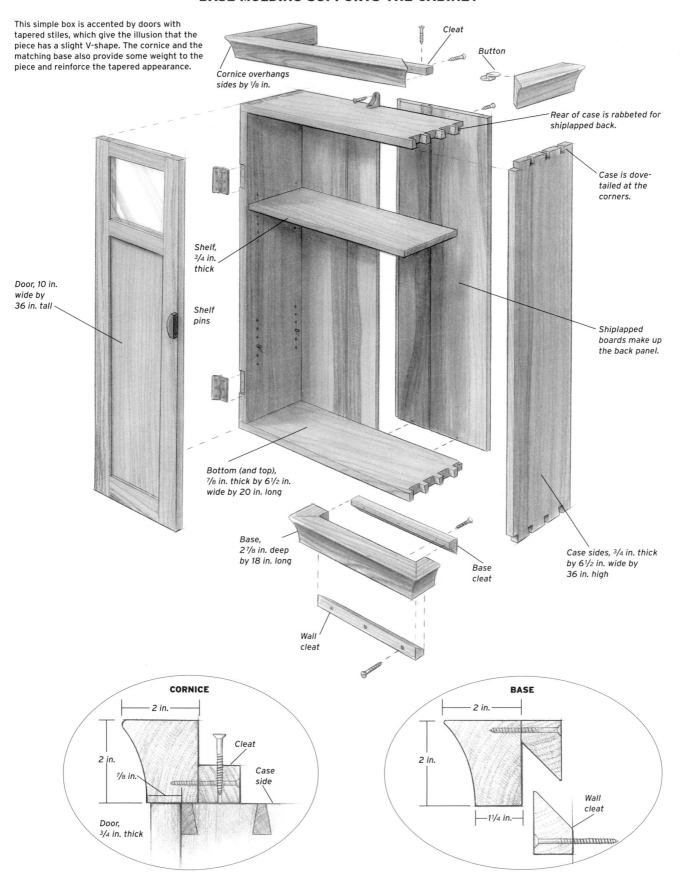

Cornice overhangs sides by 1/8 in.

Cleat

Button

Rear of case is rabbeted for shiplapped back.

Case is dove-tailed at the corners.

Shelf, 3/4 in. thick

Shelf pins

Door, 10 in. wide by 36 in. tall

Shiplapped boards make up the back panel.

Bottom (and top), 7/8 in. thick by 6 1/2 in. wide by 20 in. long

Base, 2 7/8 in. deep by 18 in. long

Base cleat

Case sides, 3/4 in. thick by 6 1/2 in. wide by 36 in. high

Wall cleat

CORNICE

2 in.

2 in.

7/8 in.

Cleat

Case side

Door, 3/4 in. thick

BASE

2 in.

2 in.

1 1/4 in.

Wall cleat

is the door style you choose. I chose overlay doors, which are attached to the outside edges of the case. One visual advantage of overlay doors is that they give the case a cleaner, less cluttered look—from the front, you see the doors, not the edges of the case. Another option is to make the top and bottom of the case wider than the sides by the thickness of the door. This allows the doors to cover the edges of the cabinet sides but fit inside the top and bottom pieces.

As for width, I wanted to fit five or six glasses side by side on each shelf. A little extra room here also is a good idea.

The carcase is just a four-sided box, dovetailed at the corners. The sides are ³/₄ in. thick, and the top and the bottom are ⁷/₈ in. thick. Although using half-blind dovetails would have kept the sides of the case cleaner, I'm still a sucker for at least some exposed joinery, so I used through-dovetails. I made the top a little thicker to allow slightly longer pins (these are cut with a 1:8 angle).

Doors Are the Focal Point

This cabinet is almost all door, so it pays to use the best wood you have for the panels and the door parts. I liked the idea of a cabinet that was tapered—slightly narrower at the top than at the bottom. But that seemed to create more problems than were worth solving, so I opted instead to taper the inside edges of the door stiles. The taper is gentle—about 1 degrees—going from 2 in. wide at the bottom of each stile to 1½ in. wide at the top. A more severe taper would have made the stile too wide at the bottom or too narrow at the top to accommodate a tenon. Each door also was fitted with a trapezoidal window roughly 7 in. on a side.

Depending on how the case is built, knife hinges would be a good choice for this cabinet. They

DOORS WITH TAPERED STILES REQUIRE CAREFUL PLANNING

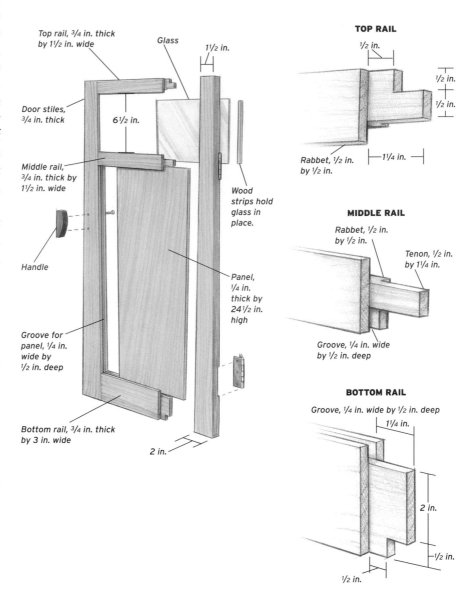

are unobtrusive and strong. I've also used crank hinges (Whitechapel Hardware; 307-739-9478), which allow doors to be folded open all the way. I decided on good-quality extruded brass butt hinges.

Because the cabinet has overlay doors, the stops are already built in. To keep the doors closed, I used small, powerful magnets sold by Lee Valley (800-871-8158). For finish, a coat of Watco™ oil brings out the wood's color, and three or four coats of blond shellac or lacquer protect it.

Scott Gibson is a freelance writer living in Maine.

HANGING CABINET

by Chris Gochnour

Like many woodworkers I know, my shop and resource library are in different locations. My detached garage serves as my shop, but I keep books and my collection of *Fine Woodworking* magazines stored in a bookcase in the basement of the house. My workshop doesn't have a shelf or cabinet big enough to store them all. I finally decided to do something about the problem and set out to design and build a cabinet deserving of the body of knowledge I've gained from *Fine Woodworking*.

The cabinet would have to hold more than 25 years, or 100 lbs., of magazines, so it had to be sturdy. I also needed it to be compact. There's not a lot of empty wall space in my shop. And most of all, I wanted the design to be minimal, something that would let beautiful wood and simple form speak for themselves and blend in nicely with my nearby tool-storage cabinets.

Durable Joinery Is Critical

I constructed the cabinet using two durable joints: through-dovetails (to attach the top to the sides) and wedged mortise and tenons (to attach the bottom to the sides). A piece of cove molding, cut on the tablesaw, serves as a crown and obscures the dovetails, which I cut quickly using a Leigh® jig.

WALL-MOUNTED CABINET CAN HANDLE A HEAVY LOAD

Made of cherry and spalted maple and constructed using through-dovetails on top and wedged mortise and tenons at the base, the cabinet can withstand heavy loads (146 issues of FWW weigh more than 100 lbs.). A French cleat provides secure mounting to a wall.

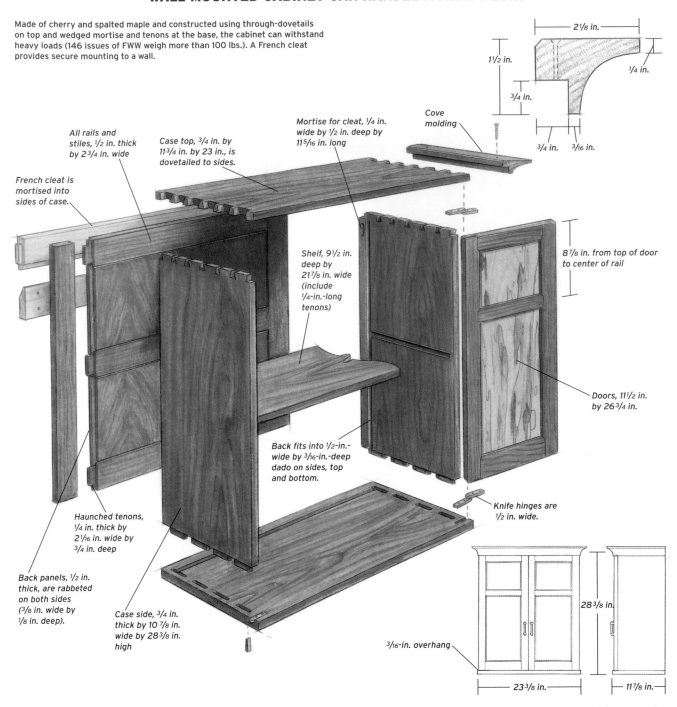

All rails and stiles, 1/2 in. thick by 2 3/4 in. wide

Case top, 3/4 in. by 11 3/4 in. by 23 in., is dovetailed to sides.

French cleat is mortised into sides of case.

Mortise for cleat, 1/4 in. wide by 1/2 in. deep by 11 5/16 in. long

Cove molding

2 1/8 in.

1 1/2 in.

3/4 in.

1/4 in.

3/4 in.

3/16 in.

Shelf, 9 1/2 in. deep by 21 7/8 in. wide (include 1/4-in.-long tenons)

8 7/8 in. from top of door to center of rail

Doors, 11 1/2 in. by 26 3/4 in.

Back fits into 1/2-in.-wide by 3/16-in.-deep dado on sides, top and bottom.

Knife hinges are 1/2 in. wide.

Haunched tenons, 1/4 in. thick by 2 1/16 in. wide by 3/4 in. deep

Back panels, 1/2 in. thick, are rabbeted on both sides (3/8 in. wide by 1/8 in. deep).

Case side, 3/4 in. thick by 10 7/8 in. wide by 28 3/8 in. high

3/16-in. overhang

28 3/8 in.

23 3/8 in.

11 7/8 in.

There were two reasons for using wedged mortise and tenons on the base. One, I wanted a continuous line with a slight overhang at the base of the cabinet. That ruled out using through-dovetails. Second, I wanted the cabinet to be tough. A wedged mortise-and-tenon joint is very strong, even if the glue fails. Sliding dovetails also would have worked, but I wanted something different. Wedged mortise and tenons work mechanically like dovetails, because the tenons are flared to fit tapered mortises (see the top drawings on the facing page). One could certainly use this joint at the top of the case, but it takes a little longer than cutting dovetails using a router jig. Before laying out and cutting the mortises and tenons for the base, I completed all of the joinery at the top, then dry-fit the assembly.

Chris Gochnour builds custom furniture in Salt Lake City, Utah.

Wedged Mortise and Tenons

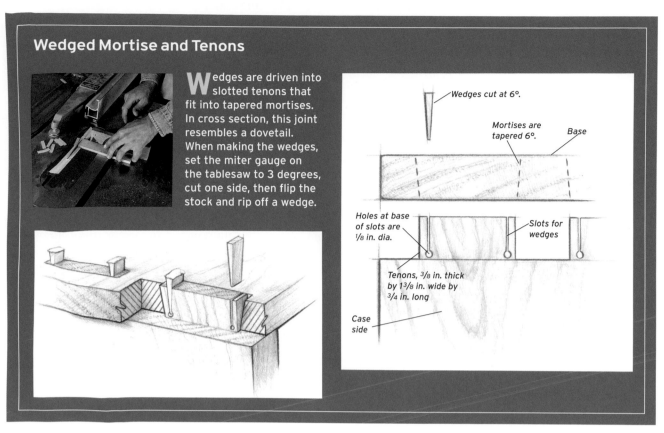

Wedges are driven into slotted tenons that fit into tapered mortises. In cross section, this joint resembles a dovetail. When making the wedges, set the miter gauge on the tablesaw to 3 degrees, cut one side, then flip the stock and rip off a wedge.

Wedges cut at 6°.

Mortises are tapered 6°.

Base

Holes at base of slots are 1/8 in. dia.

Slots for wedges

Tenons, 3/8 in. thick by 1 3/8 in. wide by 3/4 in. long

Case side

SPALTED PANELS HIGHLIGHT SIMPLE DOORS

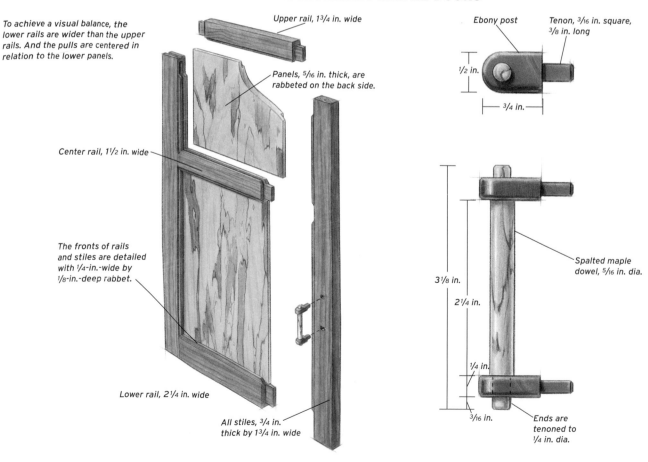

To achieve a visual balance, the lower rails are wider than the upper rails. And the pulls are centered in relation to the lower panels.

Upper rail, 1 3/4 in. wide

Panels, 5/16 in. thick, are rabbeted on the back side.

Center rail, 1 1/2 in. wide

The fronts of rails and stiles are detailed with 1/4-in.-wide by 1/8-in.-deep rabbet.

Lower rail, 2 1/4 in. wide

All stiles, 3/4 in. thick by 1 3/4 in. wide

Ebony post

Tenon, 3/16 in. square, 3/8 in. long

1/2 in.

3/4 in.

Spalted maple dowel, 5/16 in. dia.

3 1/8 in.

2 1/4 in.

1/4 in.

3/16 in.

Ends are tenoned to 1/4 in. dia.

WALL CABINET IN CHERRY

by Matthew Teague

Most every home has a narrow wall—usually at the end of a hallway or beside an entry door—where nothing seems to fit. This piece was designed for such a space. I keep tall vases in the cabinet and candles in the lower drawer, but it can be adapted easily to all sorts of needs. Add a few drawers, and you have a good spot for sewing supplies. With more shelves, this piece makes a handsome spice cabinet; the lower drawer is perfect for storing teas or loose spices.

Instead of using elaborate moldings, raised panels, or an arched door, this cabinet design highlights the basic joinery that is the standard in quality woodworking. Traditional dovetail joinery holds the case together, while sliding dovetails lock the shelves into place. The door is a simple frame-and-panel assembly, but I chose bridle joints instead of traditional mortises and tenons because the exposed joinery complements the through-dovetails on the case. Instead of cutting a raised or fielded panel, I opted for the clean look of a flat panel. By milling the rails thinner than the stiles, subtle shadowlines lend visual interest to the doors. The lower drawer inside is joined using through-dovetails at both the front and back.

I drilled an off-center ⅞-in.-dia. hole into the drawer face to serve as a finger pull. The hard edges on the finger pull are softened with a knife, and the whittled surfaces are a nice surprise when someone opens the drawer for the first time. Without fail, they pull out the drawer and take a closer look. That closer look is as near to a trophy as a woodworker gets.

Matthew Teague lives in Nashville, Tennessee, where he builds furniture and writes about woodworking.

CHERRY CABINET

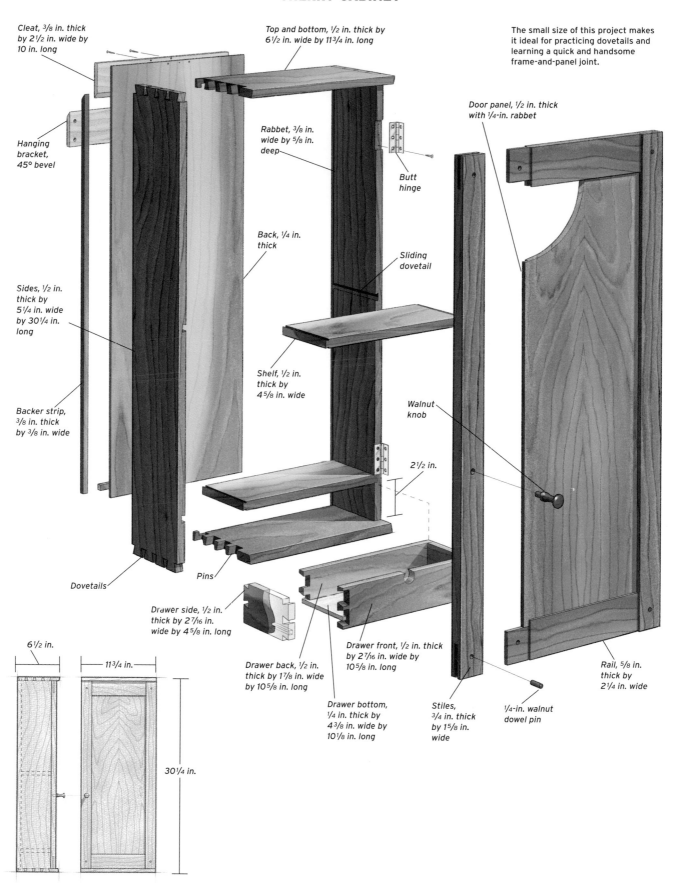

Cleat, ³/₈ in. thick by 2¹/₂ in. wide by 10 in. long

Top and bottom, ¹/₂ in. thick by 6¹/₂ in. wide by 11³/₄ in. long

The small size of this project makes it ideal for practicing dovetails and learning a quick and handsome frame-and-panel joint.

Hanging bracket, 45° bevel

Rabbet, ³/₈ in. wide by ⁵/₈ in. deep

Butt hinge

Door panel, ¹/₂ in. thick with ¹/₄-in. rabbet

Back, ¹/₄ in. thick

Sides, ¹/₂ in. thick by 5¹/₄ in. wide by 30¹/₄ in. long

Sliding dovetail

Shelf, ¹/₂ in. thick by 4⁵/₈ in. wide

Walnut knob

Backer strip, ³/₈ in. thick by ³/₈ in. wide

2¹/₂ in.

Dovetails

Pins

Drawer side, ¹/₂ in. thick by 2⁷/₁₆ in. wide by 4⁵/₈ in. long

Drawer front, ¹/₂ in. thick by 2⁷/₁₆ in. wide by 10⁵/₈ in. long

Rail, ⁵/₈ in. thick by 2¹/₄ in. wide

6¹/₂ in.

11³/₄ in.

Drawer back, ¹/₂ in. thick by 1⁷/₈ in. wide by 10⁵/₈ in. long

Drawer bottom, ¹/₄ in. thick by 4³/₈ in. wide by 10¹/₈ in. long

Stiles, ³/₄ in. thick by 1⁵/₈ in. wide

¹/₄-in. walnut dowel pin

30¹/₄ in.

BUILDING AN OPEN-PEDESTAL TABLE

by John Burchett

The open framework that supports the elliptical table seen here has a light and airy look that belies its strength. Doubled members that form the feet and tabletop rails, as shown in figure 1 on the facing page, reduce overall mass, add interesting detail, and simplify joining the legs to the feet and rails.

In addition to the elementary joinery, I used some template-shaping tricks to simplify construction. The elliptical top, with its gently curved edges, was shaped and edge-molded with a template-guided router. And the duplicate parts of the base were all quickly and easily cut on a spindle shaper using a template that rides against a special fence.

Templates are particularly useful for speedier and more accurate small production runs. I added extra length to the templates for tenons and for fixing the templates to the stock during machining. Templates that are slightly long are safer to use because they begin rubbing against the guide bearing or fence before the stock hits the cutter. Any errors in the templates will be reproduced in every cut part, so it's worth some extra time to be sure that the templates are perfect.

To simplify assembly, I glued up the base into two units, each consisting of a long foot, a pair of short feet, and a leg.

I gave the underframe a couple of coats of linseed oil and polished it off with three coats of dark wax. Because the top receives more abuse, I applied several coats of a mix of linseed oil, polyurethane, and mineral spirits as a base for 14 coats of hand-rubbed, hot, raw linseed oil applied over a month. The client continued the finishing process by applying a coat each month for the next 12 months.

John Burchett is a custom furniture maker in Copnor, Portsmouth, England.

OPEN-PEDESTAL TABLE

Straightforward joinery makes assembling this table quick and easy.

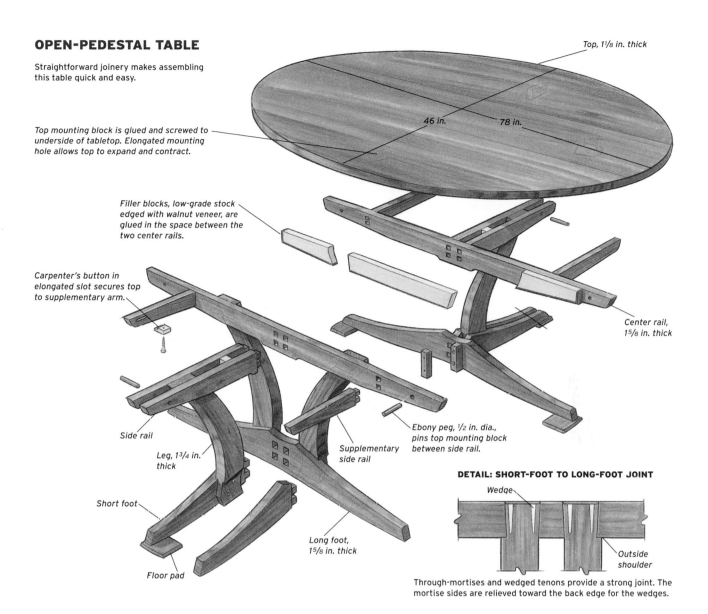

Top, 1⅛ in. thick

Top mounting block is glued and screwed to underside of tabletop. Elongated mounting hole allows top to expand and contract.

46 in.

78 in.

Filler blocks, low-grade stock edged with walnut veneer, are glued in the space between the two center rails.

Carpenter's button in elongated slot secures top to supplementary arm.

Center rail, 1⅝ in. thick

Side rail

Leg, 1¾ in. thick

Supplementary side rail

Ebony peg, ½ in. dia., pins top mounting block between side rail.

Short foot

Long foot, 1⅝ in. thick

Floor pad

DETAIL: SHORT-FOOT TO LONG-FOOT JOINT

Wedge

Outside shoulder

Through-mortises and wedged tenons provide a strong joint. The mortise sides are relieved toward the back edge for the wedges.

USING TEMPLATES

From the full-size front and side elevations of the table's base I made templates for each part from ¼-in.-thick medium-density fiberboard (MDF). I also made a quarter-arc template of an ellipse for cutting and shaping the top.

I've also found templates helpful for selecting stock and laying out the cuts. I juggled the templates around to find the most satisfying grain configuration and economical use of timber before cutting out the blanks of American walnut. Then I surfaced and thicknessed the blanks for shaping. I also machined the boards for the top, so they could settle before remachining.

SCALED TEMPLATE DRAWINGS

Templates made as shown below simplify shaping the numerous curved parts.

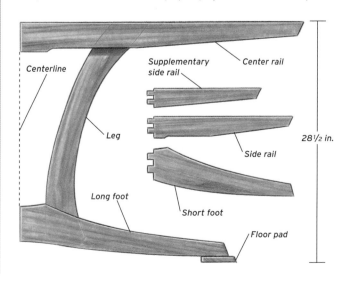

Centerline

Leg

Supplementary side rail

Center rail

Side rail

Long foot

Short foot

Floor pad

28½ in.

DINING TABLE HAS TILT TOP

by Nigel Martin

Practical and versatile, this pedestal table, shown here in cherry with ebony stringing, can be made with a round or oval top. The simple design will play as well in the den as the dining room.

The straightforward, uncluttered design of this dining table lets it fit as comfortably in a kitchen as in a formal dining room, and with its tilting top, it can be stowed against a wall in a room with multiple uses. Over the years, I've made it in cherry, as shown in the photo above, as well as chestnut, ash, elm and oak, with different finishes and detailing depending on the setting and the customer.

I think round and oval tables provide the most sociable seating arrangement, but they concentrate more knees in less space. That's why a pedestal base, with its yards of extra legroom, is such a good match for a rounded-top table. For reasons of balance and stress, a central pedestal base won't pair as well with large rectangular tops whose corners can become powerful levers. Even with a rounded top, the leg joints in a pedestal are subjected to enormous stresses. To resist those stresses, I join the legs and column of this table with tapered sliding dovetails, a very strong, self-locking joint, which I reinforce with toenailed dowels, as shown in figure 1 on the facing page.

Nigel Martin is a professional cabinetmaker in Norfolk, England.

MAKING A TILT-TOP PEDESTAL TABLE

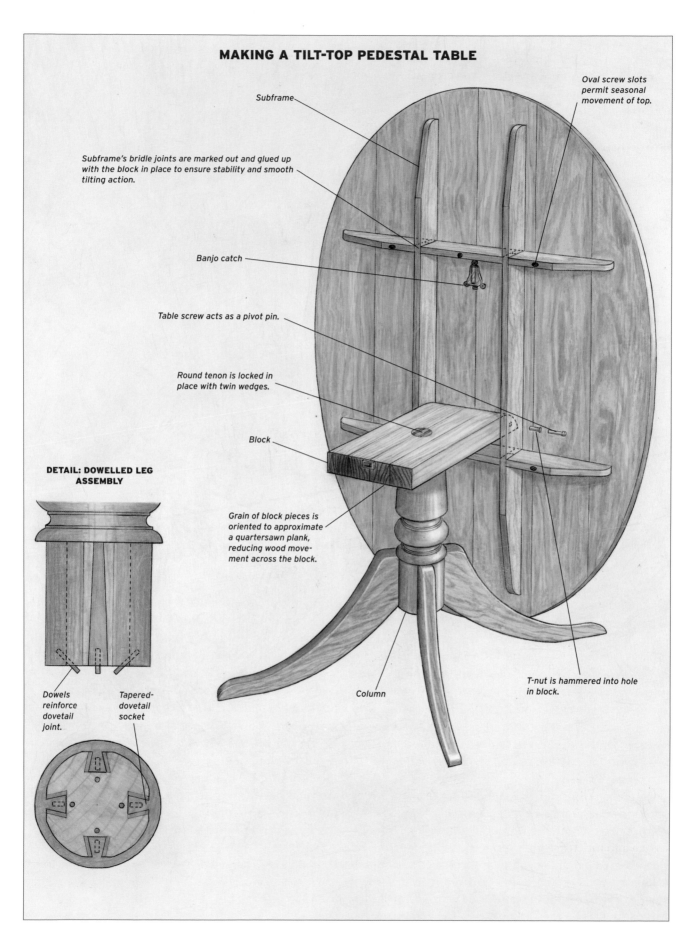

Subframe

Oval screw slots permit seasonal movement of top.

Subframe's bridle joints are marked out and glued up with the block in place to ensure stability and smooth tilting action.

Banjo catch

Table screw acts as a pivot pin.

Round tenon is locked in place with twin wedges.

Block

DETAIL: DOWELLED LEG ASSEMBLY

Grain of block pieces is oriented to approximate a quartersawn plank, reducing wood movement across the block.

Dowels reinforce dovetail joint.

Tapered-dovetail socket

Column

T-nut is hammered into hole in block.

GATE-LEG TABLE IS LIGHT BUT STURDY

by Gary Rogowski

I was shown a picture once of a gate-leg dining table. It had eight cabriole legs, and it looked like an insect with a tabletop on it. I delicately convinced my prospective clients to let me design a table with a little more grace that still had the drop leaves and gates they wanted. The tabletop was to be an oval large enough to seat eight comfortably. My concern was to lighten the base visually and still provide adequate support for the leaves. The table that resulted satisfied my clients' needs for utility and complemented its surroundings well.

Gate-leg tables were designed to save space. A leg-and-apron assembly, or gate, hinged to the table or pivoting on pins set into the table's framework, swings out to support a leaf that's hinged to the tabletop. In this way, a small table can be transformed easily into a larger one. A single gate can support a leaf on a smaller table, or double gates can be used for larger leaves, such as on this dining table. The gates can also

be on one or both sides of the table, depending on the function of the table and how much extra space is desired. When not in use, two leaves take up hardly more space than one. For the finest appearance, rule joints are used between the leaves and top. This joint looks clean and provides support for the leaves.

Double gates can pivot either toward or away from each other. I decided to have the gates pivot away from each other so that with the leaves down, the gate legs would sit side by side. Measured together, the pair of gate legs are 2½ in. wide, or the same width as one of the outer table legs. This lightens the table visually by making it look like there's only one leg in the center of the table rather than two.

Gary Rogowski designs and builds custom furniture and teaches woodworking at the Oregon School of Arts and Crafts.

CHERRY TABLE IS LIGHT BUT STURDY

The table's size, 60 in. by 84 in., seats eight, but when the leaves are down, the table is more compact and can be moved against the wall for more floor space.

GATE-LEG TABLE

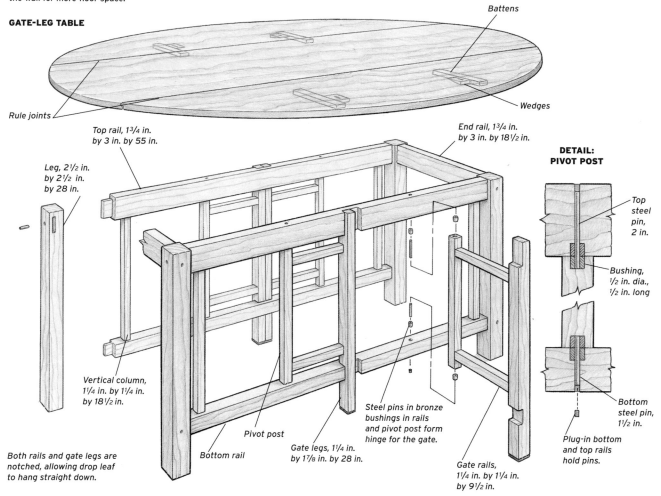

Battens

Wedges

Rule joints

Top rail, 1³/₄ in. by 3 in. by 55 in.

End rail, 1³/₄ in. by 3 in. by 18¹/₂ in.

Leg, 2¹/₂ in. by 2¹/₂ in. by 28 in.

DETAIL: PIVOT POST

Top steel pin, 2 in.

Bushing, ¹/₂ in. dia., ¹/₂ in. long

Vertical column, 1¹/₄ in. by 1¹/₄ in. by 18¹/₂ in.

Pivot post

Bottom rail

Gate legs, 1¹/₄ in. by 1⁷/₈ in. by 28 in.

Steel pins in bronze bushings in rails and pivot post form hinge for the gate.

Gate rails, 1¹/₄ in. by 1¹/₄ in. by 9¹/₂ in.

Bottom steel pin, 1¹/₂ in.

Plug-in bottom and top rails hold pins.

Both rails and gate legs are notched, allowing drop leaf to hang straight down.

MORTISING FIXTURE

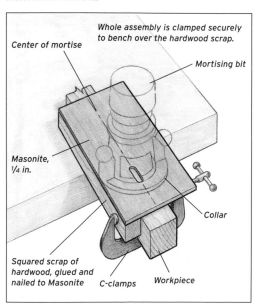

Center of mortise

Whole assembly is clamped securely to bench over the hardwood scrap.

Mortising bit

Masonite, ¹/₄ in.

Collar

Squared scrap of hardwood, glued and nailed to Masonite

C-clamps

Workpiece

Detail: Accounting for the offset distance

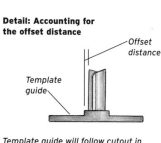

Offset distance

Template guide

Template guide will follow cutout in Masonite®, but offset between edge of bit and outside of template guide's collar must be taken into consideration. That distance must be doubled because you're routing to both sides of the bit.

TABLESAW TENONING JIG

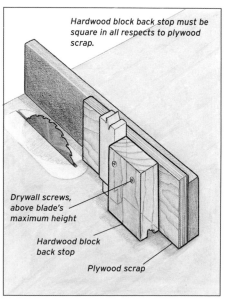

Hardwood block back stop must be square in all respects to plywood scrap.

Drywall screws, above blade's maximum height

Hardwood block back stop

Plywood scrap

HARVEST TABLE

by Christian Becksvoort

CHERRY DINING TABLE

This classic Shaker dining table features drop leaves that are supported by spinners cut into the aprons.

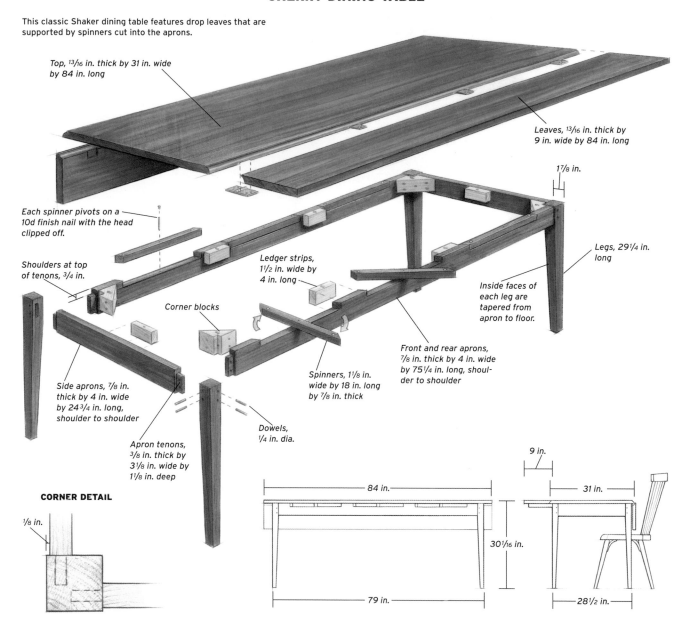

Top, ¹³/₁₆ in. thick by 31 in. wide by 84 in. long

Leaves, ¹³/₁₆ in. thick by 9 in. wide by 84 in. long

1⁷/₈ in.

Each spinner pivots on a 10d finish nail with the head clipped off.

Shoulders at top of tenons, ³/₄ in.

Ledger strips, 1½ in. wide by 4 in. long

Legs, 29¹/₄ in. long

Corner blocks

Inside faces of each leg are tapered from apron to floor.

Side aprons, ⁷/₈ in. thick by 4 in. wide by 24³/₄ in. long, shoulder to shoulder

Spinners, 1¹/₈ in. wide by 18 in. long by ⁷/₈ in. thick

Front and rear aprons, ⁷/₈ in. thick by 4 in. wide by 75¹/₄ in. long, shoulder to shoulder

Apron tenons, ³/₈ in. thick by 3¹/₈ in. wide by 1¹/₈ in. deep

Dowels, ¹/₄ in. dia.

9 in.

84 in.

31 in.

30¹/₁₆ in.

79 in.

28½ in.

CORNER DETAIL

¹/₈ in.

The drop-leaf table is one of the most versatile designs that I build. I've made small, 30-in. square end tables, 10-footers for major dinner parties, tables with drawers, tables with one leaf, and tables with leaves that hang almost to the floor. The form can be used not just for dining tables but also for side, end, serving, and couch tables.

Recently, I was commissioned to design and construct a drop-leaf table and a set of chairs to seat eight. The base should provide diners with adequate chair space, with no one straddling a leg. Figuring 24 in. (or more) per serving area, I came up with a base that's 28½ in. by 79 in.

For the top dimensions, I figured 31 in. wide by 84 in. long. The top extends beyond the base so that the two 9-in. leaves can hang below. When down, the leaves allow for chairs to be slid under them. With the leaves up, the total width of the tabletop becomes roughly 48 in. (because of the rule-joint overlap). I made this tabletop ¹³/₁₆ in. thick, but ³/₄ in. is the minimum—less than that and the quirk (or filet) on the leaf rule joint becomes too thin or fragile.

Christian Becksvoort is a contributing editor to Fine Woodworking *magazine.*

KITCHEN CLASSIC

by Thomas J. Calisto

When I was about 10 years old I saw a guy on television demonstrate how to cut through-dovetails. Fascinated by the program, I had to try it myself. I borrowed my father's jigsaw and went outside to hack up some pine shelving. I cut my first set of through-dovetails that day. The dovetails weren't pretty, but they were a great leap from nailed butt joints. I have since refined my joinery skills enough to build some furniture, so when my wife wanted a new kitchen table, I knew what my next project would be.

Most of the furniture I've built has been inspired by Shaker pieces. I like this style, but we were looking for something with a few more curves. We searched through magazines and some design books before settling on a table based on one we found in Thomas Moser's book, *Measured Shop Drawings for American Furniture* (Sterling, 1988). The table has a round apron that makes it unique, and I knew it could be scaled down to fit our kitchen.

Construction of this table is straightforward with two exceptions: the laminated curved apron and the joinery involved in connecting the apron quadrants to the legs (see the drawings at right). While the curved apron adds a little complexity to the construction, it is well within the scope of anyone who has basic joinery skills and some patience. The tenoning jig that I developed for this project greatly simplified the joinery. As with most furniture projects, it helps to draw the important views full scale. The full-scale plan view came in handy when I needed to construct the bending form and the tenoning jig for the curved apron pieces and later when I had to mark the curved aprons for length.

Thomas J. Calisto is a mechanical engineer. He spends many of his mornings and weekends in his shop in Durham, North Carolina.

A BENDING FORM FOR THE CURVED APRONS

This particleboard bending form has an outside curve that matches the inside radius of the apron quadrants. The curve of the form is larger than the finished length of the quadrants to allow some leeway when gluing up the bent laminations. Sanding sealer and wax applied to the form keep the glue from sticking to it.

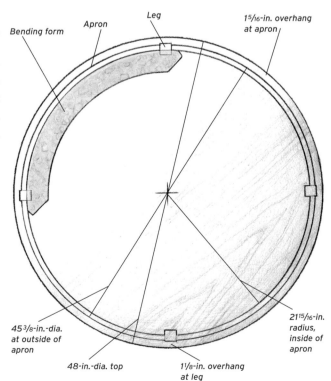

Bending form

Apron

Leg

1⁵⁄₁₆-in. overhang at apron

45³⁄₈-in.-dia. at outside of apron

48-in.-dia. top

1¹⁄₈-in. overhang at leg

21¹⁵⁄₁₆-in. radius, inside of apron

STRONG JOINERY IS HIDDEN FROM VIEW

A curved apron and tapered legs distinguish this practical and elegant table. With mortise-and-tenon joinery where apron meets leg, backed up by beefy glue blocks and cross braces, this table is strong yet lightweight.

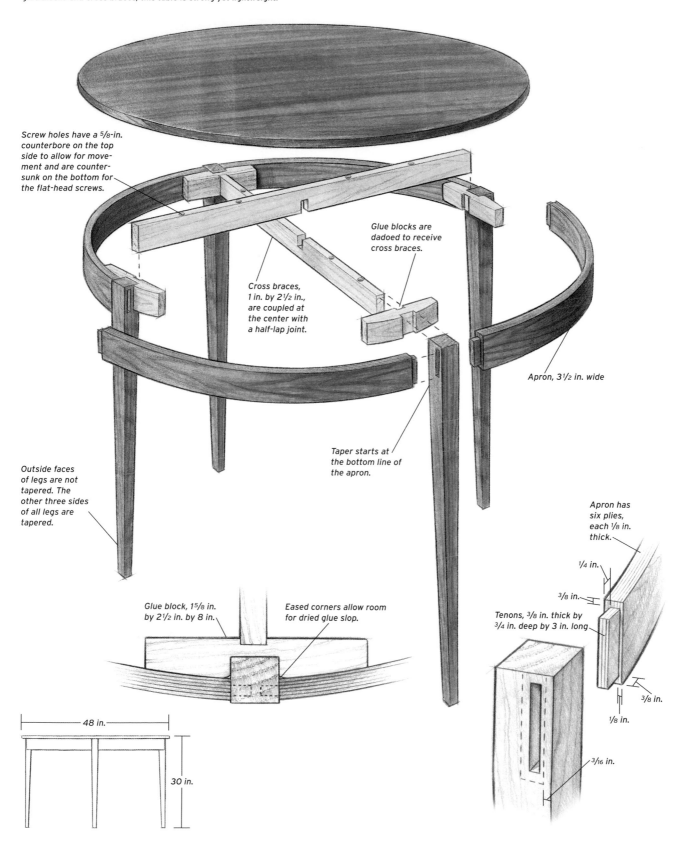

Screw holes have a 5/8-in. counterbore on the top side to allow for movement and are countersunk on the bottom for the flat-head screws.

Cross braces, 1 in. by 2 1/2 in., are coupled at the center with a half-lap joint.

Glue blocks are dadoed to receive cross braces.

Apron, 3 1/2 in. wide

Taper starts at the bottom line of the apron.

Outside faces of legs are not tapered. The other three sides of all legs are tapered.

Glue block, 1 5/8 in. by 2 1/2 in. by 8 in.

Eased corners allow room for dried glue slop.

Apron has six plies, each 1/8 in. thick.

1/4 in.

3/8 in.

Tenons, 3/8 in. thick by 3/4 in. deep by 3 in. long.

3/8 in.

1/8 in.

3/16 in.

48 in.

30 in.

AN EXPANDABLE TABLE

by William Krase

Hidden hinges.
The Soss®-brand invisible hinges face the wall when the tabletop is flded and are concealed with the top open.

A SIMPLE WAY TO EXPAND A TABLE

To convert the table from its compact mode, the top is turned 90° on the pivot carrier (see detail below); then the top is opened to full size.

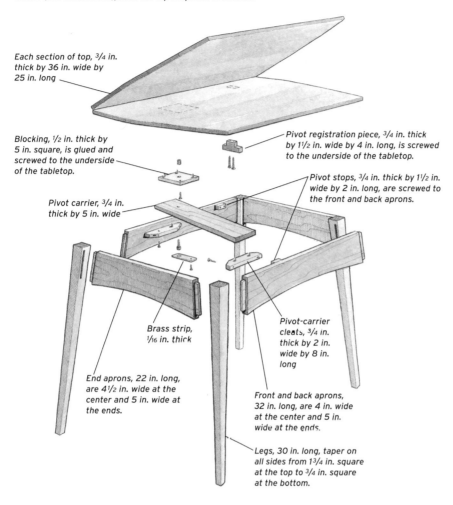

Each section of top, 3/4 in. thick by 36 in. wide by 25 in. long

Blocking, 1/2 in. thick by 5 in. square, is glued and screwed to the underside of the tabletop.

Pivot carrier, 3/4 in. thick by 5 in. wide

Pivot registration piece, 3/4 in. thick by 1 1/2 in. wide by 4 in. long, is screwed to the underside of the tabletop.

Pivot stops, 3/4 in. thick by 1 1/2 in. wide by 2 in. long, are screwed to the front and back aprons.

Brass strip, 1/16 in. thick

Pivot-carrier cleats, 3/4 in. thick by 2 in. wide by 8 in. long

End aprons, 22 in. long, are 4 1/2 in. wide at the center and 5 in. wide at the ends.

Front and back aprons, 32 in. long, are 4 in. wide at the center and 5 in. wide at the ends.

Legs, 30 in. long, taper on all sides from 1 3/4 in. square at the top to 3/4 in. square at the bottom.

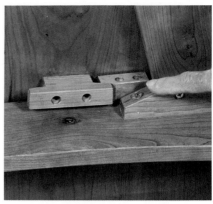

No pivoting beyond this point. The pivot stops fit snug inside the recesses of the T-shaped registration piece.

PIVOT-MECHANISM DETAIL
The tabletop rotates on a single point using a machine bolt screwed into a threaded insert.

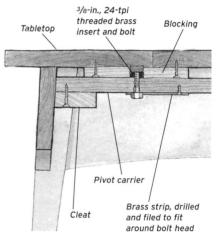

Tabletop

3/8-in., 24-tpi threaded brass insert and bolt

Blocking

Pivot carrier

Brass strip, drilled and filed to fit around bolt head

Cleat

I vividly remember the colorful language my mother used when I was a kid as she struggled to extend a removable-leaf table that was prone to jamming. So when a client asked for an expandable table, I sought a better solution. My client wanted a table that would fit against a wall and seat two and that on occasion could expand to seat six. He expected some sort of drop-leaf table, but it's difficult to sit around that kind of table when the leaves are down.

I recalled seeing a table where the top pivoted and then unfolded to double in size, a solution I thought would meet the needs of my client. The design meets several challenges inherent in this type of table. The central problem is that a fixed base must accommodate, with adequate stability, both a small top and one that is twice the size. At the same time, the footprint of the base should not extend beyond the "shadow" of the hinged top in its contracted size, lest the legs of the table conflict with the feet of the user.

The use of SOSS hinges (www.soss.com) permits the leaf to fold over 180 degrees in the closed position. When the table is open, though, the hinges are concealed. Two would have given enough strength, but I elected to use four hinges to help keep the leaves aligned.

The folding method I used is suitable for larger tables with a length-to-width ratio of 1.2 to 1.8, but it is not suitable for square, round, or oval tabletops. I made the open table boat-shaped, a design that affords everyone a better view of each other and that is conducive to conversation. The edge profile must take into account the sometimes-inverted position of one leaf. I used a simple long-radius roundover bit guided by a template.

I chose to splay the legs for extra stability and to taper them all the way to the bottom. The ends of the aprons are all 5 degrees from the vertical with the tenons cut on the tablesaw. Strictly speaking, the

Locating and Mounting the Pivot

FINDING THE PIVOT POINT

First locate the center of the hinge line in the two-seat (A) and six-seat (B) positions. Then project lines from these points at 45°. The intersection of these lines (C) is the location of the pivot point.

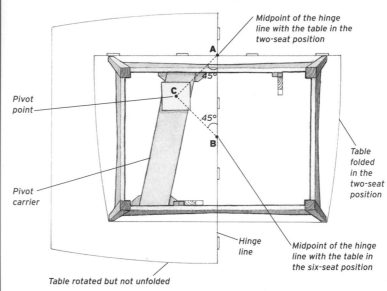

Midpoint of the hinge line with the table in the two-seat position

A

45°

C

Pivot point

45°

B

Table folded in the two-seat position

Pivot carrier

Hinge line

Midpoint of the hinge line with the table in the six-seat position

Table rotated but not unfolded

The best way to locate the pivot point is to make an accurate scale drawing of the table frame. Overlay this with a plan of the tabletop in its folded position so that you can see the relationship between the frame and the top, both in its normal position and rotated 90 degrees. Point A is the midpoint of the hinge line with the table folded in the two-seat position, while point B is the midpoint of the hinge line with the tabletop rotated and in the six-seat position. Draw lines from both points at 45 degrees to the line A-B; their intersection marks the pivot point (C). Now, the pivot carrier and the pivot stops can be drawn in.

Measurements from the scale drawing can be taken to locate the pivot point on both the pivot carrier and the tabletop.

The pivot is a 3/8-in., 24-tpi machine bolt that mates with and turns in a threaded brass insert in the tabletop. The insert is set in a block that's glued and screwed to the underside of the tabletop. The insert requires a nominal 1/2-in. pilot hole and is 5/8 in. long.

Screwing the insert into hardwood is much easier if the nominal pilot hole is enlarged by 1/32 in. To install the insert perpendicular to the surface, use an auxiliary block of wood to make things easier.

The machine bolt passes through the pivot carrier and into the threaded insert. This type of pivot should be arranged to tighten a quarter turn when the table is expanded. This will pull the parts together very slightly, so clearance over the pivot carrier should be allowed.

The final step is to add a brass strip to prevent the pivot bolt from loosening or falling out. The strip is drilled and filed to fit over the bolt head and is screwed to the pivot carrier at the other end.

---

tenons should have been cut at a compound angle due to the splay of the legs, but I didn't do this because the second angle for a 5 degrees splay is a negligible 0.2 degrees. Make a scale drawing to locate the position of the pivot point (above).

Next, the recesses for the hinges need to be cut. Because the deep recesses are awkward to cut on the edge of the large tabletop, I made a 12-in.-tall auxiliary fence for my router table.

After the aprons and legs had been assembled, I attached the pivot carrier, which provides a point on which the tabletop can turn. The pivot carrier is secured to two blocks that are screwed to the aprons.

The carrier is angled to expose the two stops that also are screwed to the aprons and limit the swivel motion. These stops register against a T-shaped piece of wood screwed to the underside of the leaf that doesn't flip over.

All tables of this design have one drawback: They cannot be lifted when the tabletop is open because the only permanent connection with the base is the pivot mechanism.

William Krase is a retired aerospace engineer who lives in Mendocino, California.

TRESTLE TABLE WITH BREADBOARD ENDS

by Charles Durfee

Mention the trestle table, and many images come to mind. It could be a Colonial family gathered for dinner around a few rough planks over a crude X-trestle. It could be Shakers in the 19th century, silent and divided by sex, eating at one of their elegant and refined but understated dining tables. For myself, it could just as easily be a double-post trestle supporting a glass top. Every large furniture manufacturer in the country now offers some version of the trestle table. Indeed, it is the very image of family life.

In the course of building many types of trestle tables, I have developed what I call my basic design and have found it to be highly adaptable. Need more width to support a heavy glass top? Double up the posts and beam. Want a desk? Add a pencil drawer, a wing, and an organizer. A workstation? Put a keyboard tray underneath the top. A trestle table can be small enough for breakfast or big enough for a grand banquet. By placing extra sets of posts and legs

along the way, a table can be stretched out to at least 12 ft., as the Shakers did.

There are limitations, of course. Although not constrained in length, the design is very much so in width. While you need a minimum width of 32 in. to 34 in. for dining—less than that becomes a knee-knocker—a top wider than 36 in. will put too much stress on the post-to-cleat joint. One solution is to adopt a double-post-and-beam design, which gives the piece a contemporary look. Several years ago, a customer requested a base design to go with a plate-glass top, to be 42 in. by 84 in. Using my basic design, I doubled the posts and beams and made the feet and cleats proportionately longer. The result turned out to be very successful—the glass nicely complemented the openness of the trestle base, which was strong enough to support the weight. A word to the wise, however: As you add width to the table and begin to approach square, the design loses its point of view

CHERRY TRESTLE TABLE

Contemporary or traditional? Which is it? Breadboard ends and chamfered edges give the table a traditional look. Leave off the breadboard ends and leave the edges crisp and square, and the table has a contemporary look. The dimensions for this table can be modified to suit the number of people who will sit at your table.

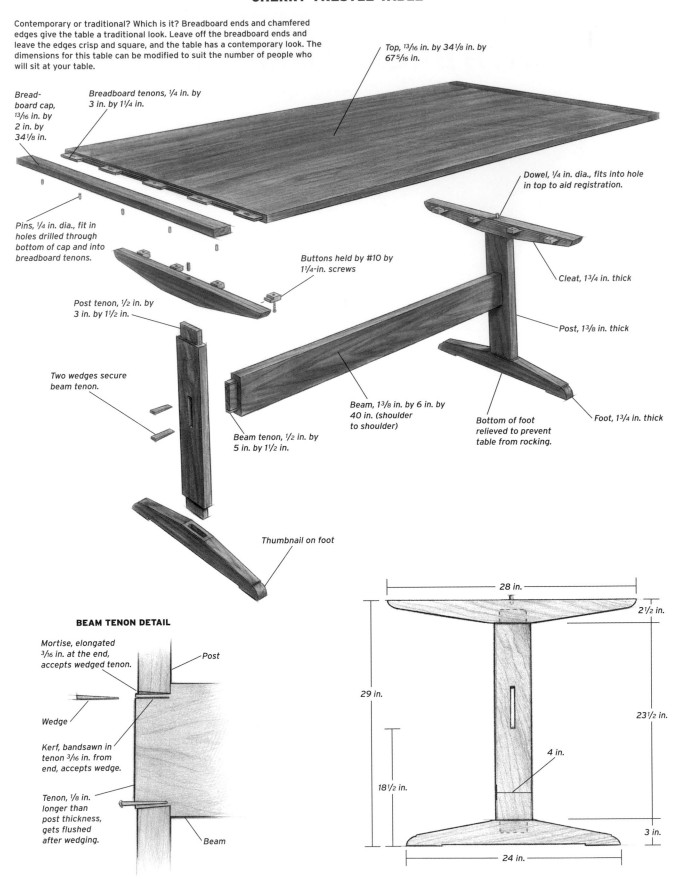

Top, ¹³/₁₆ in. by 34¹/₈ in. by 67⁵/₁₆ in.

Bread-board cap, ¹³/₁₆ in. by 2 in. by 34¹/₈ in.

Breadboard tenons, ¹/₄ in. by 3 in. by 1¹/₄ in.

Pins, ¹/₄ in. dia., fit in holes drilled through bottom of cap and into breadboard tenons.

Dowel, ¹/₄ in. dia., fits into hole in top to aid registration.

Buttons held by #10 by 1¹/₄-in. screws

Cleat, 1³/₄ in. thick

Post tenon, ¹/₂ in. by 3 in. by 1¹/₂ in.

Post, 1³/₈ in. thick

Two wedges secure beam tenon.

Beam, 1³/₈ in. by 6 in. by 40 in. (shoulder to shoulder)

Beam tenon, ¹/₂ in. by 5 in. by 1¹/₂ in.

Bottom of foot relieved to prevent table from rocking.

Foot, 1³/₄ in. thick

Thumbnail on foot

BEAM TENON DETAIL

Mortise, elongated ³/₁₆ in. at the end, accepts wedged tenon.

Post

Wedge

Kerf, bandsawn in tenon ³/₁₆ in. from end, accepts wedge.

Tenon, ¹/₈ in. longer than post thickness, gets flushed after wedging.

Beam

28 in.

2¹/₂ in.

29 in.

23¹/₂ in.

4 in.

18¹/₂ in.

3 in.

24 in.

Design decisions can be made about the base as well. The Shakers raised the standard beam out of harm's way— underneath the top. This idea makes for good leg room and gives the table a wonderfully light, almost floating, effect. You don't need to be an engineer, however, to know that this will make the base less rigid. Indeed, at least one of the Shakers' tables showed trouble in that regard. Their solution to improve this was to use a drawbolt arrangement, as I had in my reproduction of the Hancock table design. The Shakers adopted this system because they could disassemble the table and transport it to another community to be shown as a model. However, when assembled, it was surprisingly solid, with no water spilling when the turkey was being carved.

On my basic design, the beam is about two-thirds of the way off the floor, giving good leg room and avoiding the Shakers' bolted joint. The beam is 6 in. wide, through-mortised, and wedged into the post. No water spills.

Many early Colonial trestle tables had feet that were broad and flat, combined with posts nearly square in section. This setup often has problems with rigidity, however. The feet on the basic table are higher and narrower, with a post that is wider than it is thick, which affords more substantial joinery. The Hancock Shaker feet are arched and up on their toes, evoking classical styles and providing more landing for the joint. Again, the posts are wider than they are thick.

A good furniture design will work well in a variety of settings. The music of Bach has been played as jazz and pop, used and abused. So too has the trestle table. But it is healthy, and it endures. Rightfully so.

Charles Durfee lives in Woolwich, Maine, and has built furniture since 1978.

and should be abandoned in favor of a leg-and-apron, pedestal, or other type of base.

Moving out of the dining room and into the office, you can find a lovely cherry trestle table being used as a writing desk. Because you work only from one side, a width of 26 in. is fine. The height can be the same as that of a dining table, i.e., 30 in. Again, the length can be as short or long as desired. A pencil drawer hung under the top provides useful storage, and there is plenty of leg room to stretch out into as you chew on ideas. When I built the first of these desks, typewriters were still in use. Now, typewriters are only at the Smithsonian. But the trestle-table desk can be adapted to the digital age. A keyboard tray can replace the pencil drawer. Or, if you have enough room, keep the main desk for writing and set the monitor on a wing (this time kept flush with the main surface), with the keyboard tray under the wing. Wires can be clipped up under the top. Other computer components can be put on the desk or in a separate piece of furniture.

PEDESTAL TABLE

by John Zeitoun

I love flipping through books of antique furniture and looking over pieces at garage sales, and I jump at the challenge of reproducing an antique in my shop. Such was the case when a client showed me a picture of a 160-year-old French Regency pedestal table from the book *The Furniture of Old Ontario* (Macmillan, 1973) and asked if I could make it for him.

The picture didn't explain construction techniques, but using generally accepted proportions, as well as considering the space it was to occupy, I was able to reproduce the table. I was able to simplify the construction process by breaking it down into small steps and by using a few jigs. According to the book, the original table had a hardwood base with bird's-eye maple veneer and a pine tabletop. But I chose to make mine out of walnut

John Zeitoun operates a custom cabinetry shop near his hometown of Wakefield, Quebec, Canada.

The oak version of the table shown here was first featured on the cover of *Fine Woodworking* #122. That photo illustrated my article about building an Arts and Crafts side chair. After the article was published, I received many calls—not about the chair, but regarding the table.

One client wanted a lighter, more feminine pick of wood: figured maple. She chose a design I had already used for an oak table. Its inspiration came from Stickley's No. 657 library table and Frank Lloyd Wright's rectilinear furniture. With a top measuring

Subtop Keeps the Base from Racking

The subtop, a piece of ³/₄-in. plywood with solid edges glued to two sides, fits into a rabbet cut into the long upper rails of the table's base. Four large holes in the subtop house screws that hold the tabletop in place. The holes are larger at the top than at the bottom to allow the screws to move as the tabletop adjusts to seasonal changes in humidity. —R.A.

Screw and glue subtop to rails. The author squares up a slight misalignment in the base using a pipe clamp, then glues and screws the subtop in place.

48 in. by 110 in., it's meant for entertaining large groups. Bird's-eye maple was my customer's wood of choice. But I knew it would be nearly impossible to find bird's-eye in the large dimensions required: 2-in. thick and 10 ft. long. We settled on curly maple. Birds-eye was selected as a secondary wood, and its use was limited to the spindles.

Even with bulky legs to support its mass, the use of curly maple (finished in a light tone) gives the table a more feminine, lighter presence.

Rex Alexander makes furniture, cabinetry and millwork in Brethren, Michigan.

ARTS AND CRAFTS DINING TABLE

Curly and birds' eye maple lend this Arts and Crafts design a light look. The mortise-and-tenon construction is reinforced with pins and screws.

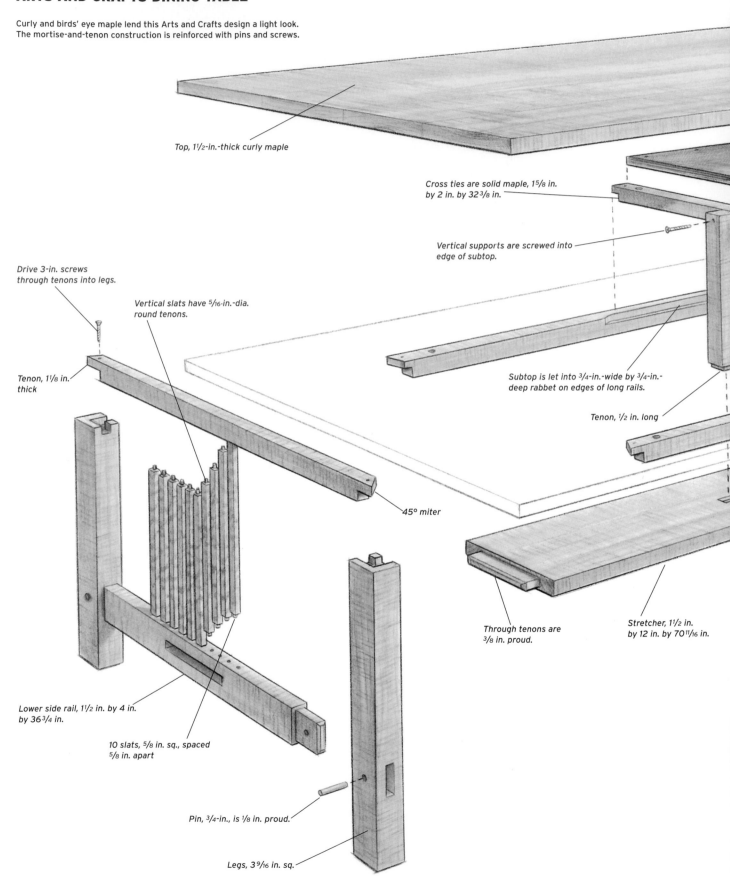

Top, 1 1/2-in.-thick curly maple

Cross ties are solid maple, 1 5/8 in. by 2 in. by 32 3/8 in.

Vertical supports are screwed into edge of subtop.

Drive 3-in. screws through tenons into legs.

Vertical slats have 5/16-in.-dia. round tenons.

Tenon, 1 1/8 in. thick

Subtop is let into 3/4-in.-wide by 3/4-in.-deep rabbet on edges of long rails.

Tenon, 1/2 in. long

45° miter

Through tenons are 3/8 in. proud.

Stretcher, 1 1/2 in. by 12 in. by 70 11/16 in.

Lower side rail, 1 1/2 in. by 4 in. by 36 3/4 in.

10 slats, 5/8 in. sq., spaced 5/8 in. apart

Pin, 3/4-in., is 1/8 in. proud.

Legs, 3 9/16 in. sq.

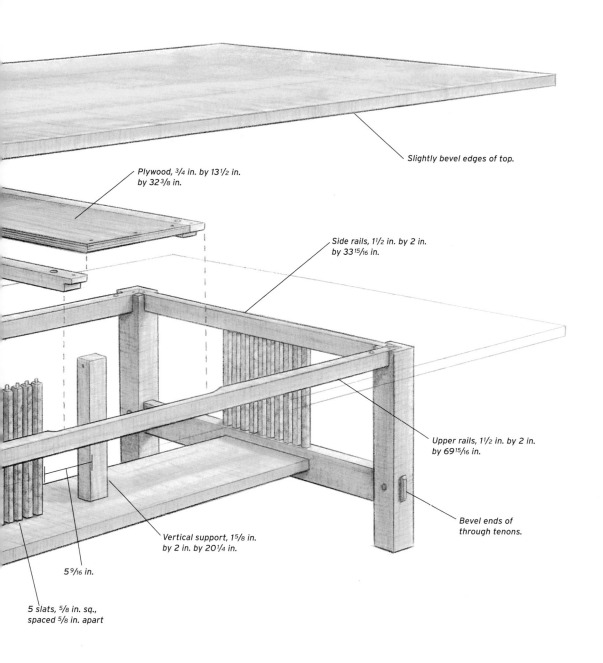

Slightly bevel edges of top.

Plywood, $^3/_4$ in. by 13$^1/_2$ in. by 32$^3/_8$ in.

Side rails, 1$^1/_2$ in. by 2 in. by 33$^{15}/_{16}$ in.

Upper rails, 1$^1/_2$ in. by 2 in. by 69$^{15}/_{16}$ in.

Bevel ends of through tenons.

Vertical support, 1$^5/_8$ in. by 2 in. by 20$^1/_4$ in.

5$^9/_{16}$ in.

5 slats, $^5/_8$ in. sq., spaced $^5/_8$ in. apart

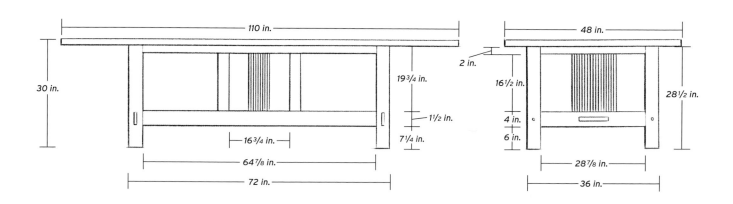

110 in.

48 in.

2 in.

30 in.

19$^3/_4$ in.

16$^1/_2$ in.

28$^1/_2$ in.

1$^1/_2$ in.

4 in.

6 in.

7$^1/_4$ in.

16$^3/_4$ in.

64$^7/_8$ in.

28$^7/_8$ in.

72 in.

36 in.

BUILD A GREENE & GREENE SIDE TABLE

by Gary Rogowski

Simple is beautiful, so they say. But I also know that simple and beautiful together are challenging to achieve. This became apparent when I set out to reproduce this Greene & Greene side table, which embodies the details and construction techniques practiced by the prolific furniture-making brothers Charles and Henry Greene in the early 20th century.

The table base is assembled with pinned mortise-and-tenon joints; square ebony plugs decorate the pinned joinery; breadboard ends keep the tabletop flat; and the piece features a cloud-lift motif.

Although the construction details are fairly simple, the challenge lay in translating the beauty of the table from photograph to the real thing. At first, I made a scale drawing from the photo, but the table looked oversize and chunky. To overcome my dilemma, I built a full-scale mock-up out of cardboard. This took only a few hours of slicing pieces of cardboard and assembling them with hot-melt glue. If a part seemed too big, I cut it down and rebuilt the model.

For the tabletop, the aprons, and the stretchers, I chose a thickness of 1 in., which matched the strong appearance of the legs. When I was happy with the look of the cloud lift, I made a template for it out of ¼-in.-thick medium-density fiberboard (MDF) and then transferred the shape to my cardboard aprons. After I drew the breadboard ends on the cardboard top, the design felt and looked right. Now it was time to mill some wood.

Gary Rogowski teaches classes at The Northwest Woodworking Studio in Portland, Oregon, where he lives.

MAHOGANY SIDE TABLE

Cloud lifts and ebony plugs decorate the piece. A signature Greene and Greene detail is the breadboard ends, which help keep the solid tabletop flat. Pinned mortise-and-tenon joints keep the table rigid yet allow for seasonal movement.

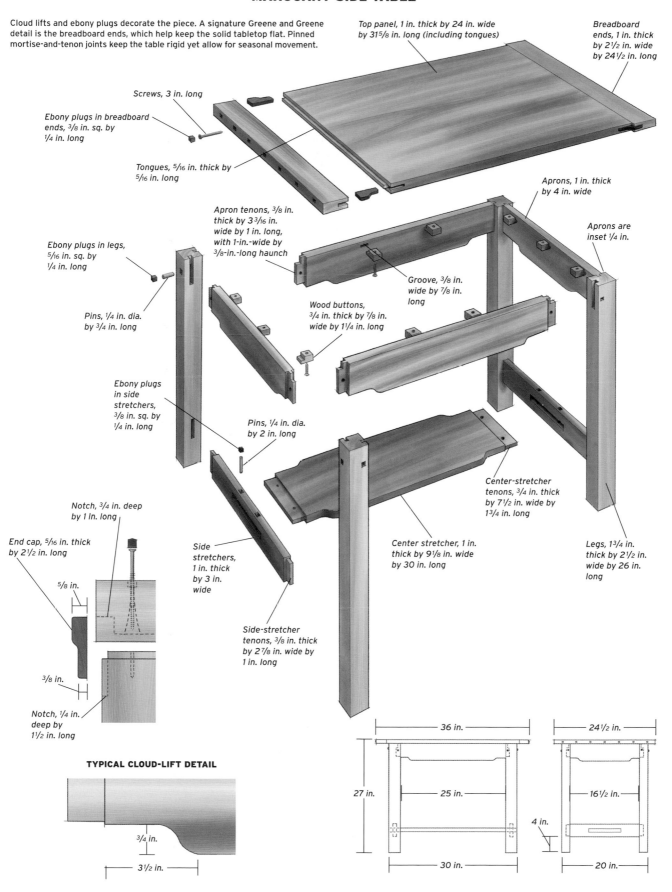

Top panel, 1 in. thick by 24 in. wide by 31⅝ in. long (including tongues)

Breadboard ends, 1 in. thick by 2½ in. wide by 24½ in. long

Screws, 3 in. long

Ebony plugs in breadboard ends, ⅜ in. sq. by ¼ in. long

Tongues, 5/16 in. thick by 5/16 in. long

Aprons, 1 in. thick by 4 in. wide

Aprons are inset ¼ in.

Apron tenons, ⅜ in. thick by 3 3/16 in. wide by 1 in. long, with 1-in.-wide by ⅜-in.-long haunch

Ebony plugs in legs, 5/16 in. sq. by ¼ in. long

Groove, ⅜ in. wide by ⅞ in. long

Pins, ¼ in. dia. by ¾ in. long

Wood buttons, ¾ in. thick by ⅞ in. wide by 1¼ in. long

Ebony plugs in side stretchers, ⅜ in. sq. by ¼ in. long

Pins, ¼ in. dia. by 2 in. long

Center-stretcher tenons, ¾ in. thick by 7½ in. wide by 1¾ in. long

Notch, ¾ in. deep by 1 in. long

End cap, 5/16 in. thick by 2½ in. long

⅝ in.

Side stretchers, 1 in. thick by 3 in. wide

Center stretcher, 1 in. thick by 9⅛ in. wide by 30 in. long

Legs, 1¾ in. thick by 2½ in. wide by 26 in. long

⅜ in.

Notch, ¼ in. deep by 1½ in. long

Side-stretcher tenons, ⅜ in. thick by 2⅞ in. wide by 1 in. long

TYPICAL CLOUD-LIFT DETAIL

¾ in.

3½ in.

36 in.

24½ in.

27 in.

25 in.

16½ in.

4 in.

30 in.

20 in.

DROP-LEAF BREAKFAST TABLE

by Robert Treanor

Modesty and majesty. *This small Queen Anne breakfast table contains a broad range of joinery. Pinned tenons, knuckle joints and half-blind dovetails connect the aprons and legs, and rule joints run between the leaves and fixed top.*

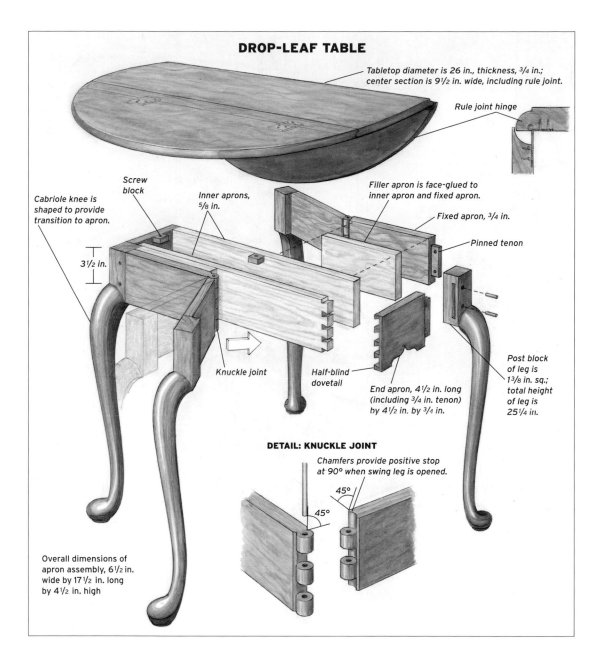

DROP-LEAF TABLE

Tabletop diameter is 26 in., thickness, ³/₄ in.; center section is 9¹/₂ in. wide, including rule joint.

Rule joint hinge

Screw block

Inner aprons, ⁵/₈ in.

Filler apron is face-glued to inner apron and fixed apron.

Fixed apron, ³/₄ in.

Cabriole knee is shaped to provide transition to apron.

3¹/₂ in.

Pinned tenon

Knuckle joint

Half-blind dovetail

End apron, 4¹/₂ in. long (including ³/₄ in. tenon) by 4¹/₂ in. by ³/₄ in.

Post block of leg is 1³/₈ in. sq.; total height of leg is 25¹/₄ in.

DETAIL: KNUCKLE JOINT

Chamfers provide positive stop at 90° when swing leg is opened.

45°

45°

Overall dimensions of apron assembly, 6¹/₂ in. wide by 17¹/₂ in. long by 4¹/₂ in. high

---

As an apartment dweller, I am constantly fighting a losing battle for space. In one small, narrow hallway in my apartment, the phone and its paraphernalia has to share space with one of the precious closets. Little room is left for a table on which to write messages or to place small items. It seemed to me that a drop-leaf table, narrow when closed, would fit the space and provide terms for a truce in my little battle. And as a peace dividend, I could always open up the table and use it elsewhere for special occasions.

The small table I made is a good example of a late Queen Anne breakfast table. The 18th-century form combines grace and versatility, and making it demands the same attributes in the craftsman. The half-blind dovetailed aprons, the rule-jointed leaves,

and the knuckle joints on the swing legs all require precise work. And shaping the compound curves of the cabriole legs needs a steady hand and eye. The skills are not difficult to master, and the effort will be rewarded with a useful and elegant table. The original on which my table is based was made of walnut, but I built mine of cherry. Maple or mahogany would also be appropriate. I used pine for the small amount of secondary wood.

I finished the table with several coats of a tung oil/ Danish oil mix. A coat of paste wax was applied after the oil finish was completely dry.

Robert Treanor is a cabinetmaker and teacher in San Francisco.

SPLAY-LEGGED TABLE

by Garrett Hack

Few furniture legs are as elegant as square, tapered ones. Splay those same legs, and your table will have a personality quite out of the ordinary. This small table is a perfect project for you to demystify tapered and splayed legs and add them to your skills as a designer and craftsperson.

I took a simplified approach to both hand and machine work. I used a pattern to lay out and build the table legs, which taper from top to bottom on all sides, creating an elegant profile.

The table is constructed using machine-cut joinery. I've even designed in cockbeads to hide any discrepancy of the mortise at the bottoms of the aprons. Finally, the tabletop features an elegant, underside bevel.

Garrett Hack is a contributing editor to Fine Woodworking *magazine.*

Tying it together. *With the base assembled and the cockbeading glued to the aprons' edges, the top is screwed into place. Heavy chamfers on the top's underside lend the piece lightness.*

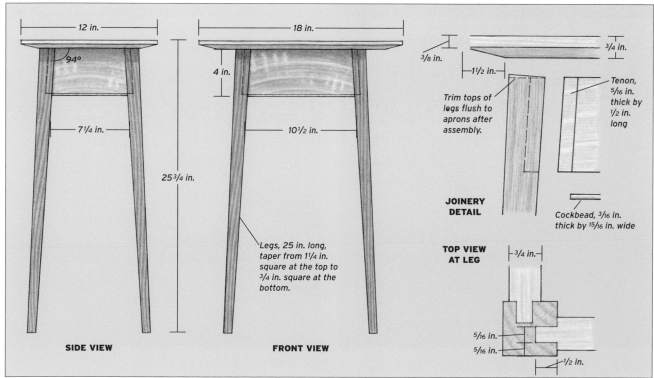

12 in. — SIDE VIEW — 94° — 7¼ in. — 25¾ in.

18 in. — FRONT VIEW — 4 in. — 10½ in.

Legs, 25 in. long, taper from 1¼ in. square at the top to ¾ in. square at the bottom.

3/8 in. — ¾ in. — 1½ in.

Trim tops of legs flush to aprons after assembly.

Tenon, 5/16 in. thick by ½ in. long

JOINERY DETAIL

Cockbead, 3/16 in. thick by 15/16 in. wide

TOP VIEW AT LEG — ¾ in. — 5/16 in. — 5/16 in. — ½ in.

COFFEE TABLE
PUTS JOINERY ON DISPLAY

by Kevin Rodel

Beveled through-tenons

Gridwork stretcher

INSIDE THE JOINERY

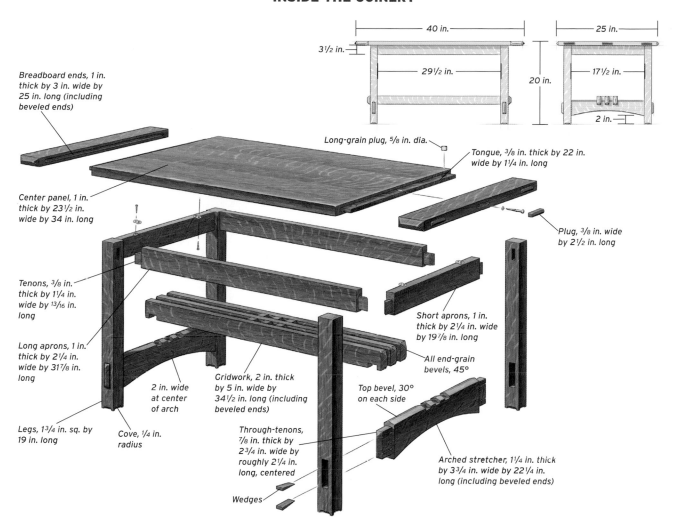

Breadboard ends, 1 in. thick by 3 in. wide by 25 in. long (including beveled ends)

40 in.

3½ in.

25 in.

29½ in.

17½ in.

20 in.

2 in.

Long-grain plug, ⅝ in. dia.

Tongue, ⅜ in. thick by 22 in. wide by 1¼ in. long

Center panel, 1 in. thick by 23½ in. wide by 34 in. long

Plug, ⅜ in. wide by 2½ in. long

Tenons, ⅜ in. thick by 1¼ in. wide by 13/16 in. long

Short aprons, 1 in. thick by 2¼ in. wide by 19⅞ in. long

Long aprons, 1 in. thick by 2¼ in. wide by 31⅞ in. long

All end-grain bevels, 45°

2 in. wide at center of arch

Gridwork, 2 in. thick by 5 in. wide by 34½ in. long (including beveled ends)

Top bevel, 30° on each side

Legs, 1¾ in. sq. by 19 in. long

Cove, ¼ in. radius

Through-tenons, ⅞ in. thick by 2¾ in. wide by roughly 2¼ in. long, centered

Arched stretcher, 1¼ in. thick by 3¾ in. wide by 22¼ in. long (including beveled ends)

Wedges

Breadboard ends with ebony accents

Arts and Crafts style is noteworthy for taking joinery—the product of the craftsman's hand—and elevating it to the level of artistic decoration. The basis of this table design is four decorative joints: through-tenons, gridwork, half-lap joints, and breadboard ends. These design elements will work beautifully together in tables of almost any size.

This Arts and Crafts coffee table is made of fumed or stained white oak. The two ends of the base—with their beveled and wedged through-tenons—are built first, and then connected by the gridwork stretcher. The top receives breadboard ends with decorative ebony details.

Although the project seen here is a coffee table, the techniques are the same for all of the tables illustrated on p. 118.

Kevin Rodel builds Arts and Crafts furniture in Pownal, Maine.

One Design, Many Tables

My goal as a furniture maker always has been to develop a design vocabulary, which in turn would allow me to create a line of furniture incorporating pieces that work well together and seem to come from a single maker. This table design is no exception. By changing the dimensions of the stock, you can build similar tables: coffee table, end table/nightstand, sofa/hall table, or dining table. Combining these pieces in a home will unify the decor. The pieces are similar enough to create a nice theme, but they're different enough to avoid the feeling of boring repetition.

One key difference is the tabletops: A simple inlay is enough for the top of the end table, while the dining table has a tile inlay. Of course, for these designs to work visually, the thicknesses of some elements must be adjusted appropriately. – K.R.

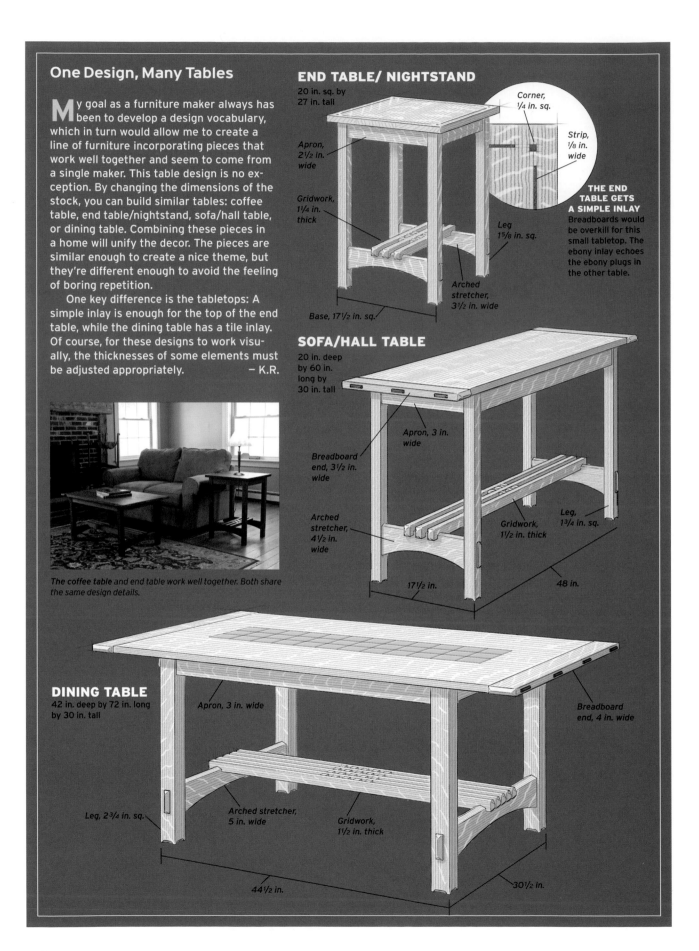

The coffee table and end table work well together. Both share the same design details.

END TABLE/ NIGHTSTAND
20 in. sq. by 27 in. tall

Corner, 1/4 in. sq.

Strip, 1/8 in. wide

Apron, 2½ in. wide

Gridwork, 1¼ in. thick

Leg 1⅝ in. sq.

Arched stretcher, 3½ in. wide

Base, 17½ in. sq.

THE END TABLE GETS A SIMPLE INLAY
Breadboards would be overkill for this small tabletop. The ebony inlay echoes the ebony plugs in the other table.

SOFA/HALL TABLE
20 in. deep by 60 in. long by 30 in. tall

Apron, 3 in. wide

Breadboard end, 3½ in. wide

Arched stretcher, 4½ in. wide

Gridwork, 1½ in. thick

Leg, 1¾ in. sq.

17½ in.

48 in.

DINING TABLE
42 in. deep by 72 in. long by 30 in. tall

Apron, 3 in. wide

Breadboard end, 4 in. wide

Leg, 2¾ in. sq.

Arched stretcher, 5 in. wide

Gridwork, 1½ in. thick

44½ in.

30½ in.

PEMBROKE TABLE

by Jefferson Kolle

My father-in-law has become one of my best friends. He always admired a Pembroke table I'd made years ago, and in fact, he commented on it almost every time he came to our house. In appreciation for all that I've learned from him—he'd been more than a surrogate father since my dad died—I made another one of the tables for him.

Pembroke tables have been around for centuries. Small and graceful, they have been made in forms simple to elaborate. The one I made is on the simple side—the only adornments being the tapered legs and the curved top. What makes the table fun to build are the moving parts: the hinged drop leaves with their attendant rule joints and the short, wood-hinged arms that support the leaves. In the drawings, I've included the dimensions for my table, which is 34¾ in. long at the center of the top. You can adjust the dimensions of the table to suit your needs. Most often, Pembroke tables are small side tables, but they were built in all sizes.

Jeff Kolle is the new product editor at the Taunton Press.

Laying Out the Tabletop

Two trammels swing different arcs. By using different center points, trammels of different lengths, and a compass, it's possible to lay out a gracefully curving tabletop of any dimension. The curves break at each corner spur, and the spurs are aligned with the table's legs.

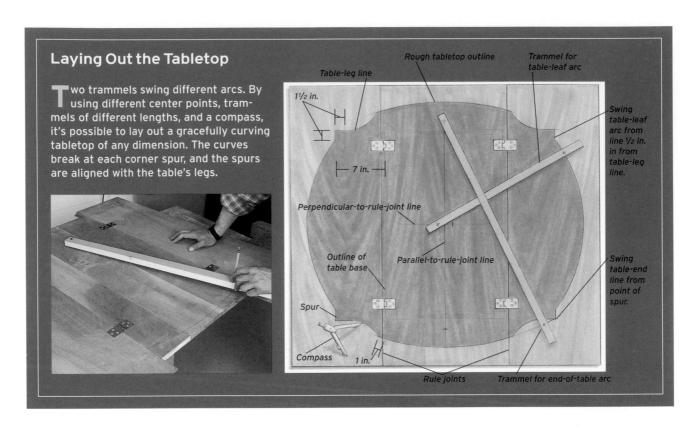

- Table-leg line
- Rough tabletop outline
- Trammel for table-leaf arc
- 1½ in.
- Swing table-leaf arc from line ½ in. in from table-leg line.
- 7 in.
- Perpendicular-to-rule-joint line
- Outline of table base
- Parallel-to-rule-joint line
- Swing table-end line from point of spur.
- Spur
- Compass
- 1 in.
- Rule joints
- Trammel for end-of-table arc

Rule Joint and Table-Leaf Hinge

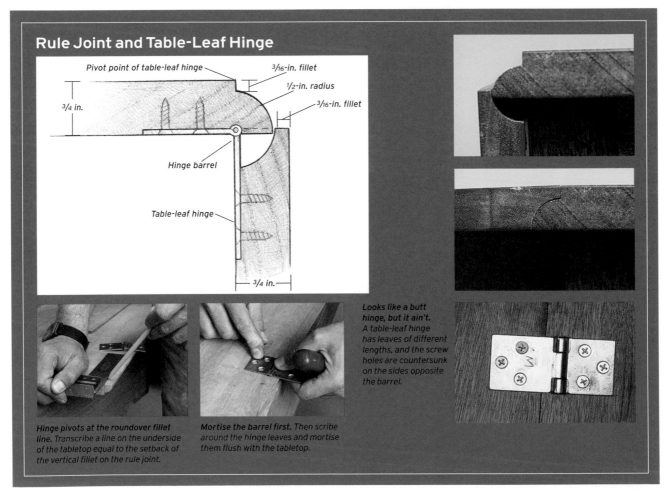

- Pivot point of table-leaf hinge
- ³⁄₁₆-in. fillet
- ½-in. radius
- ³⁄₄ in.
- ³⁄₁₆-in. fillet
- Hinge barrel
- Table-leaf hinge
- ³⁄₄ in.

Looks like a butt hinge, but it ain't. A table-leaf hinge has leaves of different lengths, and the screw holes are countersunk on the sides opposite the barrel.

Hinge pivots at the roundover fillet line. Transcribe a line on the underside of the tabletop equal to the setback of the vertical fillet on the rule joint.

Mortise the barrel first. Then scribe around the hinge leaves and mortise them flush with the tabletop.

MAHOGANY PEMBROKE TABLE

Traditionally, Pembroke tables have a wide top and shallow leaves. With the leaves open, this table's top appears almost circular with spurs making four corners. When the leaves are folded down, the spurs line up with the outside edges of the tapered legs. The leaves are held open with swinging leaf supports.

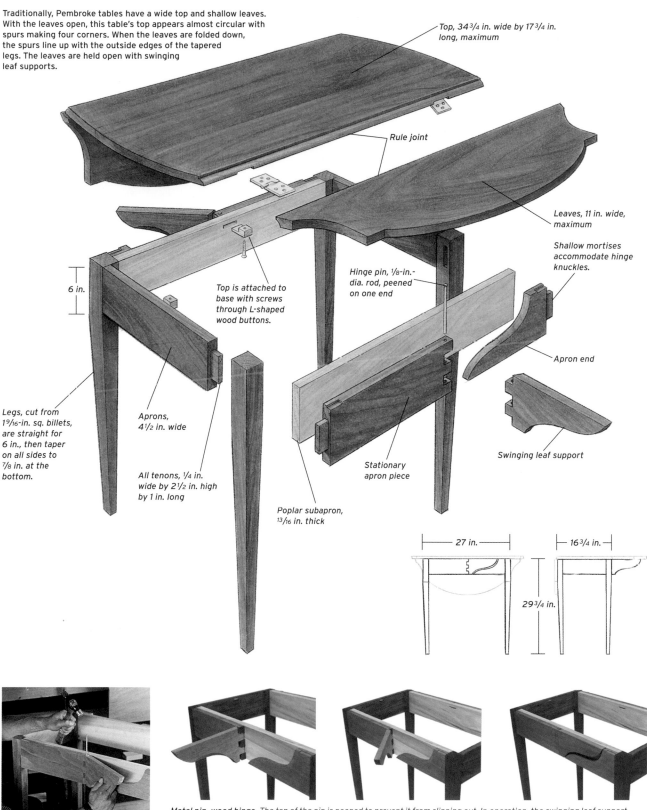

Top, 34 3/4 in. wide by 17 3/4 in. long, maximum

Rule joint

Leaves, 11 in. wide, maximum

Shallow mortises accommodate hinge knuckles.

Hinge pin, 1/8-in.-dia. rod, peened on one end

6 in.

Top is attached to base with screws through L-shaped wood buttons.

Apron end

Legs, cut from 1 9/16-in. sq. billets, are straight for 6 in., then taper on all sides to 7/8 in. at the bottom.

Aprons, 4 1/2 in. wide

All tenons, 1/4 in. wide by 2 1/2 in. high by 1 in. long

Stationary apron piece

Swinging leaf support

Poplar subapron, 13/16 in. thick

27 in. ⊢ 16 3/4 in. ⊣

29 3/4 in.

Metal pin, wood hinge. The top of the pin is peened to prevent it from slipping out. In operation, the swinging leaf support folds flat against the apron when the table leaves are down.

LOW TEA TABLE HIGHLIGHTS JOINERY

by C. Michael Vogt

The elegance of simplicity and craftsmanship. *Vogt made this table for a craft show exhibiting Japanese pottery, so he designed the walnut table just 17 in. high for floor-seated tea drinkers. To further reflect Asian lifestyle, he used simple components and traditional joinery.*

I find the dovetail an appealing joint, both aesthetically and structurally. Although its traditional use in carcase and drawer construction is well known, a sliding version of the dovetail can be used to connect furniture components such as tabletops to their bases. I relied on sliding dovetails to join a top to two upper rails in the walnut table shown in the photo above. And I used a more visible variation of the dovetail, butterfly keys, to connect the halves of the tabletop. The table is quite easy to build, but because its joinery is preeminent, the table requires craftsmanship with both machine and hand tools.

Designing a Table for Tea

When I made the table for a juried craft show, I knew it would be displayed near Japanese pottery. So when I designed the table, I envisioned it for drinking tea while seated on the floor. I borrowed traditional details, such as sliding dovetails, but I was also influenced by modern work—that of the late George Nakashima.

When making the walnut tabletop shown here, I chose rosewood for the butterfly keys. And when I built the table in red oak, I used cherry keys. In both examples, I had purposely saved small scraps of contrasting wood for the butterflies.

Inlaying Butterfly Keys

I individually mark out keys rather than use a pattern because even minute differences between key sizes or shapes will be apparent in their fit to the mortises. Using a plunge router, I waste most of the butterfly cavity to a depth of the thickness of the key less 1/32 in. Using chisels, I pare the rest of the way to the outline.

To inlay the keys, I chamfer the bottom edges so that they will just ease into the mortises. When I'm assembling the table, I tap the butterflies home with a mallet.

A Tokyo furniture-store owner once saw my table at a gallery. He picked it up and examined it closely. Then he placed it on the floor and, kneeling on the top, racked the table back and forth. His nod of approval made all the careful joinery well worthwhile.

C. Michael (Tico) Vogt is a furniture maker in Saratoga Springs, New York.

TABLE ASSEMBLY

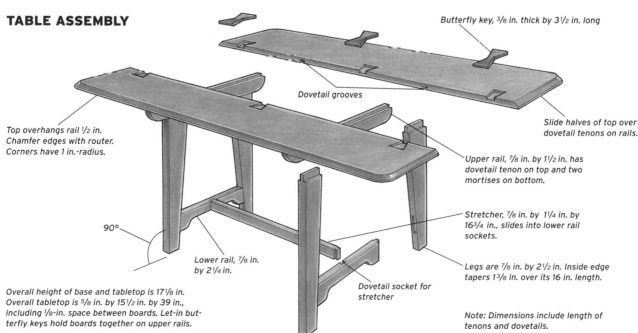

Butterfly key, 3/8 in. thick by 3 1/2 in. long

Dovetail grooves

Slide halves of top over dovetail tenons on rails.

Top overhangs rail 1/2 in. Chamfer edges with router. Corners have 1 in.-radius.

Upper rail, 7/8 in. by 1 1/2 in. has dovetail tenon on top and two mortises on bottom.

90°

Stretcher, 7/8 in. by 1 1/4 in. by 16 3/4 in., slides into lower rail sockets.

Lower rail, 7/8 in. by 2 1/4 in.

Legs are 7/8 in. by 2 1/2 in. Inside edge tapers 1 3/8 in. over its 16 in. length.

Dovetail socket for stretcher

Overall height of base and tabletop is 17 1/8 in. Overall tabletop is 5/8 in. by 15 1/2 in. by 39 in., including 1/8-in. space between boards. Let-in butterfly keys hold boards together on upper rails.

Note: Dimensions include length of tenons and dovetails.

FEDERAL CARD TABLE

by Steve Latta

Demilune card tables are a favorite project of mine because building them involves tools and techniques both traditional and modern. Their ancestry dates to the early years of American independence when they were popular all along the Eastern Seaboard. True to the neoclassic passion for symmetry, they often were made in pairs and positioned to balance a doorway, alcove, or piece of furniture.

During an age of newfound wealth and status, the nouveau riche used the ornamentation on their card tables as one way to flaunt their wealth. Price books and invoices of the time set costs for stringing, bellflowers, ornamental ovals, and the like. With the intricacy of the inlay reflecting the status of the owner, the level of embellishment on period tables varies greatly. This table, based on Baltimore pieces, is stylish enough to remain unadorned, but feel free to embellish it to your tastes and skills.

Steve Latta teaches at the Thaddeus Stevens College of Technology in Lancaster, Pennsylvania.

Stringing and Banding

You can inlay just the front faces of the legs or, as in this case, include the side faces. The same stringing is used on the apron and the legs.

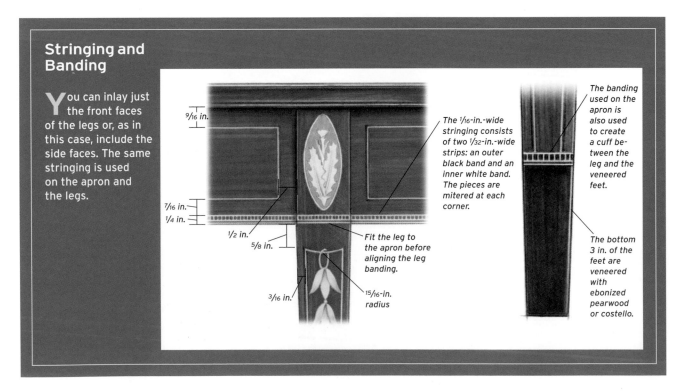

9/16 in.

7/16 in.

1/4 in.

1/2 in.

5/8 in.

3/16 in.

15/16 in. radius

Fit the leg to the apron before aligning the leg banding.

The 1/16-in.-wide stringing consists of two 1/32-in.-wide strips: an outer black band and an inner white band. The pieces are mitered at each corner.

The banding used on the apron is also used to create a cuff between the leg and the veneered feet.

The bottom 3 in. of the feet are veneered with ebonized pearwood or costello.

GATE-LEG CARD TABLE

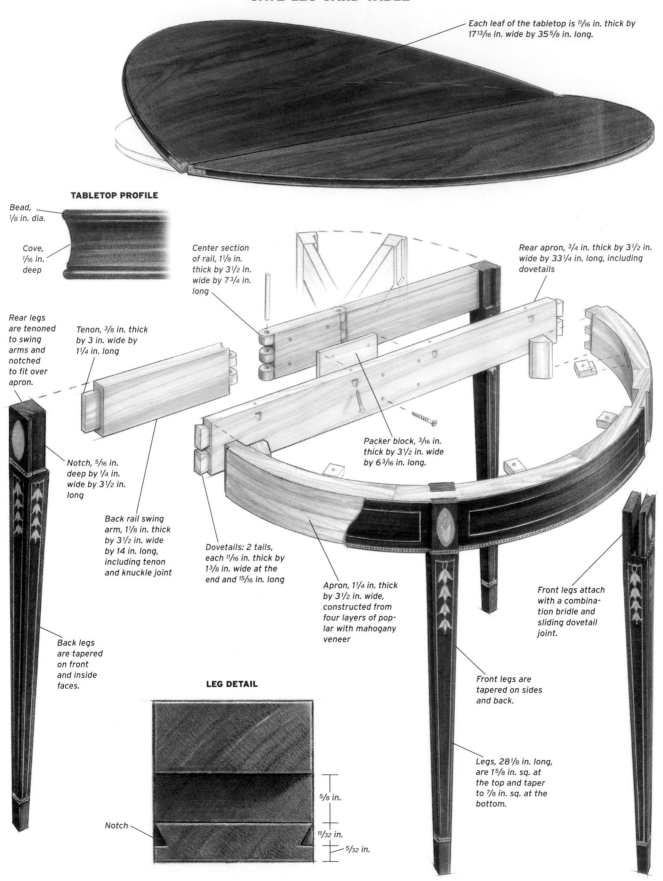

Each leaf of the tabletop is $^{11}/_{16}$ in. thick by $17^{13}/_{16}$ in. wide by $35^5/_8$ in. long.

TABLETOP PROFILE

Bead, $^1/_8$ in. dia.

Cove, $^1/_{16}$ in. deep

Center section of rail, $1^1/_8$ in. thick by $3^1/_2$ in. wide by $7^3/_4$ in. long

Rear apron, $^3/_4$ in. thick by $3^1/_2$ in. wide by $33^1/_4$ in. long, including dovetails

Rear legs are tenoned to swing arms and notched to fit over apron.

Tenon, $^3/_8$ in. thick by 3 in. wide by $1^1/_4$ in. long

Notch, $^5/_{16}$ in. deep by $^1/_4$ in. wide by $3^1/_2$ in. long

Packer block, $^3/_{16}$ in. thick by $3^1/_2$ in. wide by $6^3/_{16}$ in. long.

Back rail swing arm, $1^1/_8$ in. thick by $3^1/_2$ in. wide by 14 in. long, including tenon and knuckle joint

Dovetails: 2 tails, each $^{11}/_{16}$ in. thick by $1^3/_8$ in. wide at the end and $^{15}/_{16}$ in. long

Back legs are tapered on front and inside faces.

Apron, $1^1/_4$ in. thick by $3^1/_2$ in. wide, constructed from four layers of poplar with mahogany veneer

Front legs attach with a combination bridle and sliding dovetail joint.

Front legs are tapered on sides and back.

Legs, $28^1/_8$ in. long, are $1^5/_8$ in. sq. at the top and taper to $^7/_8$ in. sq. at the bottom.

LEG DETAIL

Notch

$^5/_8$ in.

$^{11}/_{32}$ in.

$^5/_{32}$ in.

Construction Tip: Create a Full-Size Plan

You will find it much easier to build this table if you first make a full-size plan of the table as seen from above. Draw the plan on 1/2-in.-thick plywood or MDF. Include the placement of the legs, the apron, and the location of the knuckle joints. You can use this plan as a template for shaping the two leaves of the tabletop.

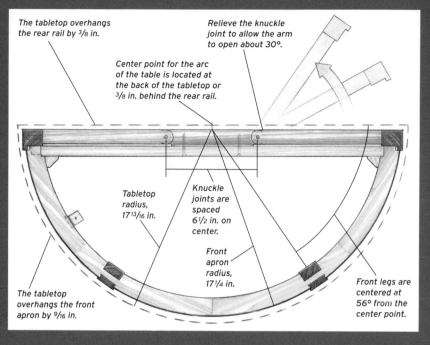

The tabletop overhangs the rear rail by 3/8 in.

Relieve the knuckle joint to allow the arm to open about 30°.

Center point for the arc of the table is located at the back of the tabletop or 3/8 in. behind the rear rail.

Tabletop radius, 17¹³/₁₆ in.

Knuckle joints are spaced 6¹/₂ in. on center.

Front apron radius, 17¹/₄ in.

The tabletop overhangs the front apron by 9/16 in.

Front legs are centered at 56° from the center point.

Segments of the Bricklaid Apron

The semicircular apron of the table has a core of four layers of ⁷/₈-in.-thick poplar laminated together. Each layer consists of three or four pieces, butted together and staggered in the manner of a mason building a brick wall. You will need a template for the three sizes of poplar sections needed to build the core. The first and third layers have three pieces: a long center section with two shorter side sections. The second and fourth layers are made of four equal sections. All the stock is 4 in. wide.

1ST AND 3RD LAYERS OF APRON

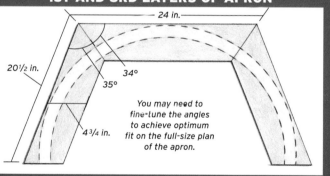

24 in.

20¹/₂ in.

34°

35°

4³/₄ in.

You may need to fine-tune the angles to achieve optimum fit on the full-size plan of the apron.

2ND AND 4TH LAYERS OF APRON

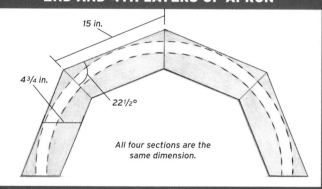

15 in.

4³/₄ in.

22¹/₂°

All four sections are the same dimension.

TILT-TOP TABLE

by Mario Rodriguez

As a woodworking instructor, I'm always looking for interesting and challenging projects to present in my classes. This Federal tilt-top tea table satisfies all of my criteria for an intermediate-level project: It's neat and compact with only a few parts, and the construction introduces students to both machine- and hand-tool techniques. The bonus is that the finished product is graceful in design and fits into almost any interior space.

In the 18th century, many of these small tables were made with local hardwoods, and there are a number of period examples in maple, walnut, and cherry. My version is made of mahogany, which is available from most commercial suppliers in the required thicknesses, from 4/4 to 12/4. I find mahogany ideal for the turning required in this project, and it takes a finish beautifully.

Mario Rodriguez is a contributing editor to Fine Woodworking *magazine.*

Sliding dovetails secure legs.

Wedge locks the pivot back.

Cleats orient the top.

MAHOGANY TEA TABLE

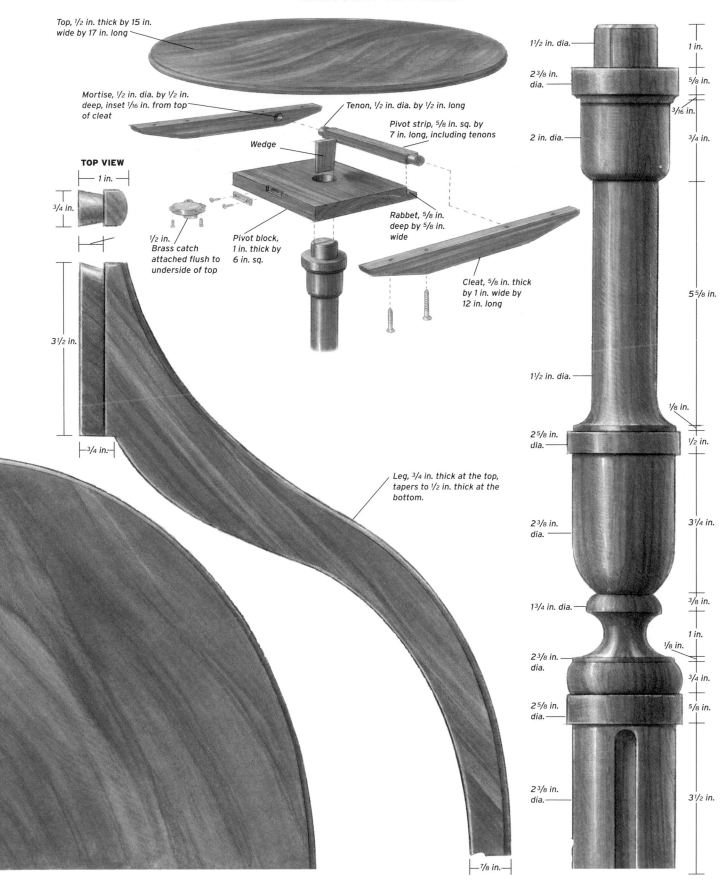

Top, 1/2 in. thick by 15 in. wide by 17 in. long

Mortise, 1/2 in. dia. by 1/2 in. deep, inset 1/16 in. from top of cleat

Tenon, 1/2 in. dia. by 1/2 in. long

Pivot strip, 5/8 in. sq. by 7 in. long, including tenons

Wedge

TOP VIEW

1 in.

3/4 in.

Rabbet, 5/8 in. deep by 5/8 in. wide

1/2 in. Brass catch attached flush to underside of top

Pivot block, 1 in. thick by 6 in. sq.

Cleat, 5/8 in. thick by 1 in. wide by 12 in. long

3 1/2 in.

3/4 in.

Leg, 3/4 in. thick at the top, tapers to 1/2 in. thick at the bottom.

7/8 in.

1 1/2 in. dia.

2 3/8 in. dia.

2 in. dia.

1 1/2 in. dia.

2 5/8 in. dia.

2 3/8 in. dia.

1 3/4 in. dia.

2 3/8 in. dia.

2 5/8 in. dia.

2 3/8 in. dia.

1 in.

5/8 in.

3/16 in.

3/4 in.

5 5/8 in.

1/8 in.

1/2 in.

3 1/4 in.

3/8 in.

1 in.

1/8 in.

3/4 in.

5/8 in.

3 1/2 in.

Framing the table.
Rosewood beading adds
definition to the top,
and wraps seamlessly
around the legs.

A place for your stuff.
The drawer blends in
with the front apron,
making it nearly
invisible. A fingerhold
in the false front is
easy to grab.

A CONTEMPORARY CORNER TABLE

by Tony O'Malley

When rough milling the wood for a table, I typically make an extra leg, in case something goes wrong while cutting the mortises or sawing the tapers. Years ago, after making a pair of Shaker-style desks, I ended up with three extra legs (I was prone to making more mistakes back then). I couldn't just toss them into the firewood pile, and I didn't want to backtrack and make a fourth leg, so I created this three-legged table.

I designed this table to fit into a corner of a dining room, where the recessed front wouldn't impede movement and an extra drawer is always useful. But the table would also work well in a narrow hallway. If you are certain that the table will stay in a corner, you can make the side rails from a secondary wood and not extend the beading beyond the front. However, in a really large room this kind of table can also anchor the corner of an area rug and be visible from all sides.

Tony O'Malley is a writer and furniture maker.

A CONCAVE CORNER TABLE

The clean lines of the exterior hide the structural complexity of the interior with its concealed drawer.

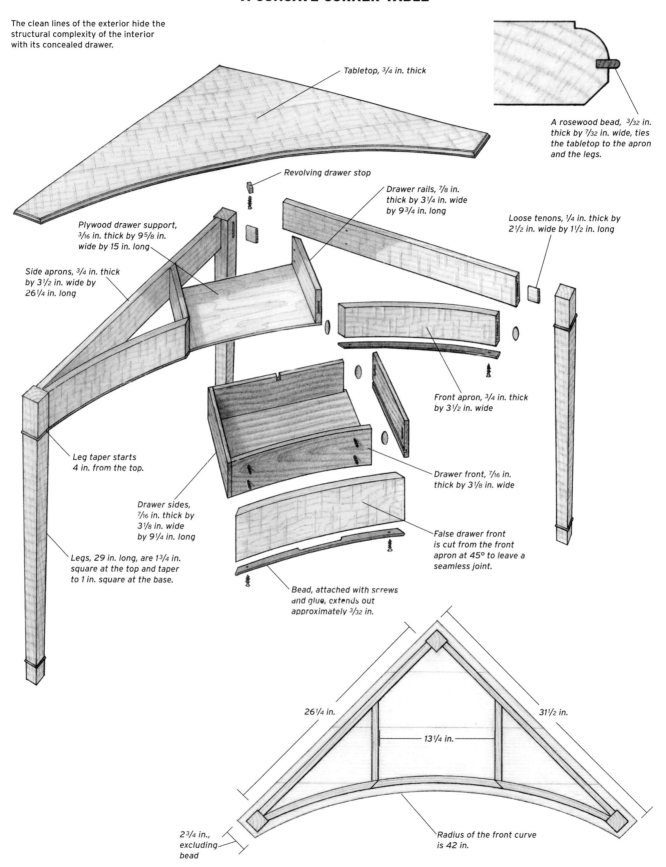

Tabletop, 3/4 in. thick

A rosewood bead, 3/32 in. thick by 7/32 in. wide, ties the tabletop to the apron and the legs.

Revolving drawer stop

Drawer rails, 7/8 in. thick by 3 1/4 in. wide by 9 3/4 in. long

Loose tenons, 1/4 in. thick by 2 1/2 in. wide by 1 1/2 in. long

Plywood drawer support, 3/16 in. thick by 9 5/8 in. wide by 15 in. long

Side aprons, 3/4 in. thick by 3 1/2 in. wide by 26 1/4 in. long

Front apron, 3/4 in. thick by 3 1/2 in. wide

Leg taper starts 4 in. from the top.

Drawer front, 7/16 in. thick by 3 1/8 in. wide

Drawer sides, 7/16 in. thick by 3 1/8 in. wide by 9 1/4 in. long

False drawer front is cut from the front apron at 45° to leave a seamless joint.

Legs, 29 in. long, are 1 3/4 in. square at the top and taper to 1 in. square at the base.

Bead, attached with screws and glue, extends out approximately 3/32 in.

26 1/4 in.

31 1/2 in.

13 1/4 in.

2 3/4 in., excluding bead

Radius of the front curve is 42 in.

COFFEE TABLE IS SPARE AND STURDY

by Lars Mikkelsen

Ever since I started building furniture, I've taken pleasure in making the many different components in a piece and seeing them all fit together like pieces of a puzzle. As I progressed as a craftsman, the joints got better and more complex, and my enjoyment of the process increased. But making a lot of tight-fitting joints can be quite time-consuming and expensive, and most of my clients have tight budgets. They have come to me because they want something more than they can get in the department store, but they can't necessarily afford to have me spend a lot of time doing greatly detailed work. I often have to find ways to compromise while still aiming to produce beautiful furniture of sound construction. I look for ways to simplify, to use what tools and materials I can afford, and to make limited resources grant handsome returns.

I recently had a challenge of this kind when a client approached me about making a coffee table. Together we settled on a basic table in the Craftsman vein and a carefully trimmed budget for the job. Two hallmarks of Craftsman furniture are pinned through-mortises

and legs coopered or veneered so quartersawn grain shows all around. But I decided to leave them out of my table, substituting the simplicity of loose-tenon joinery and solid-wood construction.

This table was my first effort in the Craftsman style. I had originally suggested this style to my client because I felt that it would fit the decor and because it stands up so well to heavy use. But while building the table, I came to appreciate the honesty with which design and construction are related in Craftsman work. There is no unnecessary ornamentation— sound structural components make the design.

For the finish, I applied three coats of Antique Minwax®. I rubbed in the final coat with fine steel wool and immediately wiped it off, leaving a beautifully smooth finish that, with occasional reoiling, will only get more beautiful with time.

Lars Mikkelsen is a furniture maker in Santa Margarita, California.

LOOSE TENONS SIMPLIFY JOINERY

Lars Mikkelsen picked the functional Craftsman style for this low table and pared it down to its essence.

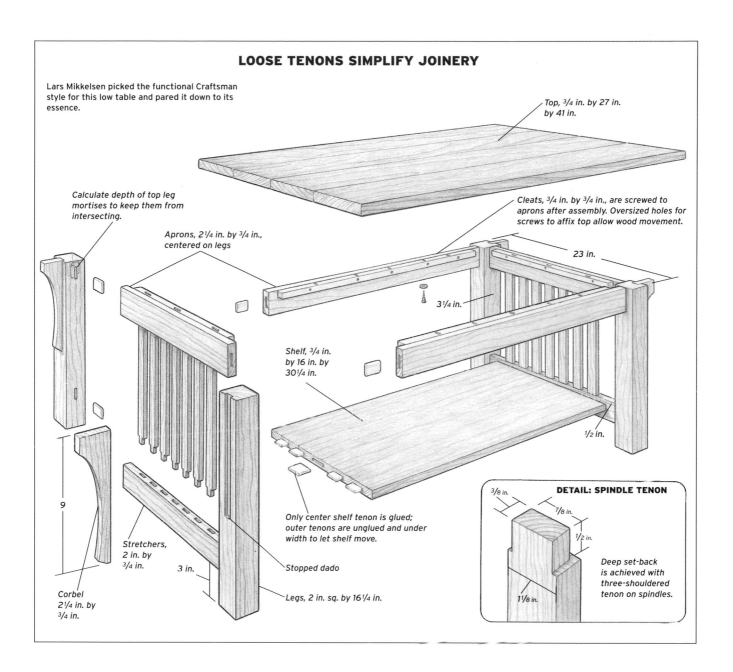

Top, 3/4 in. by 27 in. by 41 in.

Calculate depth of top leg mortises to keep them from intersecting.

Aprons, 2 1/4 in. by 3/4 in., centered on legs

Cleats, 3/4 in. by 3/4 in., are screwed to aprons after assembly. Oversized holes for screws to affix top allow wood movement.

23 in.

3 1/4 in.

Shelf, 3/4 in. by 16 in. by 30 1/4 in.

1/2 in.

9

Only center shelf tenon is glued; outer tenons are unglued and under width to let shelf move.

Stretchers, 2 in. by 3/4 in.

3 in.

Stopped dado

Corbel 2 1/4 in. by 3/4 in.

Legs, 2 in. sq. by 16 1/4 in.

DETAIL: SPINDLE TENON

3/8 in.

7/8 in.

1/2 in.

1 1/8 in.

Deep set-back is achieved with three-shouldered tenon on spindles.

SOFA TABLE COMPLEMENTS ANTIQUES

by Gene McCall

When a husband and wife asked me to design a sofa table for them, I knew that the piece would have to go with the other furniture in their living room and fit easily into the context of their home. The room in question was decorated with an eclectic mix of formal 18th-century American and English antiques. The imposing look of the room was softened by colorful floral fabrics and oriental rugs, as well as by a contemporary coffee table. Because of these things, I decided that the sofa table should incorporate different design motifs and joinery that would harmonize with the restrained elegance of the home and its furnishings.

Aside from lovely wood and a rich finish, I felt the real snap of my clients' sofa table should come from

details, like delicate moldings and lively frets. The design I arrived at (Chinese Chippendale in spirit) blends well with most any room featuring English or American period furniture.

In the corner of my shop was a particularly lovely piece of highly figured mahogany with wild dark grain streaks. It was ideal for the table's lower shelf. To make the shelf more visible and also to help maintain a feeling of lightness about the table, I chose to inset the tabletop with three pieces of glass.

Gene McCall is a furniture maker in Englewood, Florida. He also teaches sculpture at the Ringling School of Art in Sarasota.

SOFA TABLE ASSEMBLY

By skillfully combining mahogany and glass, Gene McCall met his clients' need for a sofa table that fit aesthetically within a room of mixed styles. To do this, McCall designed the piece with a variety of decoration, like the corner fret detail below.

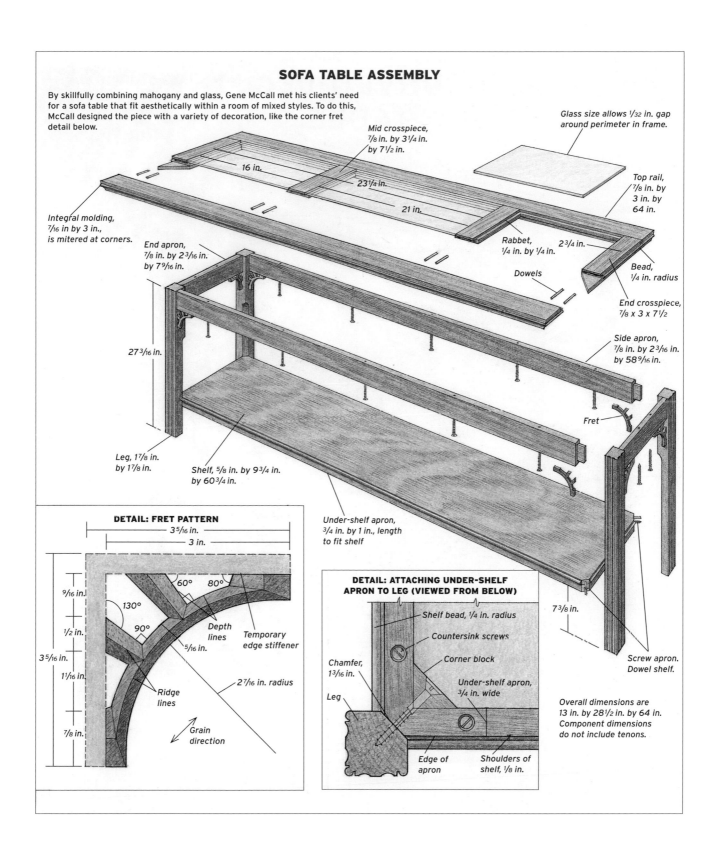

Mid crosspiece, 7/8 in. by 3 1/4 in. by 7 1/2 in.

Glass size allows 1/32 in. gap around perimeter in frame.

16 in.

23 1/4 in.

21 in.

Top rail, 7/8 in. by 3 in. by 64 in.

Integral molding, 7/16 in by 3 in., is mitered at corners.

End apron, 7/8 in. by 2 3/16 in. by 7 9/16 in.

Rabbet, 1/4 in. by 1/4 in.

2 3/4 in.

Dowels

Bead, 1/4 in. radius

End crosspiece, 7/8 x 3 x 7 1/2

Side apron, 7/8 in. by 2 3/16 in. by 58 9/16 in.

27 3/16 in.

Fret

Leg, 1 7/8 in. by 1 7/8 in.

Shelf, 5/8 in. by 9 3/4 in. by 60 3/4 in.

Under-shelf apron, 3/4 in. by 1 in., length to fit shelf

DETAIL: FRET PATTERN

3 5/16 in.

3 in.

9/16 in.

1/2 in.

3 5/16 in.

1 1/16 in.

7/8 in.

60°   80°

130°

90°

Depth lines

5/16 in.

Temporary edge stiffener

Ridge lines

Grain direction

2 7/16 in. radius

DETAIL: ATTACHING UNDER-SHELF APRON TO LEG (VIEWED FROM BELOW)

Shelf bead, 1/4 in. radius

Countersink screws

Corner block

Chamfer, 1 3/16 in.

Leg

Under-shelf apron, 3/4 in. wide

Edge of apron

Shoulders of shelf, 1/8 in.

7 3/8 in.

Screw apron. Dowel shelf.

Overall dimensions are 13 in. by 28 1/2 in. by 64 in. Component dimensions do not include tenons.

CURVED-LEG TABLE

by Don Kondra

Although I rely heavily on machines to get the job done quickly, I aim to build furniture that looks organic and invites people to touch it. That's why I've turned to using lots of curves in my work. It's true that building swoopy furniture requires more labor than making stick-straight pieces, but I think curves are appealing. And they're also more interesting from a design or construction point of view. Furniture that's square to the world bores me.

Once you get hooked on curves, a whole new world of design opens up. I always make full-sized drawings on newsprint (end rolls) that can be purchased cheaply from the local newspaper. Working from an accurate drawing is the key to finessing the joinery and accurately milling curved parts. To get consistent results and to minimize the amount of handwork required, I also make a router or shaper jig.

I've made several versions of this hall table, and no two were alike. The current version (shown here), with a walnut top and curly maple base, suits me for now. But who knows? The next one might have a different curve or two.

The two most prominent features of a hall table are the top and the legs. The top is rectangular with edges that are beveled under. The legs are curved gently and tapered, and the edges are rounded over. To ease the transition from the square, dark top to the curvy, light base, I created a gap (negative space), which makes the top appear to float. The top is secured to a pair of cross braces with four screws.

Don Kondra builds custom furniture in Saskatoon, Saskatchewan, Canada.

TABLE WITH CURVED, TAPERED LEGS

Legs are rough-cut on the bandsaw, then machined on a router table or shaper.

Top, ³/4 in. thick

Top edge is beveled under 15°.

Cutout has ³/4-in. radius.

All mortises are ¹/4 in. wide and ¹⁷/32 in. deep.

Top of cross brace is ¹/4 in. proud of rail.

Tenon on cross brace is ¹/4 in. thick by ¹/2 in. deep.

Rails, ³/4 in. thick by 3¹/8 in. wide, rise ¹/4 in. above legs.

Oversized holes for screws

Chamfer top and bottom edges of all rails 45°.

Top is attached to cross braces with four #8 screws countersunk.

Round over all edges of legs with ³/8-in. roundover bit.

Tenons on rails are ¹/4 in. thick by 2¹/16 in. wide by ¹/2 in. long.

Curved and tapered leg, 28 in. long, 1³/4 in. sq. at top, 1 in. sq. at bottom

Curve is based on arc that rises ³/8 in. over a run of 30 in.

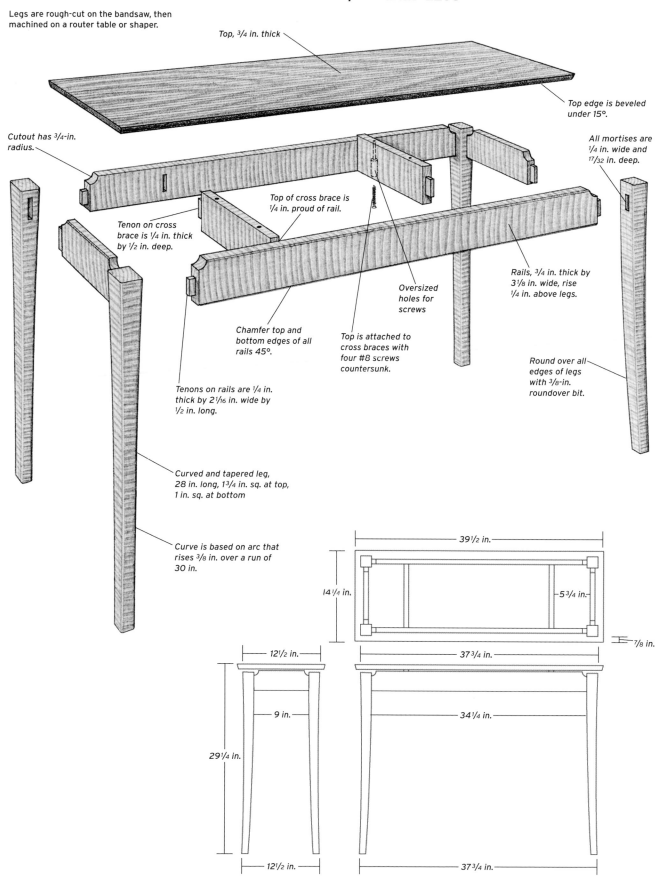

39¹/2 in.

14¹/4 in.

5³/4 in.

7/8 in.

12¹/2 in.

37³/4 in.

9 in.

34¹/4 in.

29¹/4 in.

12¹/2 in.

37³/4 in.

SOFA TABLE IN QUARTERSAWN OAK

by Scott Gibson

A couple of years ago, some friends expanded their small farmhouse by adding a wing that included a new a living/dining room. At one end they built a big fieldstone fireplace and moved in a Stickley-style sofa. The back of the sofa faces the dining-room table a half-dozen feet away. A narrow table at the back of the sofa would offer a convenient place to lay out food, plates or serving utensils, but

there was very little room to work with. The tabletop could be no deeper than 12 in. In addition, the base could not completely obscure the quartersawn oak panels in the back of the sofa.

This table was designed to fit that space. Its top is exactly 1 ft. deep and 60 in. wide, big enough to be useful but not wide enough to block traffic. Its drawers are shallow—just 3 in. deep inside—so the upper part

of the table presents a low profile. To keep it from looking too spindly, I added a curved steel stretcher at the base. The table fits the spot perfectly, but it also could work in any long, narrow space, like an entrance hall.

Nothing about the construction is complicated, although two components—the legs and the steel stretcher—require more than their fair share of planning.

Making the Legs

Gustav Stickley's Craftsman furniture gets a good deal of its charm from its simple, rectilinear lines and the rays exposed on the radial face of the white oak he typically used. To make the legs, Stickley milled an interlocking profile into the edges of four pieces of 4/4 quartersawn stock and glued them together so the distinctive figure showed on all four sides. There is more than one way to make the legs this way (see the drawings on p. 140–141), so choose an option that works best for you.

Making the Steel Stretcher

Stickley furniture has mostly straight lines. This table does, too, but I thought a curved stretcher at the bottom of the table would

relieve some of that monotony. Making it from a completely different material was appealing, too. My son, Ben, fabricated these two curved pieces from mild steel, heating the pieces in a coal forge and hammering them into shape over a pine log. The two pieces are joined at the center by a pair of ¼-in. steel rivets.

Ben had to make the stretcher fit exactly between the legs of the table base. To guarantee a good fit, I drew the stretcher full scale on a piece of plywood. That gave Ben a reference against which to check his work. At the ends of the stretcher pieces, he formed ½-in.-long tenons that fit into mortises drilled into the inside faces of the legs. The stretcher is glued to the legs with epoxy. Finding

Where metal and wood meet. *The two pieces of curved steel that form the bottom stretcher are tenoned on both ends. The tenons, shaped with a hacksaw and a mill file, fit into holes drilled by hand, on an angle, into the legs.*

Finding a Blacksmith

The heyday of the village smithy may be long past, but there still are thousands of skilled artisans capable of fabricating custom iron or steel furniture components. One place to look is on the website of the Artist-Blacksmith's Association of North America (www.abana.org; 706-310-1030). The organization claims a membership of 4,500 in the United States, Canada, New Zealand, and Australia. Although individual members are not listed, the site gives names, phone numbers, and e-mail addresses for chapter presidents by state and region. They should be able to recommend someone local.

Jonathan Nedbor, president of the Northeastern Blacksmiths Association, said a blacksmith probably can offer ideas on how metal can be worked to complement a piece of furniture in ways a woodworker might not think of. Although he would rather fabricate metal parts with the piece of furniture in his shop, Nedbor said he also can work from scale drawings.

Nedbor said it's important to find a blacksmith who is competent and has a similar design sense to yours. "There's no way to know until you really look at their work and do a little research talking with them," he said.

Steel is relatively cheap, but labor rates vary considerably. Full-time smiths are likely to charge more because they carry higher overhead than do weekend or evening blacksmiths who hold down day jobs. Sound familiar? Labor rates also vary by region. Nedbor's shop rate is $58 an hour.

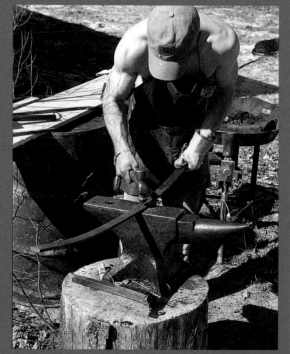

Texturing the stretcher. *Blacksmith Ben Gibson uses a ball-peen hammer to create a dimpled texture in the stretcher.*

a blacksmith to make parts such as this is not always easy, but a national organization of blacksmiths can help (see p. 139). This table also can be made using wooden stretchers.

This table is stained to the same reddish brown of the sofa. The stain color is a 50-50 mix of two Minwax stains, ipswich pine and puritan pine. The topcoat is Tried & True varnish oil.

Scott Gibson is a furniture maker and freelance writer living in Maine.

A CONTEMPORARY TWIST ON AN ARTS AND CRAFTS DESIGN

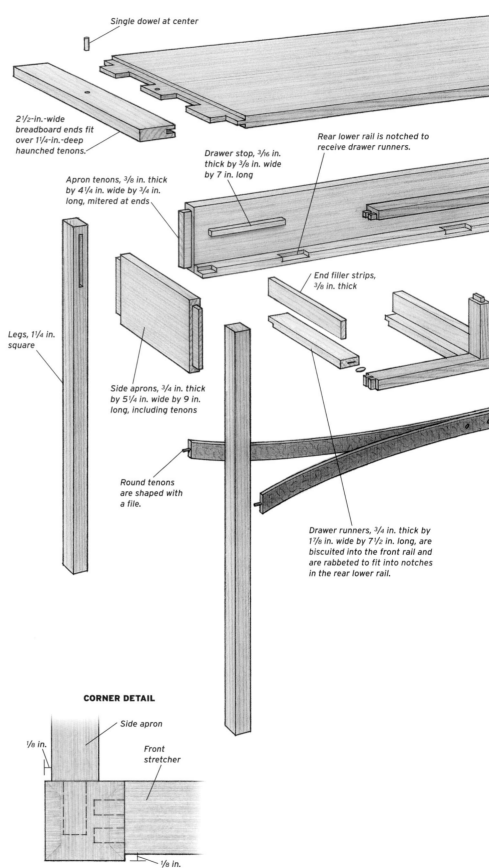

Single dowel at center

2 1/2-in.-wide breadboard ends fit over 1 1/4-in.-deep haunched tenons.

Apron tenons, 3/8 in. thick by 4 1/4 in. wide by 3/4 in. long, mitered at ends

Drawer stop, 3/16 in. thick by 3/8 in. wide by 7 in. long

Rear lower rail is notched to receive drawer runners.

End filler strips, 3/8 in. thick

Legs, 1 1/4 in. square

Side aprons, 3/4 in. thick by 5 1/4 in. wide by 9 in. long, including tenons

Round tenons are shaped with a file.

Drawer runners, 3/4 in. thick by 1 7/8 in. wide by 7 1/2 in. long, are biscuited into the front rail and are rabbeted to fit into notches in the rear lower rail.

DOUBLE MORTISE-AND-TENON JOINERY

For strength, the upper and lower rails are joined to the legs with double tenons.

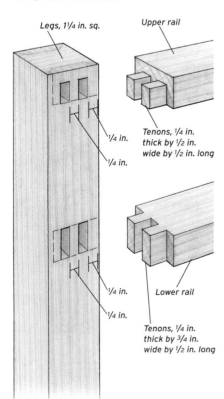

Legs, 1 1/4 in. sq.

Upper rail

Tenons, 1/4 in. thick by 1/2 in. wide by 1/2 in. long

1/4 in.

1/4 in.

Lower rail

Tenons, 1/4 in. thick by 3/4 in. wide by 1/2 in. long

1/4 in.

1/4 in.

CORNER DETAIL

Side apron

1/8 in.

Front stretcher

1/8 in.

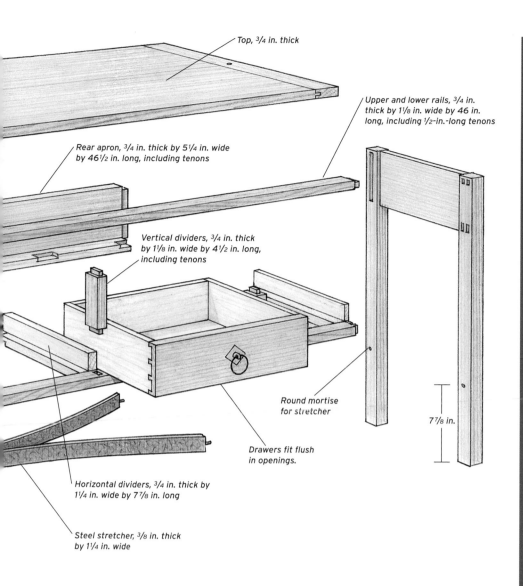

Top, 3/4 in. thick

Upper and lower rails, 3/4 in. thick by 1 1/8 in. wide by 46 in. long, including 1/2-in.-long tenons

Rear apron, 3/4 in. thick by 5 1/4 in. wide by 46 1/2 in. long, including tenons

Vertical dividers, 3/4 in. thick by 1 1/8 in. wide by 4 1/2 in. long, including tenons

Round mortise for stretcher

7 7/8 in.

Drawers fit flush in openings.

Horizontal dividers, 3/4 in. thick by 1 1/4 in. wide by 7 7/8 in. long

Steel stretcher, 3/8 in. thick by 1 1/4 in. wide

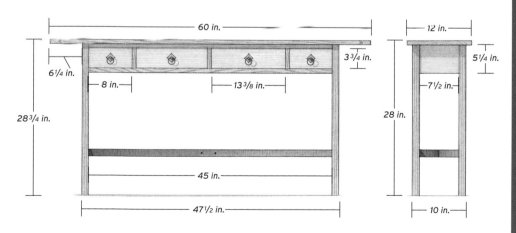

60 in.

3 3/4 in.

6 1/4 in.

8 in.

13 3/8 in.

12 in.

5 1/4 in.

7 1/2 in.

28 3/4 in.

28 in.

45 in.

47 1/2 in.

10 in.

Four Ways to Make a Quartersawn Leg

Quartersawn legs are a signature of Arts and Crafts furniture. Here are four ways to make them.

MITERED ASSEMBLY
Set up your tablesaw at 45 degree, miter all four pieces and glue them together.

LOCK MITER
With a lock-miter router bit, assembly can be easier and the leg stronger.

VENEER ON TWO FACES
A simple solution is to cut the leg 1/4 in. undersize and glue on two 1/8-in.-thick quartersawn veneers. The glueline virtually disappears, especially if the edges are chamfered.

AUTHOR'S SOLUTION
Gibson starts with a leg that is 1/8 in. oversize. Then he makes 45 degree cuts in the four corners and plows out the middle of two faces with a dado blade. He uses epoxy to glue in oversize wedges with quartersawn faces, then planes all four sides down to size.

House and furniture share common elements. Working with large timbers raised concerns for the author. What appears to be a solid-board top is actually a clever sandwich of MDF and veneer. Through-mortised legs are another clever deception. The breadboard ends (facing page) also have an unusual design.

CHERRY SOFA TABLE

by Eric Keil

Of the 23 pieces of furniture I made for a house in the Pennsylvania Poconos, this sofa table was the most gratifying to build and the best designed. Large members make up the tabletop and legs, and a 5/4 cabinet rests below. It's a hefty design built in a light, natural cherry, with unique exposed joinery that complements other furniture I installed in the home. The table's effect is at once traditional and contemporary, as are the processes used to build it.

The sofa table is my favorite piece in the house, but I did have a few concerns with the initial design. I spoke with Robert McLaughlin, the architect who designed the table, and it was apparent that he had a lot of woodworking savvy. He anticipated many of my concerns and accepted some compromises to improve the joinery and chances that the table age gracefully.

As I looked at the preliminary drawings, there were three unconventional design elements that seemed troublesome. The configuration of the boards that made up the top was specific and unusual: two 2-in. by 5-in. pieces surrounded by a butt-jointed frame. Instead of a traditional breadboard design, the long outermost side boards sandwiched the end boards. This kind of joinery

with solid lumber would have caused the joints between the end boards and the center of the table to fail over time. The architect had no problem with my solution to replace the center pieces with a stable substrate and veneer.

A concern was that the design called for the legs to come through

Breadboards with a twist. *The unique breadboard design of the tabletop calls for the long side boards to sandwich the short end boards.*

the top in a full through-tenon. Even if I consistently and accurately cut the mortises and through-tenons on the legs, I couldn't glue and clamp the top to the assembled cabinet and legs below. And housing the solid legs in a veneered substrate wouldn't allow for seasonal wood movement. We decided to make the tenons false. The legs would butt the bottom of the tabletop, and corresponding end-grain inserts could be carefully fit to shallow mortises on the top of the table.

The carcase of the cabinet itself was to be made of 5/4 solid cherry boards. The design called for the cabinet to be joined at the corners with an oversize finger or box joint. The fingers were 4 in. wide, corresponding with the seams between each 4-in.-wide board and its neighbor. The problem with this design was that the only long-grain-to-long-grain glue bond occurs every 4 in., which simply isn't sufficient. I added two biscuits to each finger (dowels or splines could have been used instead), which solved the problem of insufficient bonding surface but created another dilemma that I will address later.

The tabletop's 2-in.-thick center was made by laminating three pieces of medium-density fiberboard (MDF)— two pieces ¾ in. thick and one piece ⅜ in. thick—then skinning both sides with ¹/₁₆-in.-thick cherry veneer. I glued up the veneer in two pieces so that it appears to be two 5-in.-wide boards. The veneer was cut about ¾ in. oversized on the tablesaw and then seamed. Making the substrate, cauls, and veneer the same approximate size allowed for easy alignment and control of the pieces as they went into the vacuum bag. It was also quicker and less obnoxious to trim the ¾-in. oversize panels on a tablesaw than it would have been

Veneer sandwiches MDF. Three layers of MDF and two layers of veneer are all coated in glue and set into the vacuum bag at the same time. Glued up slightly oversize, the entire center panel of the tabletop is later trimmed to size on the tablesaw.

to trim glue squeeze-out and oversize veneer with a router and trimmer bit.

Placing the vacuum bag on an absolutely flat surface and laminating multiple layers of the substrate material produced a flat panel with no warp, cup, or twist.

The 16-in.-deep cabinet under the sofa table was the most labor intensive part of the project. It was made by stacking four 4-in.-deep butt-jointed boxes. Alternately butted and stacked, the boxes create a strong cabinet. The legs were doweled to the cross member that supports the cabinet, then set into place under the tabletop.

When I reflect on this project, I still get gratification from how tightly crafted this table is. Another thing that makes this table so intriguing is the weight of the large cherry timbers and Robert McLaughlin's design. In the large room where it lives, the table appears to grow gracefully from the floor.

Eric Keil designs and builds custom furniture in Wilkes-Barre, Pennsylvania.

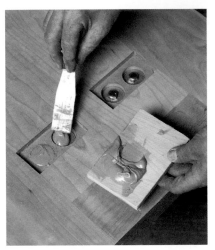

The tabletop is secured to the legs with 6-in. lag screws, then covered with auto-body filler. More common wood fillers might shrink, leaving depressions in the tabletop. End-grain inserts are coated with polyurethane glue and then tapped into place.

A Word From the Architect
by Robert McLaughlin

I've always tried to create houses and furniture that express the nature of both the materials and the construction process. Whether it's exposing bolts in steelwork or leaving the joinery uncovered in wood, the effect is always powerful.

The monumental scale of some of the rooms in the house led principal architect Peter Bohlin and me to these furniture designs. We needed sizable legs and cross members so that the furniture wouldn't seem lost against the 9-in. square columns that frame the house. We also designed overlapping and penetrating connections to match the Arts and Crafts or Japanese-like joinery seen throughout the home.

It was clear early on that Eric Keil understood the styles that we were trying to create.

One aspect of this project that was amazingly successful was the collaboration between an owner, a craftsman, and designers. Often, when too many people become involved in a project, the outcome becomes diluted. But that

never happened. All parties were involved at each phase of the work, including full-size mock-ups to see how the pieces would fit in the room. The work between Eric and me was almost always hands-on. I'd visit his shop at least every other week, and sometimes more.

Toward the end of the project, our sketches to

WORKING HEAVY STOCK

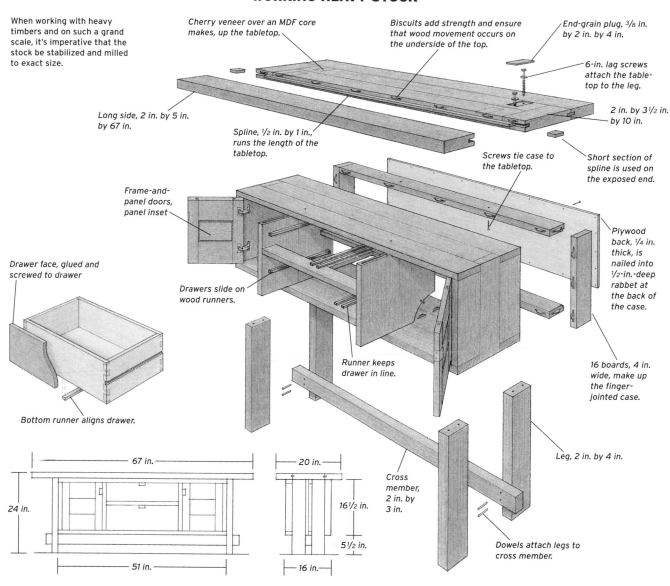

When working with heavy timbers and on such a grand scale, it's imperative that the stock be stabilized and milled to exact size.

Cherry veneer over an MDF core makes, up the tabletop.

Biscuits add strength and ensure that wood movement occurs on the underside of the top.

End-grain plug, 3/8 in. by 2 in. by 4 in.

6-in. lag screws attach the table-top to the leg.

Long side, 2 in. by 5 in. by 67 in.

Spline, 1/2 in. by 1 in., runs the length of the tabletop.

2 in. by 3 1/2 in. by 10 in.

Screws tie case to the tabletop.

Short section of spline is used on the exposed end.

Frame-and-panel doors, panel inset

Plywood back, 1/4 in. thick, is nailed into 1/2-in.-deep rabbet at the back of the case.

Drawer face, glued and screwed to drawer

Drawers slide on wood runners.

Runner keeps drawer in line.

16 boards, 4 in. wide, make up the finger-jointed case.

Bottom runner aligns drawer.

Cross member, 2 in. by 3 in.

Leg, 2 in. by 4 in.

Dowels attach legs to cross member.

67 in.

20 in.

24 in.

16 1/2 in.

5 1/2 in.

51 in.

16 in.

Eric consisted only of the major dimensions and no notes. Eric knew what we wanted, and we trusted his judgment, so we didn't have to waste time mapping out every detail. This process led to the successful execution of all of the furniture, including this sofa table.

Robert McLaughlin, formerly with Bohlin Cywinski Jackson Architects in Wilkes-Barre, Pa., is now principal of McLaughlin Design Associates in Kansas City, Kansas.

A meeting of minds. Furniture maker Eric Keil (right) and architect Robert McLaughlin discuss concerns about the sofa table's design.

A LIGHT SETTEE IN CHERRY

by Matthew Teague

I can't draw well, but it's never kept me from trying—on newspapers, leases, whatever happens to be in front of me. And when I needed a coffee table, I was drawing them everywhere. One design began on a Post-it Note® while I was on the phone—which may explain, in retrospect, its odd transformation. When one table leg turned out a little canted, I drew another line off the back, making it a chair. Then when I tried to turn the chairlike doodle into a perspective drawing, the lines were too long—yet further proof that I can't draw. But when I looked back down, my coffee table had turned into a vaguely elegant settee. I drew little cross-hatched lines across the seat and was rather pleased.

A BENCH FOR TWO

This design uses mortise-and-tenon joinery throughout, with square walnut pegs to accent the light cherry. Seat rails are rounded over to accommodate a woven seat.

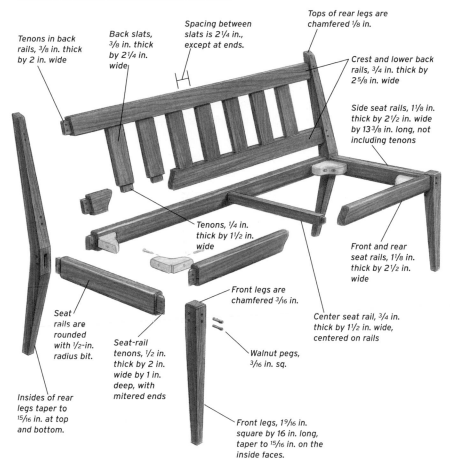

Tenons in back rails, 3/8 in. thick by 2 in. wide

Back slats, 3/8 in. thick by 2 1/4 in. wide

Spacing between slats is 2 1/4 in., except at ends.

Tops of rear legs are chamfered 1/8 in.

Crest and lower back rails, 3/4 in. thick by 2 5/8 in. wide

Side seat rails, 1 1/8 in. thick by 2 1/2 in. wide by 13 3/8 in. long, not including tenons

Tenons, 1/4 in. thick by 1 1/2 in. wide

Front and rear seat rails, 1 1/8 in. thick by 2 1/2 in. wide

Seat rails are rounded with 1/2-in. radius bit.

Seat-rail tenons, 1/2 in. thick by 2 in. wide by 1 in. deep, with mitered ends

Front legs are chamfered 3/16 in.

Center seat rail, 3/4 in. thick by 1 1/2 in. wide, centered on rails

Walnut pegs, 3/16 in. sq.

Insides of rear legs taper to 15/16 in. at top and bottom.

Front legs, 1 9/16 in. square by 16 in. long, taper to 15/16 in. on the inside faces.

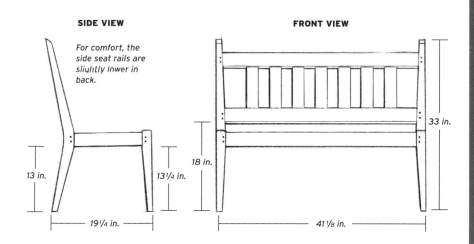

SIDE VIEW

For comfort, the side seat rails are slightly lower in back.

13 in.

13 1/4 in.

18 in.

19 1/4 in.

FRONT VIEW

33 in.

41 1/8 in.

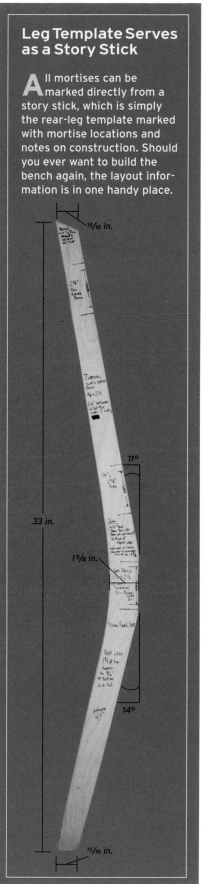

Leg Template Serves as a Story Stick

All mortises can be marked directly from a story stick, which is simply the rear-leg template marked with mortise locations and notes on construction. Should you ever want to build the bench again, the layout information is in one handy place.

15/16 in.

11°

33 in.

1 5/8 in.

14°

15/16 in.

Weaving a Reed Seat

Right-side up. By bending the reed to a tight curve, one side will fray while the other won't. Orient the frayed side so that it can't be seen.

Securing the reed. Begin by tacking a length of reed to the seat rail at the rear left corner of the seat.

Beginning the warp. The first length of reed goes under the front seat rail and over the back and continues in this way to the end of the seat.

Herringbone Weave

Woven of $^5/_8$-in. reeds, this herringbone pattern makes an attractive and comfortable seat. Though the weave may appear complicated at first glance, it is nothing more than a repeating pattern weave of over three, under three. After the first six rows, the pattern repeats itself to the front of the seat. To ensure that the seat stays tight, the same pattern is repeated on the bottom of the seat.

Ending the warp. When you reach the side rail, pull the reed underneath the seat and use a #3 upholsterer's tack to secure it to the seat rail.

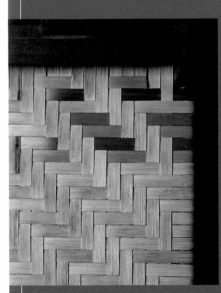

The first and last weavers are fill-in strips. Instead of wrapping around the seat rails, 6 in. to 8 in. of extra length is simply tucked inside the seat—the tightness of the weave will hold the fill-in strips in place. Before weaving the last rows, add another fill-in strip between the front legs.

Weaving begins underneath the seat at the rear left corner. Instead of tacking the reed into place, simply fold under the first 6 in. or 8 in.

1. The first row, a fill-in strip, skips two warps

2. Under one warp

3. Over three warps

4. Over two warps

5. Over one warp

6. Under three warps

7. Repeat the pattern from the fill-in strip.

Weaving a herringbone pattern. As you continue weaving the pattern into the seat, the weave gets tighter. You'll need to guide the last few rows using a dull knife.

I spent a bit more time on later drawings: I designed a stretcher system, tried two dozen shapes for the back and various seat treatments, but in the end I kept returning to the Post-it Note sketch of my coffee table. I liked its lightness and the simplicity of its straight lines. I bumped up the size of the seat rails to avoid using stretchers and to give the undercarriage a more delicate look. And I chose to use a woven seat for its light appearance.

My settee appears rooted in the Shaker and Arts and Crafts traditions, but the woven seat and walnut accents lend the piece a contemporary look, which suits my tastes. It's a small, low bench, perfect for an entryway or along a short wall.

Building this settee calls for only about 15 bd. ft. of wood—8/4 for the legs, 5/4 for the seat rails, and 4/4 for the back. I chose cherry because it is easily worked with hand tools and because its light color lends the unimposing look that I wanted the piece to have. But the design would work just as well using other woods.

Matthew Teague designs and builds furniture in Nashville, Tennessee.

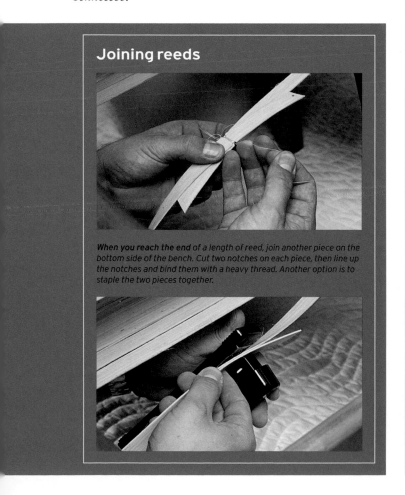

Joining reeds

When you reach the end of a length of reed, join another piece on the bottom side of the bench. Cut two notches on each piece, then line up the notches and bind them with a heavy thread. Another option is to staple the two pieces together.

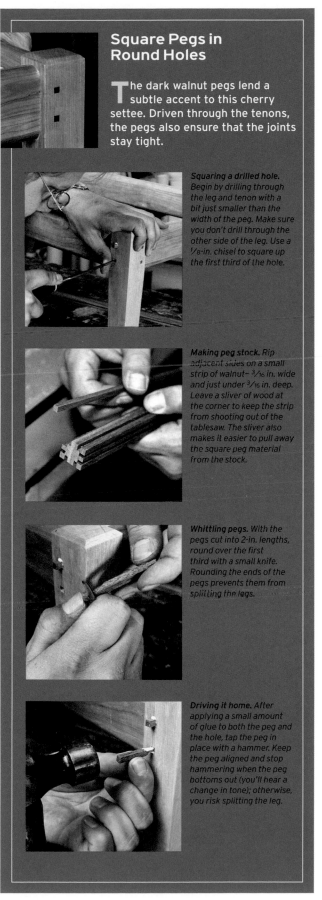

Square Pegs in Round Holes

The dark walnut pegs lend a subtle accent to this cherry settee. Driven through the tenons, the pegs also ensure that the joints stay tight.

Squaring a drilled hole. Begin by drilling through the leg and tenon with a bit just smaller than the width of the peg. Make sure you don't drill through the other side of the leg. Use a 1/8-in. chisel to square up the first third of the hole.

Making peg stock. Rip adjacent sides on a small strip of walnut– 3/16 in. wide and just under 3/16 in. deep. Leave a sliver of wood at the corner to keep the strip from shooting out of the tablesaw. The sliver also makes it easier to pull away the square peg material from the stock.

Whittling pegs. With the pegs cut into 2-in. lengths, round over the first third with a small knife. Rounding the ends of the pegs prevents them from splitting the legs.

Driving it home. After applying a small amount of glue to both the peg and the hole, tap the peg in place with a hammer. Keep the peg aligned and stop hammering when the peg bottoms out (you'll hear a change in tone); otherwise, you risk splitting the leg.

SHAKER ROCKER

by Ernie Conover

The Shaker rocker is one of the most recognized rocking-chair designs, and rightfully so. It has simple and attractive lines, it is economical to build, and, if designed properly, it can be very comfortable.

This chair also is a wonderful project in my woodworking classes because it introduces students to spindle turning, steam-bending, and a few important hand-tool techniques. The plans I use in class are an amalgamation of an early brethren's rocker, which is detailed in John Kassay's *The Book of Shaker Furniture*, and the rocking chairs made later at the famous Shaker production shop at Mount Lebanon in New York state.

I made a number of modifications to improve the strength of the chair, taking into account modern-day physiques. The original 1³⁄₈-in.-thick back posts are beefed up to 1⁹⁄₁₆ in. thick, and all of the seat rails and stretchers are about ⅛ in. larger in diameter than those on classic examples of the chair.

I also took some historical liberties with its design, incorporating features from various chairs produced by different Shaker communities. The arms and rockers are ½ in. thick and book-matched from the same figured maple board. The front arm posts have a ginger-jar profile and attach to the arms with a through-tenon and a mushroom cap. Finally, the back is woven with one curved back slat above.

My wife, Susan, who is a fiber artist, weaves the Shaker-tape seats and backs on my chairs. However, most of my students find that weaving is part of the fun of making a Shaker rocking chair. You'll need about 80 yd. of 1-in.-wide tape to complete this chair.

Ernie Conover is a regular contributor to Fine Woodworking *who teaches woodworking at his workshop in Parkman, Ohio.*

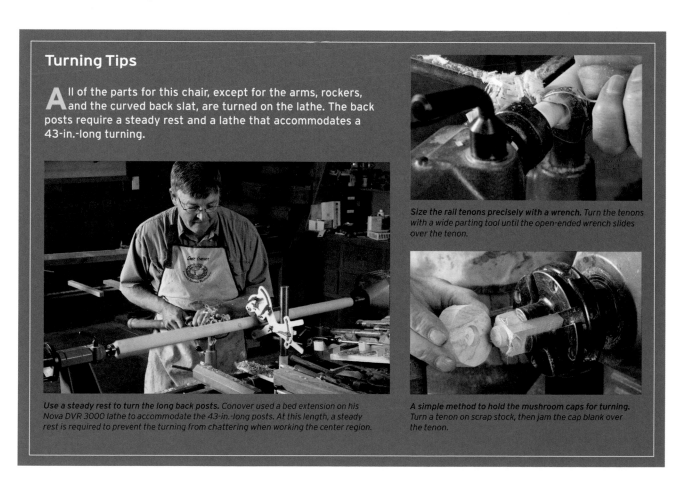

Turning Tips

All of the parts for this chair, except for the arms, rockers, and the curved back slat, are turned on the lathe. The back posts require a steady rest and a lathe that accommodates a 43-in.-long turning.

Size the rail tenons precisely with a wrench. Turn the tenons with a wide parting tool until the open-ended wrench slides over the tenon.

Use a steady rest to turn the long back posts. Conover used a bed extension on his Nova DVR 3000 lathe to accommodate the 43-in.-long posts. At this length, a steady rest is required to prevent the turning from chattering when working the center region.

A simple method to hold the mushroom caps for turning. Turn a tenon on scrap stock, then jam the cap blank over the tenon.

SHAKER ROCKER

The chair is made from roughly 8 bd. ft. of hard maple. Conover used curly or figured wood as much as possible, except for the seat rails and stretchers, where straight-grain stock is necessary for strength. All of the finished dimensions include tenons.

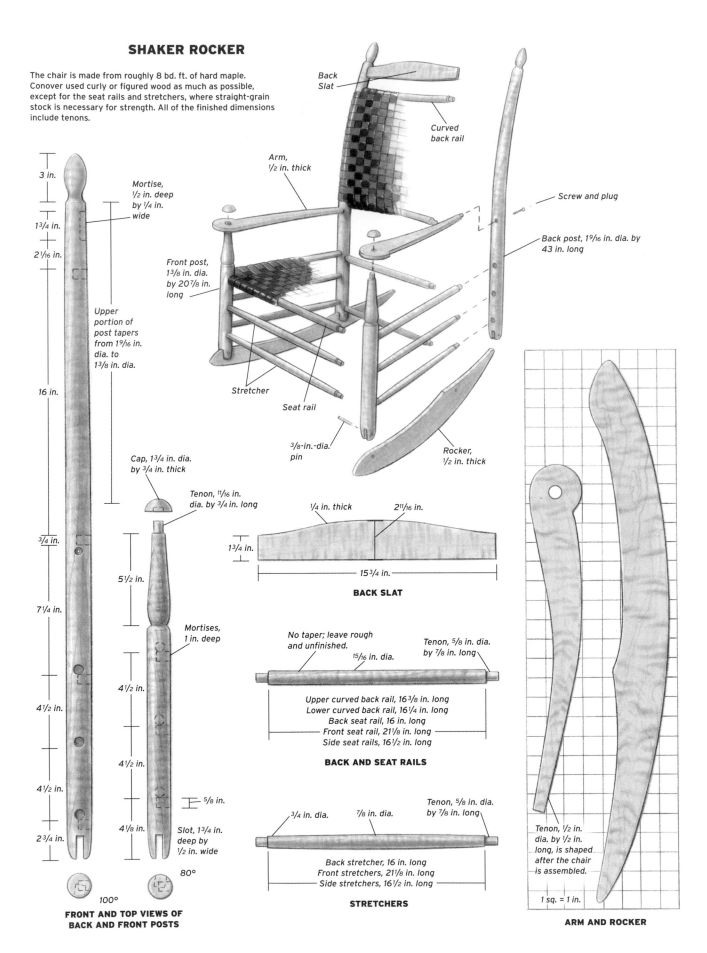

Back Slat

Arm, 1/2 in. thick

Curved back rail

Screw and plug

Back post, 1 9/16 in. dia. by 43 in. long

Front post, 1 3/8 in. dia. by 20 7/8 in. long

Stretcher

Seat rail

Rocker, 1/2 in. thick

3/8-in.-dia. pin

3 in.

1 3/4 in.

2 1/16 in.

Mortise, 1/2 in. deep by 1/4 in. wide

Upper portion of post tapers from 1 9/16 in. dia. to 1 3/8 in. dia.

16 in.

Cap, 1 3/4 in. dia. by 3/4 in. thick

Tenon, 11/16 in. dia. by 3/4 in. long

3/4 in.

5 1/2 in.

7 1/4 in.

Mortises, 1 in. deep

4 1/2 in.

4 1/2 in.

4 1/2 in.

4 1/2 in.

4 1/8 in.

5/8 in.

2 3/4 in.

Slot, 1 3/4 in. deep by 1/2 in. wide

100°

80°

**FRONT AND TOP VIEWS OF
BACK AND FRONT POSTS**

1/4 in. thick

2 11/16 in.

1 3/4 in.

15 3/4 in.

BACK SLAT

No taper; leave rough and unfinished.

15/16 in. dia.

Tenon, 5/8 in. dia. by 7/8 in. long

Upper curved back rail, 16 3/8 in. long
Lower curved back rail, 16 1/4 in. long
Back seat rail, 16 in. long
Front seat rail, 21 1/8 in. long
Side seat rails, 16 1/2 in. long

BACK AND SEAT RAILS

3/4 in. dia.

7/8 in. dia.

Tenon, 5/8 in. dia. by 7/8 in. long

Back stretcher, 16 in. long
Front stretchers, 21 1/8 in. long
Side stretchers, 16 1/2 in. long

STRETCHERS

Tenon, 1/2 in. dia. by 1/2 in. long, is shaped after the chair is assembled.

1 sq. = 1 in.

ARM AND ROCKER

Steam-Bending Made Simple

The bending of the back posts, the back slat, and the back rails is done by heating the parts in a steambox and then clamping them to a form.

To do the job, I use a shopmade steambox composed of a propane outdoor stove that boils water in a 5-gal. gas tank and then sends steam through a radiator hose into a 4-in.-dia. Schedule-80 drainpipe. The back posts should steam in the box for about an hour at a temperature around 200°F to become flexible enough to bend. The back slat and rails need to steam for only about 15 to 20 minutes. Once a part is removed from the steambox, you have about 30 to 60 seconds to clamp it to a form.

Just like a teapot, the steambox must leak steam to prevent it from exploding under pressure. Also, it must be positioned on a slope so that condensation inside the box can drain into the water tank. Always wear heavy gloves and eye protection when operating the steambox and shuttling parts to the bending jigs. An extra pair of hands is a big help.

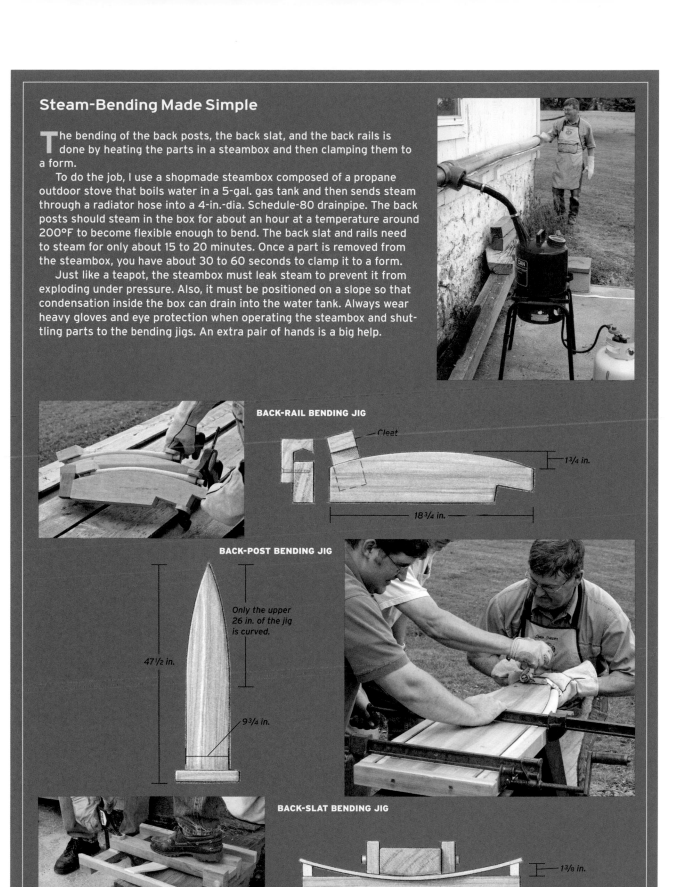

BACK-RAIL BENDING JIG

Cleat

1³/4 in.

18³/4 in.

BACK-POST BENDING JIG

Only the upper 26 in. of the jig is curved.

47¹/2 in.

9³/4 in.

BACK-SLAT BENDING JIG

1³/8 in.

18³/4 in.

CONTEMPORARY CHAIR IN ASH

by Garrett Hack

Even the most basic chair must support a body comfortably and be strong enough to take lots of rocking and rolling. This likely involves angled joinery; add some grace to the design, and you're probably working with curved parts as well. A lot of woodworkers shy away from making chairs, but there are many good reasons for building them. Design a dining table or a desk, and it seems only fitting to complete the project by building the chairs, too. Dealing with angled joinery and curved parts exposes you to making patterns, full-scale drawings, mock-ups, and thinking in three dimensions. Also, chairs are great for improving hand skills such as fitting joints and smoothing curves.

By design, this chair is not overwhelming in its joinery or curves. Rather than steam-bending or laminating parts, I designed the curves to be sawn from 8/4 stock. To splay the back toward the top, I used a common design trick: rotating the curved rear legs inward by 4 degrees. Also, the seat narrows toward the back to give it a graceful look and tilts slightly backward for comfort.

By carefully working out the curve of the rear legs, the tilt of the seat, and the taper and angle of the front legs, I was able to keep the joinery square in the side view, avoiding compound angles in most cases. This type of chair requires a slip seat, basically an upholstered platform that sits in a rabbet in the seat rails.

Garrett Hack is a contributing editor to Fine Woodworking.

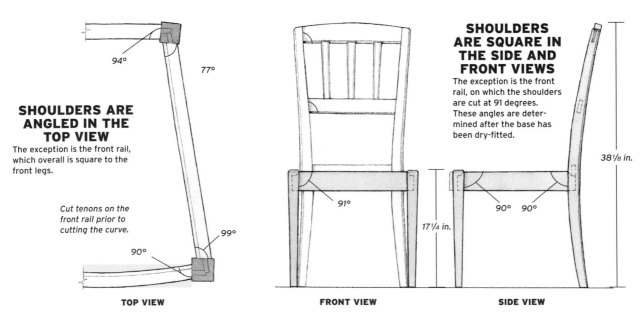

SHOULDERS ARE ANGLED IN THE TOP VIEW
The exception is the front rail, which overall is square to the front legs.

Cut tenons on the front rail prior to cutting the curve.

94°

77°

90°

99°

TOP VIEW

91°

17¼ in.

FRONT VIEW

SHOULDERS ARE SQUARE IN THE SIDE AND FRONT VIEWS
The exception is the front rail, on which the shoulders are cut at 91 degrees. These angles are determined after the base has been dry-fitted.

38⅛ in.

90°   90°

SIDE VIEW

FULL-SIZE DRAWINGS AND TEMPLATES AID CONSTRUCTION

Building a comfortable, attractive chair is never easy, but these joints have been simplified as much as possible. Most are angled in only one direction. In the front seat rail, the curve is cut after the joinery has been laid out and cut. Make a full-size drawing and templates for each part to keep track of lengths, curves, and joinery. The lengths of the upper rails and slats are determined after the base of the chair has been built and dry-fitted.

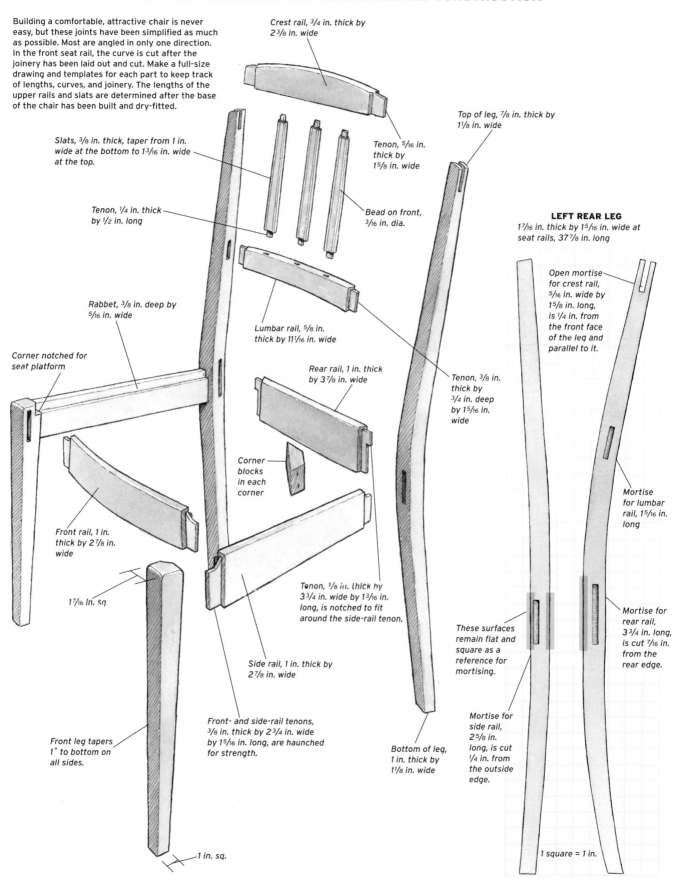

Crest rail, 3/4 in. thick by 2 3/8 in. wide

Slats, 3/8 in. thick, taper from 1 in. wide at the bottom to 1 3/16 in. wide at the top.

Tenon, 1/4 in. thick by 1/2 in. long

Tenon, 5/16 in. thick by 1 5/8 in. wide

Top of leg, 7/8 in. thick by 1 1/8 in. wide

Bead on front, 3/16 in. dia.

LEFT REAR LEG
1 7/16 in. thick by 1 5/16 in. wide at seat rails, 37 7/8 in. long

Rabbet, 3/8 in. deep by 5/16 in. wide

Lumbar rail, 5/8 in. thick by 11 1/16 in. wide

Open mortise for crest rail, 5/16 in. wide by 1 5/8 in. long, is 1/4 in. from the front face of the leg and parallel to it.

Corner notched for seat platform

Rear rail, 1 in. thick by 3 7/8 in. wide

Tenon, 3/8 in. thick by 3/4 in. deep by 1 5/16 in. wide

Mortise for lumbar rail, 1 5/16 in. long

Corner blocks in each corner

Front rail, 1 in. thick by 2 7/8 in. wide

Mortise for rear rail, 3 3/4 in. long, is cut 7/16 in. from the rear edge.

1 7/16 in. sq.

These surfaces remain flat and square as a reference for mortising.

Tenon, 3/8 in. thick by 3 3/4 in. wide by 1 3/16 in. long, is notched to fit around the side-rail tenon.

Side rail, 1 in. thick by 2 7/8 in. wide

Mortise for side rail, 2 5/8 in. long, is cut 1/4 in. from the outside edge.

Front leg tapers 1° to bottom on all sides.

Front- and side-rail tenons, 3/8 in. thick by 2 3/4 in. wide by 1 5/16 in. long, are haunched for strength.

Bottom of leg, 1 in. thick by 1 1/8 in. wide

1 in. sq.

1 square = 1 in.

MORRIS CHAIR

by Gene Lehnert

The Morris-style spindle chair is my favorite Gustav Stickley piece. In his popular *Craftsman* magazine, Stickley wrote, "No better or more comfortable and useful chair was ever designed." The chair, which features pinned through-tenon joinery, makes a comfortable, adjustable-back chair in the Craftsman tradition. I worked up this version (see the photo below) after looking at a lot of museum pieces and studying examples in Stickley's *Craftsman* magazine, books and other magazine articles.

Although Stickley sometimes used other woods, his primary choice was quartersawn white oak, which he darkened by fuming with ammonia. Even in his day, Stickley commented that quartersawing was a wasteful method of woodcutting. Today, the wood is rather difficult to find. However, larger retail suppliers sell it by the board foot. It should be selected for color match and figure. Sapwood should be eliminated as it tends not to darken when fumed with ammonia, Stickley's choice for finishing.

Gene Lehnert teaches vocational cabinetmaking/millwork and builds furniture in La Marque, Texas.

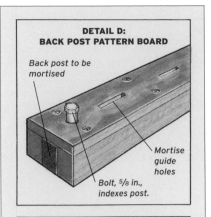

DETAIL D:
BACK POST PATTERN BOARD

Back post to be mortised

Mortise guide holes

Bolt, 5/8 in., indexes post.

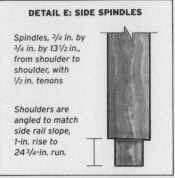

DETAIL E: SIDE SPINDLES

Spindles, 3/4 in. by 3/4 in. by 13 1/2 in., from shoulder to shoulder, with 1/2 in. tenons

Shoulders are angled to match side rail slope, 1-in. rise to 24 3/4-in. run.

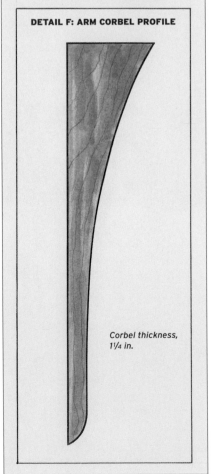

DETAIL F: ARM CORBEL PROFILE

Corbel thickness, 1 1/4 in.

MAKING A MORRIS CHAIR

Forerunner of today's recliners, this Morris chair built in the Craftsman tradition features an adjustable reclining back. The back, which pivots on pegs, rests on removable pins that slide into holes on the inside of the arms. To recline the back, simply move the adjustment pins to different holes in the arms. To make his chair even more comfortable, the author also built a matching footstool.

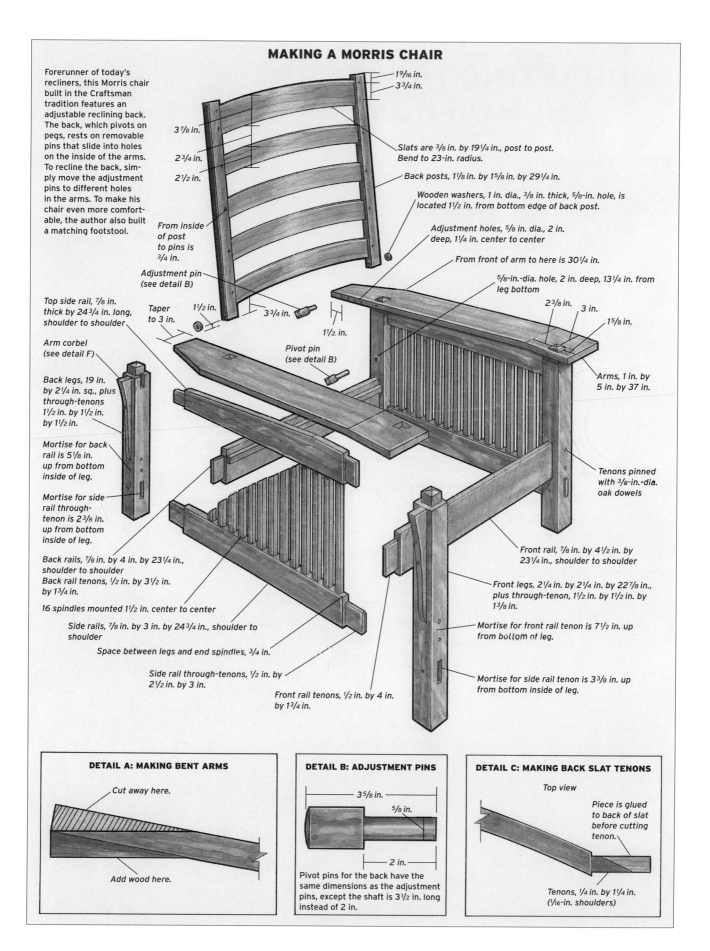

1⁹/₁₆ in.

3³/₄ in.

3⁷/₈ in.

2³/₄ in.

2¹/₂ in.

Slats are ³/₈ in. by 19¹/₄ in., post to post. Bend to 23-in. radius.

Back posts, 1¹/₈ in. by 1⁵/₈ in. by 29¹/₄ in.

Wooden washers, 1 in. dia., ³/₈ in. thick, ⁵/₈-in. hole, is located 1¹/₂ in. from bottom edge of back post.

Adjustment holes, ⁵/₈ in. dia., 2 in. deep, 1¹/₄ in. center to center

From front of arm to here is 30¹/₄ in.

⁵/₈-in.-dia. hole, 2 in. deep, 13¹/₄ in. from leg bottom

2³/₈ in.   3 in.

1⁵/₈ in.

From inside of post to pins is ³/₄ in.

Adjustment pin (see detail B)

1¹/₂ in.

3³/₄ in.

1¹/₂. in.

Pivot pin (see detail B)

Arms, 1 in. by 5 in. by 37 in.

Top side rail, ⁷/₈ in. thick by 24³/₄ in. long, shoulder to shoulder

Taper to 3 in.

Arm corbel (see detail F)

Back legs, 19 in. by 2¹/₄ in. sq., plus through-tenons 1¹/₂ in. by 1¹/₂ in. by 1¹/₂ in.

Mortise for back rail is 5¹/₈ in. up from bottom inside of leg.

Mortise for side rail through-tenon is 2³/₈ in. up from bottom inside of leg.

Back rails, ⁷/₈ in. by 4 in. by 23¹/₄ in., shoulder to shoulder
Back rail tenons, ¹/₂ in. by 3¹/₂ in. by 1³/₄ in.

16 spindles mounted 1¹/₂ in. center to center

Side rails, ⁷/₈ in. by 3 in. by 24³/₄ in., shoulder to shoulder

Space between legs and end spindles, ³/₄ in.

Side rail through-tenons, ¹/₂ in. by 2¹/₂ in. by 3 in.

Front rail tenons, ¹/₂ in. by 4 in. by 1³/₄ in.

Tenons pinned with ³/₈-in.-dia. oak dowels

Front rail, ⁷/₈ in. by 4¹/₂ in. by 23¹/₄ in., shoulder to shoulder

Front legs, 2¹/₄ in. by 2¹/₄ in. by 22⁷/₈ in., plus through-tenon, 1¹/₂ in. by 1¹/₂ in. by 1³/₈ in.

Mortise for front rail tenon is 7¹/₂ in. up from bottom of leg.

Mortise for side rail tenon is 3³/₈ in. up from bottom inside of leg.

DETAIL A: MAKING BENT ARMS

Cut away here.

Add wood here.

DETAIL B: ADJUSTMENT PINS

3⁵/₈ in.

⁵/₈ in.

2 in.

Pivot pins for the back have the same dimensions as the adjustment pins, except the shaft is 3¹/₂ in. long instead of 2 in.

DETAIL C: MAKING BACK SLAT TENONS

Top view

Piece is glued to back of slat before cutting tenon.

Tenons, ¹/₄ in. by 1¹/₄ in. (¹/₁₆-in. shoulders)

A DRAFTING TABLE FOR SHOP OR HOME

by Cameron Russell

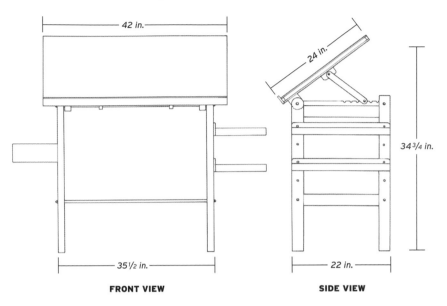

FRONT VIEW

42 in.

35 1/2 in.

SIDE VIEW

24 in.

34 3/4 in.

22 in.

Accessory trays for drafting supplies

The drafting room at the college where I teach furniture making had long been a sore spot with me. The tables we used were industrial-type library tables, not designed for drawing. The students who used them were far from comfortable. For hours at a time, they hunched over a flat surface that was at the wrong height. It made drafting a pain.

To solve that problem, I designed and built the prototype shown in the top photo on the facing page.

The construction process is simple, and the hardware we used is readily available from hardware stores or mail-order supply houses. The knockdown design makes it easy to disassemble the table for storage or moving. The torsion-box top is rigid and dead flat, yet light and portable.

The key hardware components holding the table together are four threaded rods that fit within metal pipes. The nuts and washers on the ends of the threaded rods pull the leg assemblies firmly together while the rigid lengths of pipe keep the two sides apart. This combination of tension and resistance to compressive forces stiffens the structure. The smooth cylindrical surface of the metal pipe also provides an ideal pivot pin for the tilting top.

The design for the top guarantees that it will be lightweight, dead flat, and strong. The outside skins of 1/4-in. plywood are glued to the narrow surfaces of an internal wood frame, and the considerable overall surface area makes a healthy bond. As with any face-to-face gluing of wood, this construction process offers a lot of resistance to twisting forces, making the panel very rigid for its size and weight.

I built this tabletop 24 in. wide by 42 in. long, but the lower structure could easily handle a top up to 30 in. wide by 60 in. long.

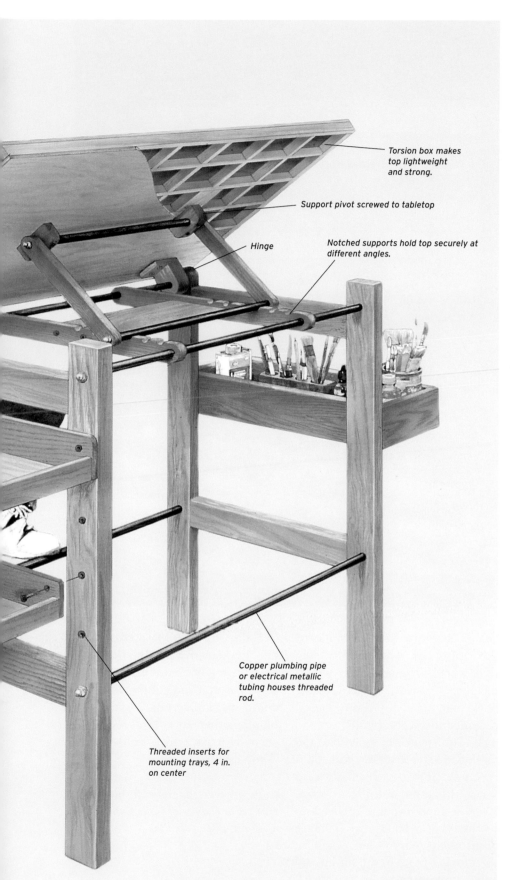

Torsion box makes top lightweight and strong.

Support pivot screwed to tabletop

Hinge

Notched supports hold top securely at different angles.

Copper plumbing pipe or electrical metallic tubing houses threaded rod.

Threaded inserts for mounting trays, 4 in. on center

Built with common materials and knockdown hardware, this table is inexpensive and easy to make. Movable hinged supports make it possible to adjust the top to different angles. Accessory trays mounted on the sides provide plenty of storage space for drafting materials.

Each side of the table is made with a front and rear leg joined by two rails, as shown in the drawings on p. 161. We used mortise-and-tenon joints to connect legs and rails, but either dowels or biscuits also could be used.

The size of the table calls for standard lengths of 36-in. threaded rod. The pipe can be either thin-walled, $^1/_2$-in. EMT (electrical metallic tubing) or $^1/_2$-in. copper plumbing pipe. The copper is much more expensive, but it can be polished and clear coated for a visually pleasing finish.

Once you've fabricated and finished all the pieces, putting them all together is a cinch. Start with the legs and notched support-

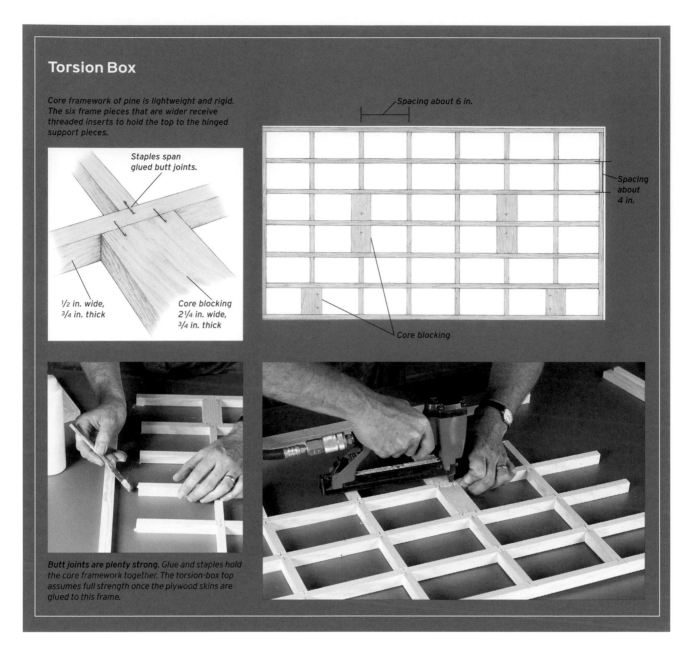

Torsion Box

Core framework of pine is lightweight and rigid. The six frame pieces that are wider receive threaded inserts to hold the top to the hinged support pieces.

Staples span glued butt joints.

½ in. wide, ¾ in. thick

Core blocking 2¼ in. wide, ¾ in. thick

Spacing about 6 in.

Spacing about 4 in.

Core blocking

Butt joints are plenty strong. Glue and staples hold the core framework together. The torsion-box top assumes full strength once the plywood skins are glued to this frame.

rail assembly. It's important to remember to slip the hinge-block pieces over the pipe as you do this, so the hinge blocks are in place when you want to secure the top later. The only tools you'll need to set up this table (or take it apart) are a box wrench, a ratchet for the threaded rods with acorn nuts, and an Allen wrench for the connector bolts.

The small blocks of wood that allow the top to pivot and to be supported at different angles are bolted through into threaded inserts set into the underside of the top. For applications like this, where I thought parts would have to be taken apart and put back together many times, I used threaded inserts and bolts.

If you plan to assemble the table and leave it set up, you could certainly substitute regular wood screws for some of this hardware. Keep in mind, though, that ready-to-assemble hardware makes adjustments easy when aligning the moving parts of the tilting and supporting pieces.

I also installed threaded inserts on the outsides of the legs for rearranging or adding accessory trays for drafting equipment. You could customize your own table to handle other specific accessories, such as a paper-roll holder or a T-square rack.

Cameron Russell teaches furniture making at Camosun College in Victoria, B.C., Canada.

CONSTRUCTION DETAILS

These drawings show the important details of parts that connect the top to the lower frame. For rigidity, the holes for the metal pipe should have flat bottoms and furnish a snug fit. If you use a spade bit (left), you may have to grind it down.

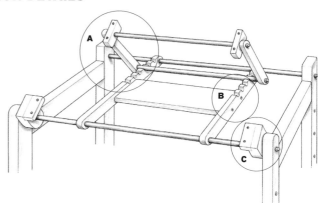

A

B

C

A. SECTION THROUGH TOP PROP

Threaded insert

Core blocking

Connector bolt

Pivot support piece

11³/₈ in.

Top prop piece

Acorn nut with washer

Threaded rod

Metal pipe

¹/₂ in.

Ends cut at ¹¹/₁₆ in. radius.

Counterbored hole for pipe is not drilled all the way through.

1³/₈ in.

C. SECTION THROUGH TOP HINGE MOUNT

Threaded insert

Core blocking

Threaded rod

Acorn nut with washer

Metal pipe

Hinge

1¹/₂ in.

Leg

1¹/₂ in.

Cross dowel and connector bolts secure notched supports to rail.

B. SECTION THROUGH NOTCHED SUPPORTS

³/₄ in. radius

1¹/₂ in.

⁵/₁₆ in. radius

1¹/₂ in.

19¹/₂ in.

21 in.

18TH-CENTURY PENNSYLVANIA SECRETARY

by Lonnie Bird

During the 18th century, building a secretary was often considered the culmination of a cabinetmaker's skill. But for years I've taught inexperienced students to build the secretary seen on these pages. The key to building a large, complex piece, such as this reproduction of a Pennsylvania desk—with more than 100 parts and nearly that many joints—is to break down the process into small, easy steps. This secretary, like all case-work, is just a series of boxes fitted within largerboxes. The moldings, curves, feet, and other details are easily made and make the completed piece visually stimulating.

I have a great appreciation for 18th-century design, aesthetics and joinery, but I don't restrict myself to building absolute reproductions. I study related examples beforehand and combine the best elements to come up with a piece that's my own. And I don't copy mistakes. If a door proportion doesn't work or a glue block was attached cross-grain, I'll make the necessary changes. I want my furniture to capture the spirit of period furniture without the shortcomings.

Lonnie Bird teaches woodworking at his shop in Dandridge, Tennessee.

The 18th-Century Aesthetic

My eye has always been drawn toward the stylistic elements of American period furniture. But rather than make exact copies, I prefer to make subtle changes within the parameters of the style. Before building a piece, I study several related examples (other Pennsylvania secretaries, for instance) and borrow the best elements, such as the foot from one piece and perhaps the door from another. For example, the serpentine gallery on this secretary is common to many Pennsylvania secretaries, and the foot is a somewhat unique version from another Pennsylvania antique.

If I'm not comfortable with an original proportion, I change it. In my mind, no matter how fine the workmanship or dramatic the figure in a door panel, if proportions are clumsy, the piece isn't successful. To ensure that the piece looks balanced, I use one of several proportioning systems. I've measured enough antiques to be convinced that period craftspeople used them, too. The golden rectangle and ratios of whole numbers are very useful.

On this piece, for example, I chose the popular tombstone panel for the gallery's prospect door and divided the height by the golden ratio (1.618) to determine the width. The top drawer in the gallery measures 2 in. by 6 in., a ratio of whole numbers; and the drawer below it graduates by ¼ in., roughly the thickness of the divider.

Using design elements from related examples allows me to keep in harmony with the Colonial cabinetmakers from a specific geographical region while building a piece of furniture that is distinctly my own.

FRONT VIEW

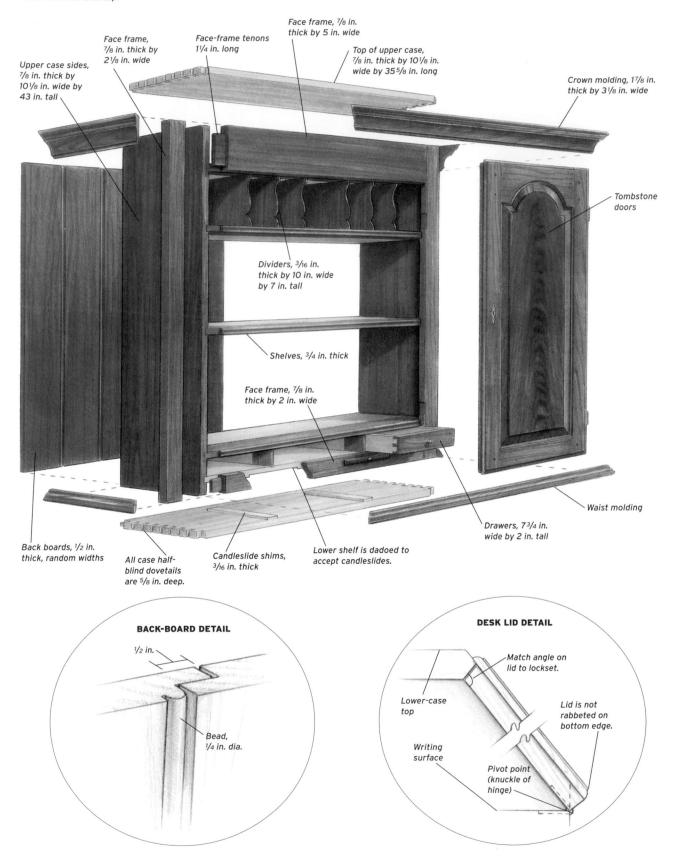

Lonnie Bird designed this 18th-century Pennsylvania secretary after studying many examples from the period. It features a fold-down lid that becomes part of the writing surface, a gallery with drawers and pigeonholes, and traditional tombstone doors on top.

Face frame, 7/8 in. thick by 5 in. wide

Face-frame tenons 1 1/4 in. long

Top of upper case, 7/8 in. thick by 10 1/8 in. wide by 35 5/8 in. long

Face frame, 7/8 in. thick by 2 1/8 in. wide

Crown molding, 1 7/8 in. thick by 3 1/8 in. wide

Upper case sides, 7/8 in. thick by 10 1/8 in. wide by 43 in. tall

Tombstone doors

Dividers, 3/16 in. thick by 10 in. wide by 7 in. tall

Shelves, 3/4 in. thick

Face frame, 7/8 in. thick by 2 in. wide

Waist molding

Drawers, 7 3/4 in. wide by 2 in. tall

Back boards, 1/2 in. thick, random widths

All case half-blind dovetails are 5/8 in. deep.

Candleslide shims, 3/16 in. thick

Lower shelf is dadoed to accept candleslides.

BACK-BOARD DETAIL

1/2 in.

Bead, 1/4 in. dia.

DESK LID DETAIL

Match angle on lid to lockset.

Lower-case top

Lid is not rabbeted on bottom edge.

Writing surface

Pivot point (knuckle of hinge)

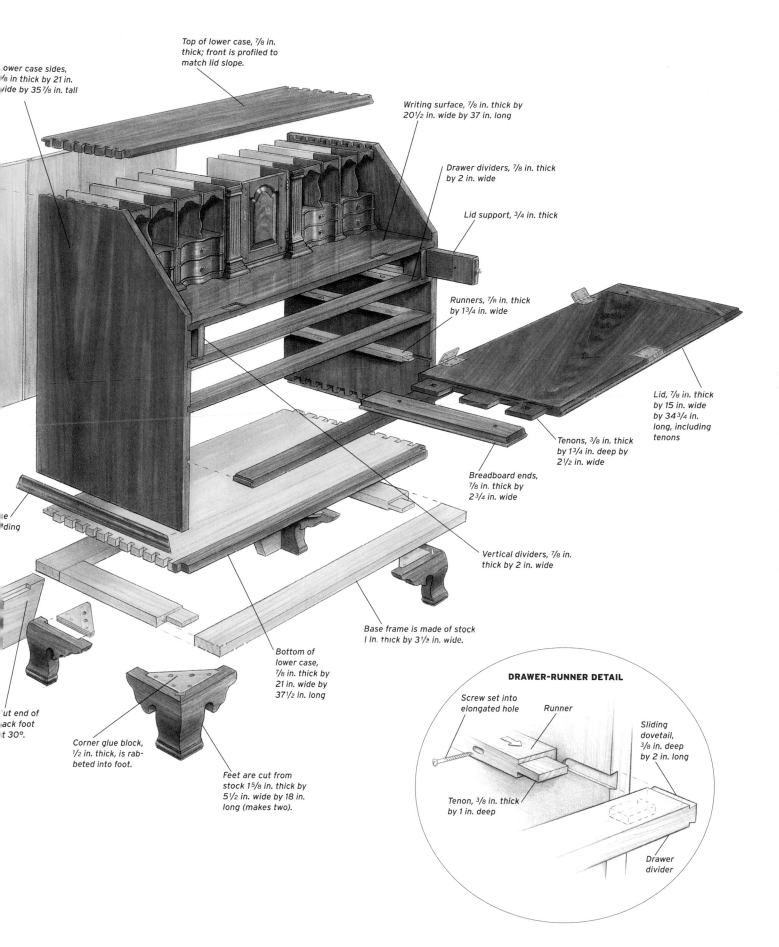

Top of lower case, 7/8 in. thick; front is profiled to match lid slope.

ower case sides, /8 in thick by 21 in. /ide by 35 7/8 in. tall

Writing surface, 7/8 in. thick by 20 1/2 in. wide by 37 in. long

Drawer dividers, 7/8 in. thick by 2 in. wide

Lid support, 3/4 in. thick

Runners, 7/8 in. thick by 1 3/4 in. wide

Lid, 7/8 in. thick by 15 in. wide by 34 3/4 in. long, including tenons

Tenons, 3/8 in. thick by 1 3/4 in. deep by 2 1/2 in. wide

Breadboard ends, 7/8 in. thick by 2 3/4 in. wide

e ding

Vertical dividers, 7/8 in. thick by 2 in. wide

Base frame is made of stock 1 In. thick by 3 1/2 in. wide.

Bottom of lower case, 7/8 in. thick by 21 in. wide by 37 1/2 in. long

ut end of ack foot t 30°.

Corner glue block, 1/2 in. thick, is rab- beted into foot.

Feet are cut from stock 1 5/8 in. thick by 5 1/2 in. wide by 18 in. long (makes two).

DRAWER-RUNNER DETAIL

Screw set into elongated hole

Runner

Sliding dovetail, 3/8 in. deep by 2 in. long

Tenon, 3/8 in. thick by 1 in. deep

Drawer divider

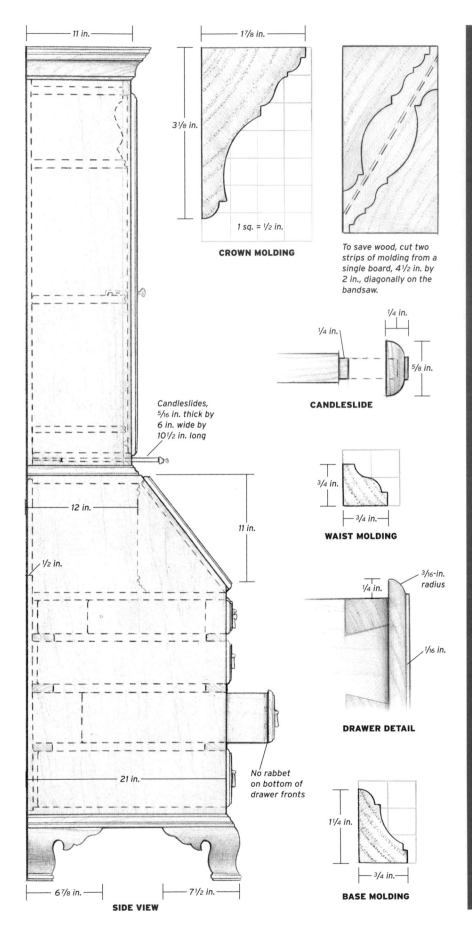

— 11 in. —

— 1 7/8 in. —

3 1/8 in.

1 sq. = 1/2 in.

CROWN MOLDING

To save wood, cut two
strips of molding from a
single board, 4 1/2 in. by
2 in., diagonally on the
bandsaw.

1/4 in.

1/4 in.

5/8 in.

CANDLESLIDE

Candleslides,
5/16 in. thick by
6 in. wide by
10 1/2 in. long

12 in.

11 in.

1/2 in.

3/4 in.

3/4 in.

WAIST MOLDING

1/4 in.

3/16-in.
radius

1/16 in.

DRAWER DETAIL

No rabbet
on bottom of
drawer fronts

21 in.

1 1/4 in.

3/4 in.

BASE MOLDING

— 6 7/8 in. —   — 7 1/2 in. —

SIDE VIEW

Old Style, New Methods

It's difficult to improve on many 18th-century joinery techniques. Dovetails are still the best choice for constructing drawers and casework, and no modern joinery method comes close to the strength of a door frame joined with pinned mortise-and-tenon joints. But a closer look at many antiques reveals that 18th-century craftspeople did not always choose the best construction methods to allow for seasonal movement. You'll often find drawer runners that were simply nailed to the sides of casework and ogee feet that were thin facades held together with a cross-grain glue block. Such practices have resulted in split case sides and cracked feet.

Today, craftspeople who choose to work in 18th-century styles must make choices about how far they will duplicate the work of the period. Because I want my furniture to have the look and feel of the originals, I work diligently to reproduce more of the lines, proportions, and details. This often requires a great deal of painstaking handwork, such as planing and scraping surfaces or sawing dovetails by hand. But I don't feel a compulsion to duplicate the construction techniques that lead a piece to self-destruct.

This is why I fasten drawer runners with screws driven through elongated holes. And, if necessary, I beef up the construction a bit. For example, I added the dovetail dividers at the back of the lower case to help withstand the pressure of an upper case loaded with books. The result is a piece of furniture that's true to the style without some of the shortcomings.

MAKING BRACKET FEET

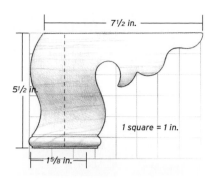

7½ in.

5½ in.

1 square = 1 in.

1⅝ in.

Feet are mitered, splined and cut to shape. With the blade set to 45 degrees, the mitered ends of the foot stock are cut to accept a hardwood spline. Before assembly, feet are bandsawn to shape.

Quick jig helps profile the feet. With the feet clamped to an elevated jig, rough out the side profile of the feet on the bandsaw.

Follow the glueline. Once the first profile has been cut, simply follow the exposed glueline to make sure the two sides match.

Veneering Drawer Fronts

Resawn drawer fronts match perfectly. Bird chooses a nice piece of crotch wood and resaws drawer fronts on the bandsaw.

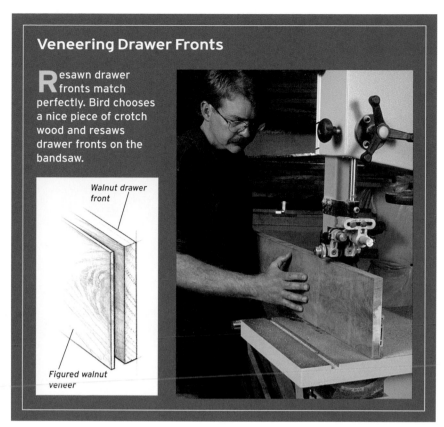

Walnut drawer front

Figured walnut veneer

Pilaster Conceals a Drawer

Document drawers of the period were often disguised by applying a decorative pilaster to the drawer fronts. This version also features a false bottom and back, creating a hidden compartment accessible from the rear.

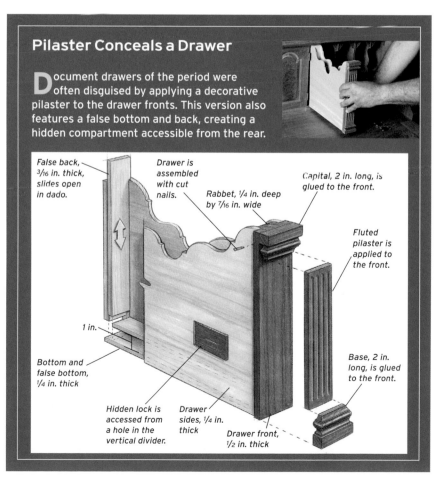

False back, ³⁄₁₆ in. thick, slides open in dado.

Drawer is assembled with cut nails.

Rabbet, ¼ in. deep by ⁷⁄₁₆ in. wide

Capital, 2 in. long, is glued to the front.

Fluted pilaster is applied to the front.

1 in.

Bottom and false bottom, ¼ in. thick

Hidden lock is accessed from a hole in the vertical divider.

Drawer sides, ¼ in. thick

Drawer front, ½ in. thick

Base, 2 in. long, is glued to the front.

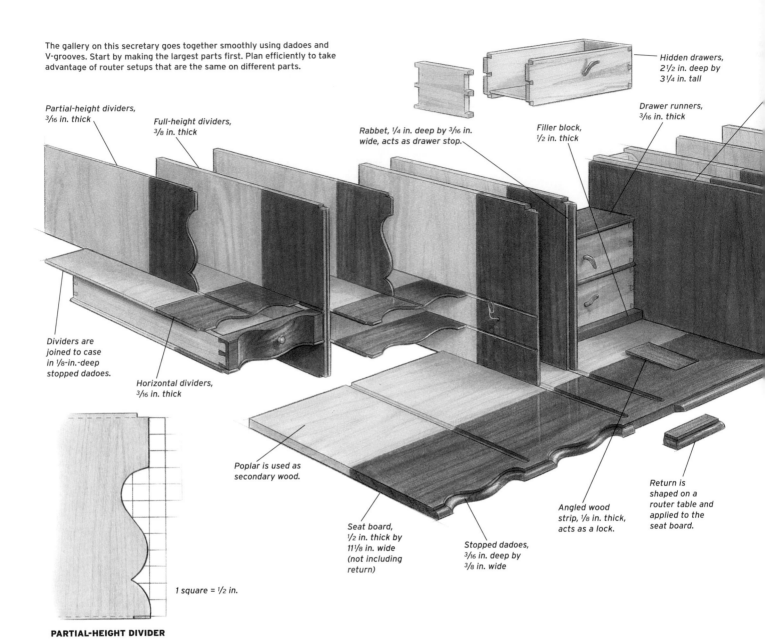

The gallery on this secretary goes together smoothly using dadoes and V-grooves. Start by making the largest parts first. Plan efficiently to take advantage of router setups that are the same on different parts.

Hidden drawers, 2½ in. deep by 3¼ in. tall

Partial-height dividers, 3/16 in. thick

Full-height dividers, 3/8 in. thick

Rabbet, ¼ in. deep by 3/16 in. wide, acts as drawer stop.

Filler block, ½ in. thick

Drawer runners, 3/16 in. thick

Dividers are joined to case in ⅛-in.-deep stopped dadoes.

Horizontal dividers, 3/16 in. thick

Poplar is used as secondary wood.

1 square = ½ in.

PARTIAL-HEIGHT DIVIDER

Seat board, ½ in. thick by 11⅛ in. wide (not including return)

Stopped dadoes, 3/16 in. deep by 3/8 in. wide

Angled wood strip, ⅛ in. thick, acts as a lock.

Return is shaped on a router table and applied to the seat board.

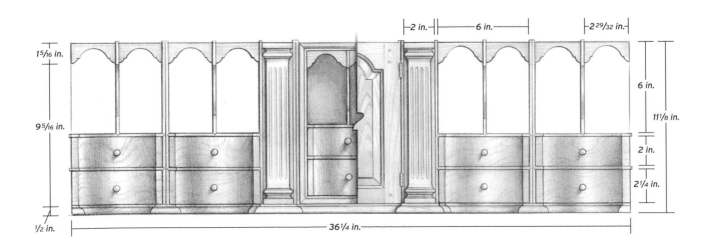

2 in.

6 in.

2 29/32 in.

1 5/16 in.

9 5/16 in.

½ in.

6 in.

11⅛ in.

2 in.

2¼ in.

36¼ in.

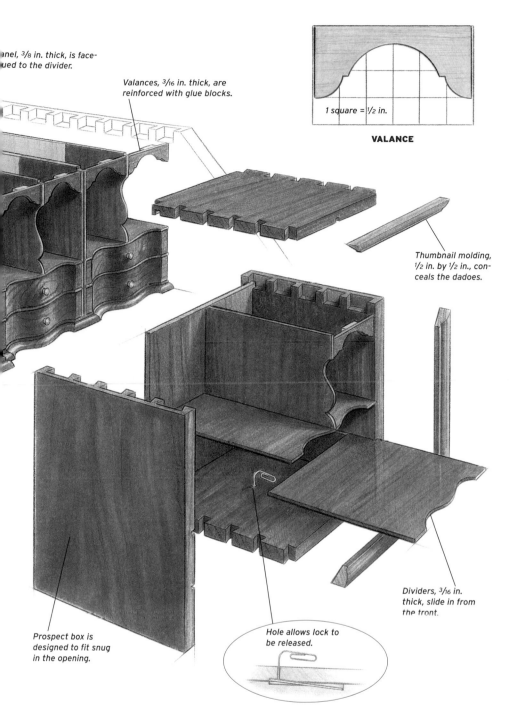

anel, ³/₈ in. thick, is face-
ued to the divider.

Valances, ³/₁₆ in. thick, are
reinforced with glue blocks.

1 square = ½ in.

VALANCE

Thumbnail molding,
½ in. by ½ in., con-
ceals the dadoes.

Prospect box is
designed to fit snug
in the opening.

Hole allows lock to
be released.

Dividers, ³/₁₆ in.
thick, slide in from
the front.

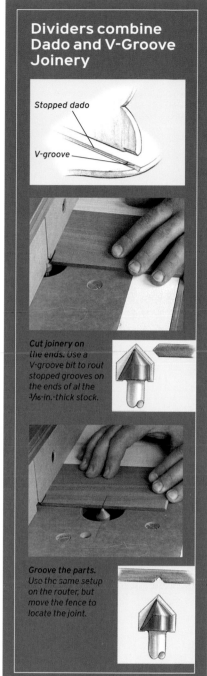

Dividers combine Dado and V-Groove Joinery

Stopped dado

V-groove

**Cut joinery on
the ends.** Use a
V-groove bit to rout
stopped grooves on
the ends of al the
³/₁₆-in.-thick stock.

Groove the parts.
Use the same setup
on the router, but
move the fence to
locate the joint.

MAKING THE SEAT BOARD

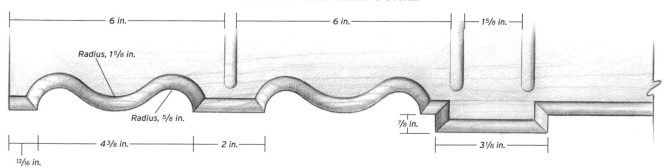

6 in.

6 in.

1⁵/₈ in.

Radius, 1⁵/₈ in.

Radius, ⁵/₈ in.

7/8 in.

4³/₈ in.

2 in.

3¹/₈ in.

¹³/₁₆ in.

THUMBNAIL DRESSES UP THE FRAME

The thumbnail profile on the inside edge of the frame requires a miter where the rails and stiles meet.

A 3/8-in. radius cove bit in a table-mounted router is used to mill the inner faces of the rails and stiles.

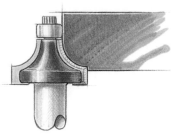

A 1/4-in. groove is routed along the rails and stiles.

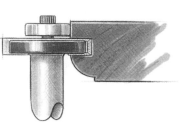

Tombstone Panel Requires Handwork

Carve the Corners. *Use a square and compass to mark out the corners of the arch (left). Scoring with a knife provides a solid reference line. Bird walks a chisel across the area to be removed, leaving less room for error (above). Use a skew chisel to get into the corners (below).*

Offset, Doors Require Extra Care in Sizing

Bird's tombstone doors are rabbeted to overlay the frame. They are also offset, meaning they close proud of the frame.

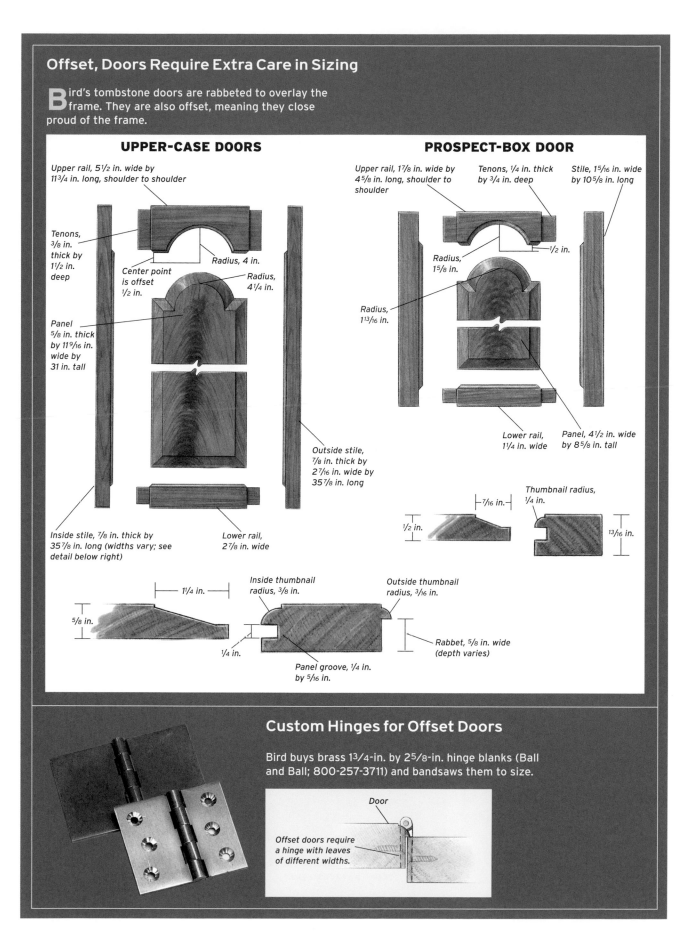

UPPER-CASE DOORS

Upper rail, 5½ in. wide by 11¾ in. long, shoulder to shoulder

Tenons, ⅜ in. thick by 1½ in. deep

Center point is offset ½ in.

Radius, 4 in.

Radius, 4¼ in.

Panel ⅝ in. thick by 11 9/16 in. wide by 31 in. tall

Outside stile, ⅞ in. thick by 2 7/16 in. wide by 35⅞ in. long

Inside stile, ⅞ in. thick by 35⅞ in. long (widths vary; see detail below right)

Lower rail, 2⅞ in. wide

1¼ in.

⅝ in.

¼ in.

Inside thumbnail radius, ⅜ in.

Outside thumbnail radius, 3/16 in.

Panel groove, ¼ in. by 5/16 in.

Rabbet, ⅝ in. wide (depth varies)

PROSPECT-BOX DOOR

Upper rail, 1⅞ in. wide by 4⅝ in. long, shoulder to shoulder

Tenons, ¼ in. thick by ¾ in. deep

Stile, 1 5/16 in. wide by 10⅝ in. long

Radius, 1⅝ in.

½ in.

Radius, 1 13/16 in.

Lower rail, 1¼ in. wide

Panel, 4½ in. wide by 8⅝ in. tall

7/16 in.

½ in.

Thumbnail radius, ¼ in.

13/16 in.

Custom Hinges for Offset Doors

Bird buys brass 1¾-in. by 2⅝-in. hinge blanks (Ball and Ball; 800-257-3711) and bandsaws them to size.

Door

Offset doors require a hinge with leaves of different widths.

FILE AND MEDIA STORAGE

HIDDEN KEYBOARD TRAY

PULL-OUT WORK SURFACE

CHERRY COMPUTER DESK

by Charles Durfee

In my study at home stands a lovely, tall secretary desk with bookcase, glowing beautifully in its 20-year-old patina. For the past several years it's been piled high with papers, notes, photos, stuff and more stuff. I make periodic assaults on the piles, but the fact of the matter is that I don't work at the desk anymore. I now work—doing letters, bills, e-mail—about 8 ft. away at a small table that holds the computer, with storage in a cabinet below. On some KMart[SM]-bought shelves lie a printer, scanner, files, and books.

Whether you have made the plunge into working from a home office or just find yourself using the computer more often, maybe it's time to give the computer a real place in your home on a piece of furniture that works well, is built to last, and is a pleasure to live with.

My original plan was for a cabinet similar to an entertainment center that could house the whole system and be closed up when not in use. But I suspect that many people work with their computer in short bursts throughout the day and week and want it out and accessible. Also, today's computers look much more stylish than the gray boxes of a few years ago.

Another problem with a cabinet design that closes everything away is that by necessity it becomes quite large and rather awkward-looking, especially if your computer has a large monitor.

That's how I arrived at an unobstructed tabletop, with enough room for equipment and workspace.

CASE-SIDE ASSEMBLY

The case sides are frame-and-panel construction, with thumbnail moldings on the inside edges of the frames. The panels have the bevel facing inward, in the Shaker style.

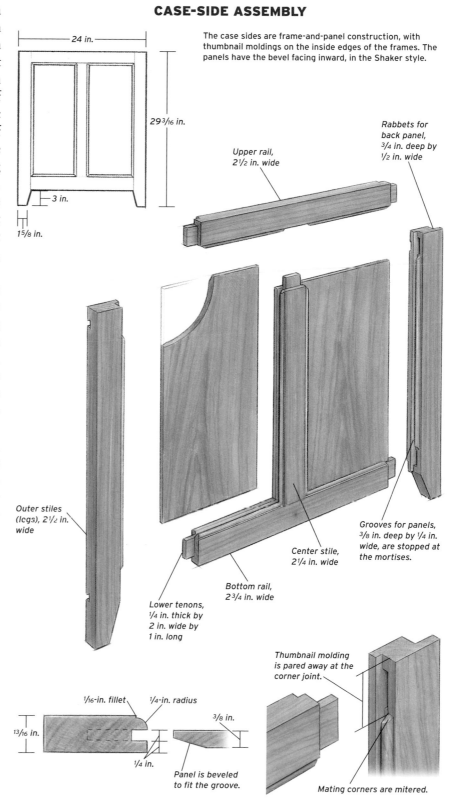

24 in.

29 3/16 in.

3 in.

1 5/8 in.

Upper rail, 2 1/2 in. wide

Rabbets for back panel, 3/4 in. deep by 1/2 in. wide

Outer stiles (legs), 2 1/2 in. wide

Grooves for panels, 3/8 in. deep by 1/4 in. wide, are stopped at the mortises.

Center stile, 2 1/4 in. wide

Bottom rail, 2 3/4 in. wide

Lower tenons, 1/4 in. thick by 2 in. wide by 1 in. long

1/16-in. fillet   1/4-in. radius

13/16 in.

1/4 in.

3/8 in.

Panel is beveled to fit the groove.

Thumbnail molding is pared away at the corner joint.

Mating corners are mitered.

CABINET PLAN

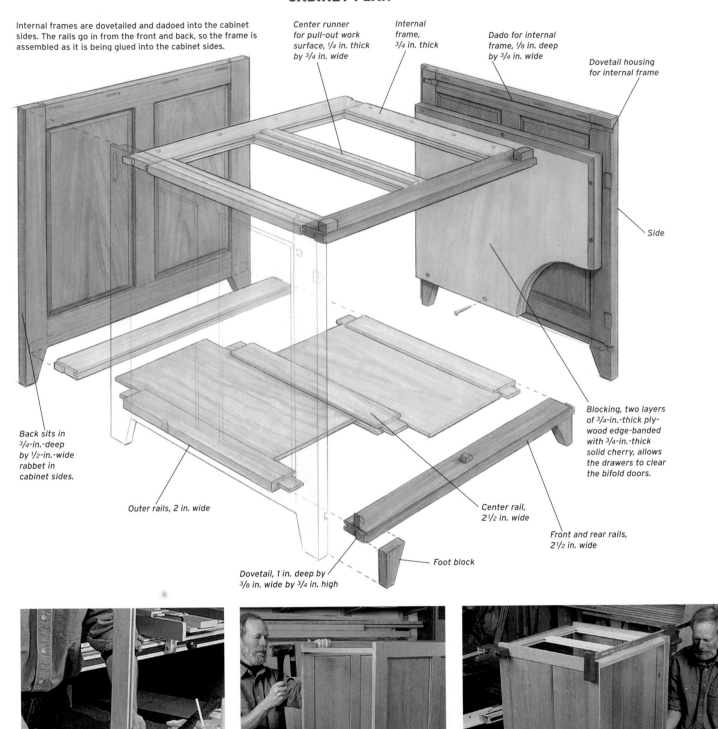

Internal frames are dovetailed and dadoed into the cabinet sides. The rails go in from the front and back, so the frame is assembled as it is being glued into the cabinet sides.

Center runner for pull-out work surface, ¼ in. thick by ¾ in. wide

Internal frame, ¾ in. thick

Dado for internal frame, ⅛ in. deep by ¾ in. wide

Dovetail housing for internal frame

Side

Blocking, two layers of ¾-in.-thick plywood edge-banded with ¾-in.-thick solid cherry, allows the drawers to clear the bifold doors.

Back sits in ¾-in.-deep by ½-in.-wide rabbet in cabinet sides.

Outer rails, 2 in. wide

Center rail, 2½ in. wide

Front and rear rails, 2½ in. wide

Dovetail, 1 in. deep by ⅜ in. wide by ¾ in. high

Foot block

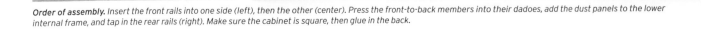

Order of assembly. Insert the front rails into one side (left), then the other (center). Press the front-to-back members into their dadoes, add the dust panels to the lower internal frame, and tap in the rear rails (right). Make sure the cabinet is square, then glue in the back.

An additional pull-out worksurface is handy. Add an adaptable storage cabinet below and a keyboard tray behind a traditional drawer front, and presto, I had my solution.

Major components—monitor, processor, and printer—go on top. The processor could also go on the floor, either in the footwell or up on brackets. Wires are bundled and routed out of the way.

Think Function First

This is a classic case of inside-out design: Begin with the function and work from there. The height is 30 in., though tall people may want to add an inch or two. The keyboard pulls out at approximately 26 in., a comfortable height. The length of the desk is 60 in. but could be extended. Stretchers support the legs at the open end and tie the design together by continuing the lower line of the cabinet.

In keeping with a Shaker aesthetic, the cabinet and doors are of frame-and-panel construction with thumbnail molding (also called sticking) on the inside edge of the frame. Classic Shaker style almost always left door panels flat (with the beveled side facing inward). The desktop edge gets a slight bullnose profile. In a departure from the Shaker style, I used brass knobs.

An additional worksurface pulls out to the right, closer at hand than the desktop when you are using the keyboard (lefties might want to reverse the entire desk). The pencil drawer, not covered by the doors, is easily accessible.

I chose bifold doors over single or double doors. A single door would stick out too far when open, which it often will be when you are working at the desk. And double doors would block access to the cabinet from a sitting position.

Bring it together. Once the cabinet base is assembled, the author uses long barclamps to glue the open base to the cabinet base.

Sources for Hardware

DRAWER SLIDES
Full extension, 22 in., ebony color, Model KV 8400
Woodworker's Supply (800-645-9292; www.woodworker.com)

KEYBOARD SLIDE
Variable height, 16 in., black color, Model KV 8150
Woodworker's Supply

BUTT HINGES
2 in. by 1½ in., "standard" finish, Part No. 142H5
Whitechapel Ltd. (800-468-5534; www.whitechapel-ltd.com)

DROP-LEAF TABLE HINGES
3 in. by 1½ in., "standard" finish, Part No. 166H17
Whitechapel Ltd.

KNOBS
Sold as desk interior knobs, ¾ in. (except ⅝-in. size on pull-out surface), semibright
Horton Brasses (800-754-9127; www.horton-brasses.com)

HOME-OFFICE HARDWARE
File-drawer fittings, wrist rest, media storage, wire managers, grommets
Rockler Woodworking and Hardware (800-279-4441; www.rockler.com)

TABLETOP FASTERNERS
Rockler Woodworking and Hardware

Behind the doors are two small drawers above a file drawer. The top drawer holds paper, print cartridges, and the like, or even a flatbed scanner. The middle drawer can hold CDs and other supplies. The file drawer is the lateral type, easier to access while seated at the desk. Closing the doors covers up all of this neatly. The drawers are hung on full-extension slides. These screw-mounted commercial slides allow the components to be moved easily in the future. I used finger joints in the drawers, which are easier to make than dovetails and are in keeping with the utilitarian nature of this desk.

A wood keyboard tray is mounted on special pull-out hardware that's attached to the underside of the desktop. The tray is hidden behind a drawer front that folds down.

For this cherry piece, I chose an oil finish, which is excellent for bringing out cherry's rich, mellow tone. I prefer an oil-varnish mix, which gives a bit more surface durability and is easy to wipe on and repair. You can mix your own, though for years I have used Minwax Antique Oil with satisfaction. If you want a more durable worksurface, use varnish. I have read that lacquer and plastic will stick together over time, making lacquer a poor choice for a computer desk.

Charles Durfee is a furniture maker in Woolwich, Maine.

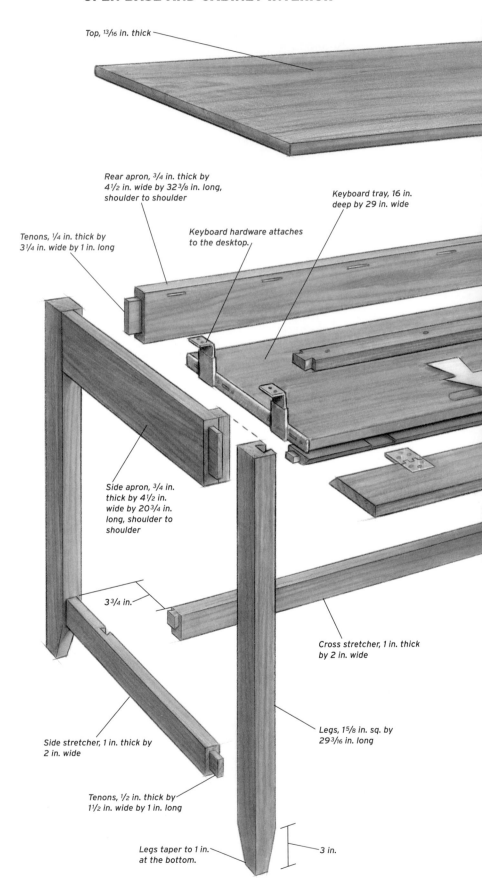

OPEN BASE AND CABINET INTERIOR

Top, 13/16 in. thick

Rear apron, 3/4 in. thick by 4 1/2 in. wide by 32 3/8 in. long, shoulder to shoulder

Keyboard tray, 16 in. deep by 29 in. wide

Tenons, 1/4 in. thick by 3 1/4 in. wide by 1 in. long

Keyboard hardware attaches to the desktop.

Side apron, 3/4 in. thick by 4 1/2 in. wide by 20 3/4 in. long, shoulder to shoulder

3 3/4 in.

Cross stretcher, 1 in. thick by 2 in. wide

Legs, 1 5/8 in. sq. by 29 3/16 in. long

Side stretcher, 1 in. thick by 2 in. wide

Tenons, 1/2 in. thick by 1 1/2 in. wide by 1 in. long

Legs taper to 1 in. at the bottom.

3 in.

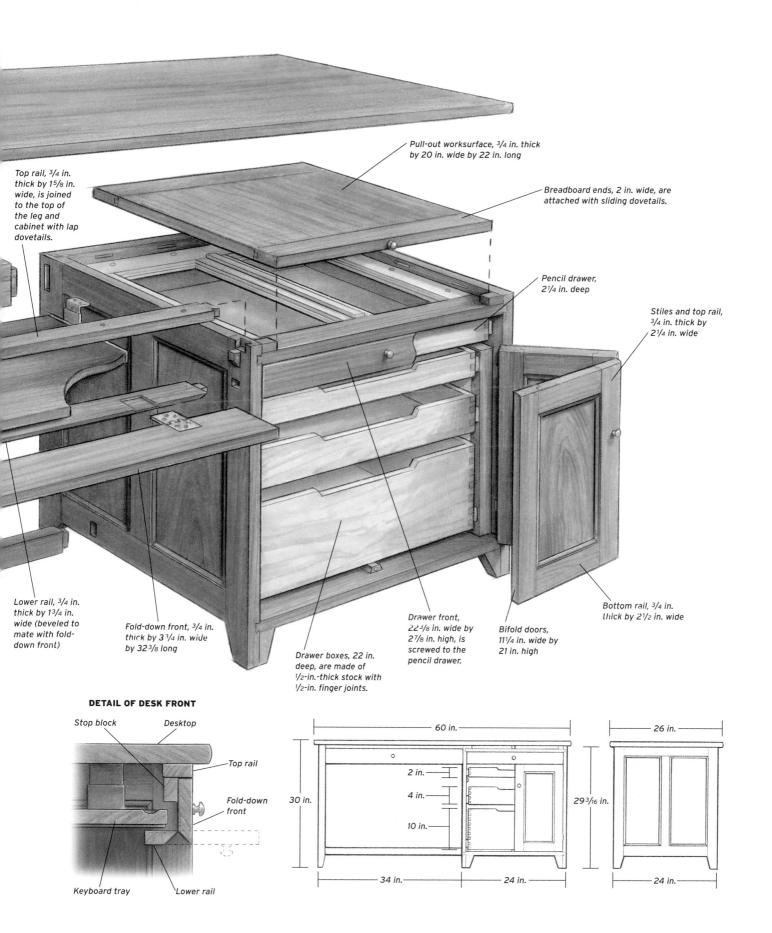

Pull-out worksurface, 3/4 in. thick by 20 in. wide by 22 in. long

Top rail, 3/4 in. thick by 1 5/8 in. wide, is joined to the top of the leg and cabinet with lap dovetails.

Breadboard ends, 2 in. wide, are attached with sliding dovetails.

Pencil drawer, 2 1/4 in. deep

Stiles and top rail, 3/4 in. thick by 2 1/4 in. wide

Lower rail, 3/4 in. thick by 1 3/4 in. wide (beveled to mate with fold-down front)

Fold-down front, 3/4 in. thick by 3 3/4 in. wide by 32 3/8 long

Drawer boxes, 22 in. deep, are made of 1/2-in.-thick stock with 1/2-in. finger joints.

Drawer front, 22 3/8 in. wide by 2 7/8 in. high, is screwed to the pencil drawer.

Bifold doors, 11 1/4 in. wide by 21 in. high

Bottom rail, 3/4 in. thick by 2 1/2 in. wide

DETAIL OF DESK FRONT

Stop block

Desktop

Top rail

Fold-down front

Keyboard tray

Lower rail

60 in.

2 in.

4 in.

10 in.

30 in.

34 in.

24 in.

26 in.

29 3/16 in.

24 in.

AN ARTS AND CRAFTS LIBRARY TABLE

by Eric Keil

I've never seen the virtues of building a table with drawers in the traditional way—with a double-tenoned stretcher below the drawer and a dovetailed top rail. It just seems like unnecessary work. I've developed methods for building a table with drawers that are faster and, to my mind, stronger. It's the same approach I use when building a chest of drawers. I build frames to go over and under the drawers, then simply attach them to preassembled ends. This approach makes the entire project more manageable and all but guarantees a smooth and square glue-up.

This library table is adapted from various Stickley catalogs from the turn of the 20th century. It would work well as a writing desk or as a reading table. My approach to the construction of this traditional Arts and Crafts piece is straightforward. I used quartersawn stock, hand-hammered hardware, and a slightly lighter finish than is customary for this style.

The Best Boards Go on Top

For this project, I ordered 100 bd. ft. of oak, then riffled through to choose boards for specific parts. Once all of the boards had been surfaced, I designated the best of the lot for the tabletop, which I typically glue together. It was easiest to glue up the table upside down on a flat surface. One nice thing about using preassembled frames is that, at glue-up, it took only a few clamps to pull everything closed.

The tabletop itself was screwed directly to the frames. It was fixed at the center with screws, and then the front and back were screwed into elongated holes—which allow for seasonal movement—through the upper frame. The drawer fronts, likewise, were simply attached with screws.

A final touch was the hand-hammered copper pulls from Gerald Rucks. With the solid drawers, the smooth-running glides, and the authentic pulls, the desk is a pleasure to use.

Eric Keil builds custom furniture and cabinetry in Wilkes-Barre, Pennsylvania.

TABLE-END GLUE-UP

Fill-in strip, 5/8 in. thick by 3/4 in. wide

Tenon at back of table is mitered.

Side apron, 5 1/8 in. wide by 21 3/4 in. long, shoulder to shoulder

Tenon, 1/2 in. thick by 3 in. wide by 1 1/2 in. deep

Distance between slats, 7/8 in.

Leg is assembled from 5/8-in.-thick mitered stock wrapped around a solid core.

Tenon, 3/8 in. thick by 3 in. wide by 1 in. deep

Slat, 5/8 in. thick by 3 3/4 in. wide by 16 1/4 in. long, shoulder to shoulder

Through-mortise, 1/2 in. wide by 7 in. long

Lower rail, 3 in. wide by 21 3/4 in. long, shoulder to shoulder

Tenon, 1/2 in. thick by 2 1/2 in. wide by 2 1/2 in. deep

Leg, 2 1/4 in. square by 29 in. long

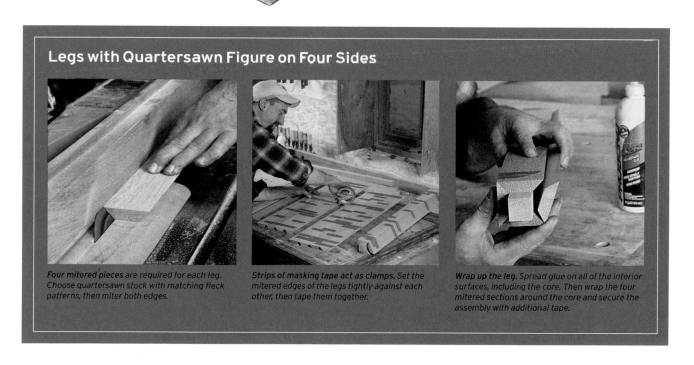

Legs with Quartersawn Figure on Four Sides

Four mitered pieces are required for each leg. Choose quartersawn stock with matching fleck patterns, then miter both edges.

Strips of masking tape act as clamps. Set the mitered edges of the legs tightly against each other, then tape them together.

Wrap up the leg. Spread glue on all of the interior surfaces, including the core. Then wrap the four mitered sections around the core and secure the assembly with additional tape.

SHELF AND DRAWER ASSEMBLY JOIN THE TWO ENDS

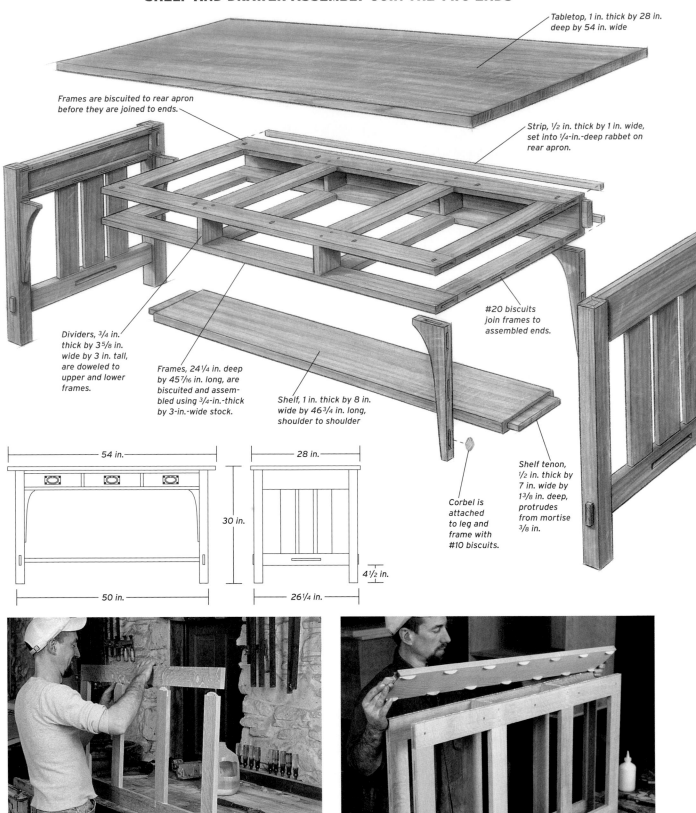

Tabletop, 1 in. thick by 28 in. deep by 54 in. wide

Frames are biscuited to rear apron before they are joined to ends.

Strip, 1/2 in. thick by 1 in. wide, set into 1/4-in.-deep rabbet on rear apron.

#20 biscuits join frames to assembled ends.

Dividers, 3/4 in. thick by 3 5/8 in. wide by 3 in. tall, are doweled to upper and lower frames.

Frames, 24 1/4 in. deep by 45 7/16 in. long, are biscuited and assembled using 3/4-in.-thick by 3-in.-wide stock.

Shelf, 1 in. thick by 8 in. wide by 46 3/4 in. long, shoulder to shoulder

Corbel is attached to leg and frame with #10 biscuits.

Shelf tenon, 1/2 in. thick by 7 in. wide by 1 3/8 in. deep, protrudes from mortise 3/8 in.

54 in.

28 in.

30 in.

50 in.

26 1/4 in.

4 1/2 in.

Frames are the starting point. *The author constructs two frames that will go above and below the drawers. The frames are simply biscuited together.*

The rear apron is biscuited to the frame assembly. *Note that the drawer dividers are already in place.*

INSTALL DRAWER BLOCKING AND GLIDES LAST

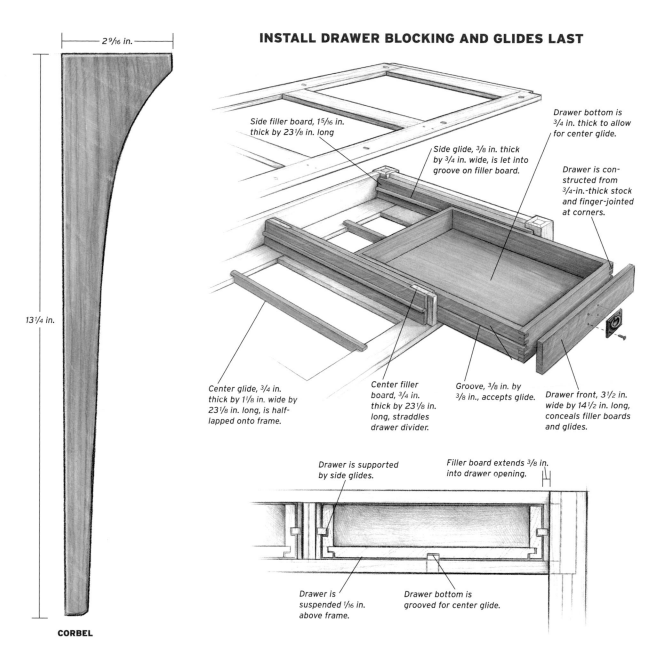

2⁹/₁₆ in.

13¹/₄ in.

CORBEL

Side filler board, 1⁵/₁₆ in. thick by 23¹/₈ in. long

Side glide, ³/₈ in. thick by ³/₄ in. wide, is let into groove on filler board.

Drawer bottom is ³/₄ in. thick to allow for center glide.

Drawer is constructed from ³/₄-in.-thick stock and finger-jointed at corners.

Center glide, ³/₄ in. thick by 1¹/₈ in. wide by 23¹/₈ in. long, is half-lapped onto frame.

Center filler board, ³/₄ in. thick by 23¹/₈ in. long, straddles drawer divider.

Groove, ³/₈ in. by ³/₈ in., accepts glide.

Drawer front, 3¹/₂ in. wide by 14¹/₂ in. long, conceals filler boards and glides.

Drawer is supported by side glides.

Filler board extends ³/₈ in. into drawer opening.

Drawer is suspended ¹/₁₆ in. above frame.

Drawer bottom is grooved for center glide.

Bring it all together. *The through-tenoned shelf, the biscuited frames, and the ends are all assembled in one operation. The glue-up proceeds easily when it is done with the table upside down on a flat surface.*

Block out the ends. *The ends of the table are blocked out with a board grooved to accept the drawer glides.*

KNOCKDOWN TRESTLE TABLE WORKS WELL INDOORS OR OUT

by Tony Konovaloff

This red-cedar table's mass is lightened visually by its gently rounded and bevel-edged top, tapered foot, and thin, slightly tapered wedges. Just the same, the table is built solidly to withstand years of use and abuse, both inside and out.

When I was a student at James Krenov's woodworking program at the College of the Redwoods, money was tight. Having virtually no furniture, though, I needed to make some basic utilitarian pieces, including a kitchen table. I went to the local lumberyard and purchased just enough 2x stock to make a trestle table like the one in the photo above. I liked that first table's lines and wanted to try it in a nicer wood, so I chose clear, vertical-grained red cedar because it's highly rot-resistant: The table can be used outside as well as in the kitchen or dining room.

Building this table can be done just as easily with power tools as with hand tools and may even be slightly quicker. But the scale of the joinery and the simplicity of the design also make this an ideal project on which to practice cutting joints by hand.

I use hand tools exclusively, partially because acquiring and practicing hand-tool skills is what initially attracted me to woodworking. But mostly I use hand tools because I really enjoy planing and cutting joinery by hand, and I really don't enjoy the scream of electric saws, routers, and sanders.

I used dimensional red cedar for this project, which I cut to length, planed smooth, and laid out for mortises and tenons. I clamped each of the trestle members in my bench vise and bored holes for the mortises using a brace and expansion bit.

I built the two trestles first, then the related pieces (stretcher, wedges, and battens) and, finally, the top. By having the trestles and related pieces ready when I finish the top, I can attach the battens to the underside of the top right away, connecting top and base before there's any chance of major wood movement. If I built the top first, it could have warped while I was building the base, making it difficult to connect the two.

Tony Konovaloff is a professional furniture maker in Bellingham, Washington.

INDOOR/OUTDOOR TRESTLE DINING TABLE

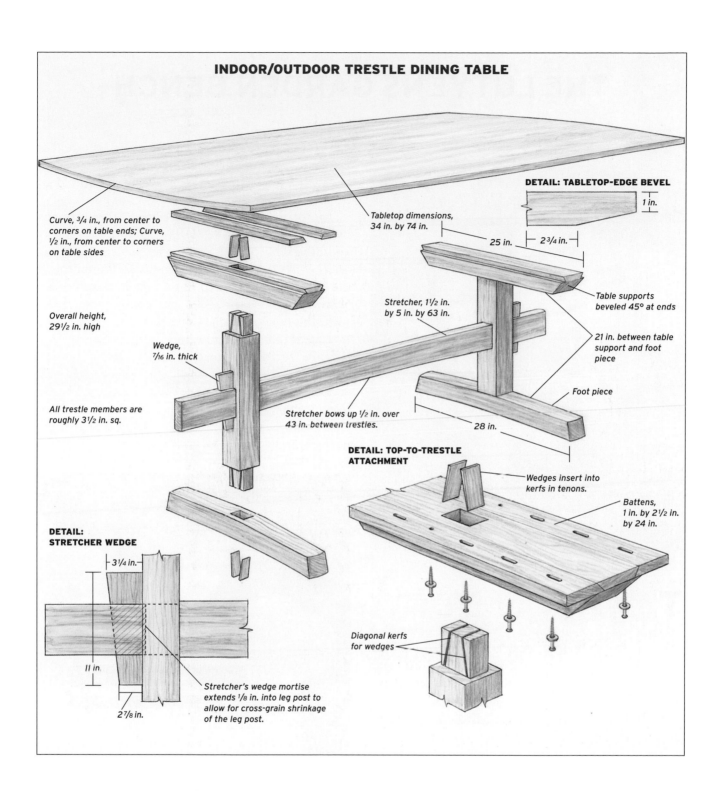

DETAIL: TABLETOP-EDGE BEVEL

1 in.

25 in.

2 3/4 in.

Curve, 3/4 in., from center to corners on table ends; Curve, 1/2 in., from center to corners on table sides

Tabletop dimensions, 34 in. by 74 in.

Table supports beveled 45° at ends

Overall height, 29 1/2 in. high

Stretcher, 1 1/2 in. by 5 in. by 63 in.

21 in. between table support and foot piece

Wedge, 7/16 in. thick

All trestle members are roughly 3 1/2 in. sq.

Stretcher bows up 1/2 in. over 43 in. between trestles.

Foot piece

28 in.

DETAIL: TOP-TO-TRESTLE ATTACHMENT

Wedges insert into kerfs in tenons.

Battens, 1 in. by 2 1/2 in. by 24 in.

DETAIL: STRETCHER WEDGE

3 1/4 in.

11 in.

2 7/8 in.

Stretcher's wedge mortise extends 1/8 in. into leg post to allow for cross-grain shrinkage of the leg post.

Diagonal kerfs for wedges

THE LUTYENS GARDEN BENCH

by Tony O'Malley

garden bench in a catalog. The bench had the kind of distinctive elegance that I wanted my garden to have, but with a price tag nearing $2,000 in the catalog, I decided to make one myself.

The original bench was designed 100 years ago by Edwin Lutyens (1869–1944), a British architect and designer. The bench's curvaceous crest rail and lollipop-like front legs form a whimsical frame around the classically regimented slats of the back and rolled armrests. An eye-catching and comfortable three-seater, it's no wonder the Lutyens bench is still copied by dozens of outdoor furniture manufacturers.

Some reproductions I've seen have no bottom stretcher at the front or back, and others have both. As I sketched and worked through drawings, I began to notice that a bottom stretcher even with the front legs would restrict a sitter's feet from going where they naturally want to go—under the seat a few

Turning our little yard into a landscaped garden retreat has been one of those back-burner projects my wife and I have managed to avoid since buying our house six years ago. It's been easy to do because neither of us is a gardener. As a woodworker, I'm always able to find constructive projects somewhere inside the house that are better suited to my skills than moving earth and planting flowers. Plus, I've decided that a proper garden should evolve slowly over the years— four years ago we planted a Japanese maple under the fringe of the huge Sycamore that dominates the yard, and last summer I laid down a brick patio outside the back porch. Good things shouldn't be rushed, I tell myself.

Now that I work primarily from home, the prospect of taking daily work breaks in a more pleasant backyard nook has me thinking more about the gardening part of our imaginary garden. But over the winter months all I could do was plan, dream, and defer. Then I saw a picture of the Lutyens

inches. As a compromise, I positioned a stretcher under the middle of the seat, tenoned into the bottom side stretchers.

I worked out the details of the entire bench using full-size drawings. I drew the bench, at various views, directly onto ¼-in. plywood. Because of the myriad joints, angles, and curves in this design, full-size drawings were crucial to making the project run smoothly. The drawings helped me not only to refine the design of the bench before committing any cuts to lumber but also to figure out the construction and necessary order of assembly.

Choose an Appropriate Wood for Outdoor Use

Reproductions of the Lutyens garden bench are typically made of teak, but I ruled that out immediately due to the cost. My bench would sit outside permanently because I didn't have a place to store it indoors over the winter, so weather resistance was a main requirement. Spanish cedar is a good mahogany-colored wood that weathers better than real mahogany, but I couldn't find any locally. I looked at several imported hardwoods being marketed for

deck building—ipe from South America and jarrah from Australia among them—but these woods are very heavy, quite abrasive to tools, and generally hard to work. High weight also helped me rule out locally grown woods like white oak and locust.

I settled on cypress for its light weight, good moisture resistance, and moderate hardness. It was also available from a local supplier at a good price and in thicknesses that would work—I used 8/4 material for the bench frame and 4/4 material for the seat boards, arm slats, and back slats, but cypress is available as dimensional lumber from many suppliers of deck-building materials.

My garden retreat is still composed of a brick patio, a Japanese maple, and a few potted plants. Only now it's also graced by a quite comfortable and distinctive bench. But I'm afraid it will take some inspired landscaping and probably more than a few years to develop a garden that's worthy of the bench.

Tony O'Malley is an editor, writer and woodworker in Emmaus, Pennsylvania.

FULL-SIZE DRAWINGS AID LAYOUT

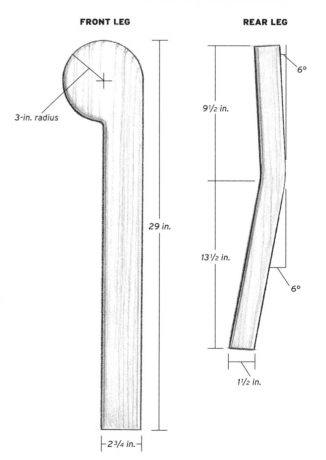

FRONT LEG

3-in. radius

29 in.

2 ¾ in.

REAR LEG

6°

9½ in.

13½ in.

6°

1½ in.

AN OUTDOOR FAVORITE

This classic bench design was built from cypress to endure all four seasons. Loose tenons and dowel joints were all joined with a slow-setting, waterproof epoxy so that the entire bench could be assembled at once.

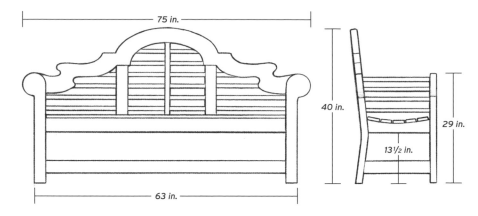

75 in.

40 in.

29 in.

13½ in.

63 in.

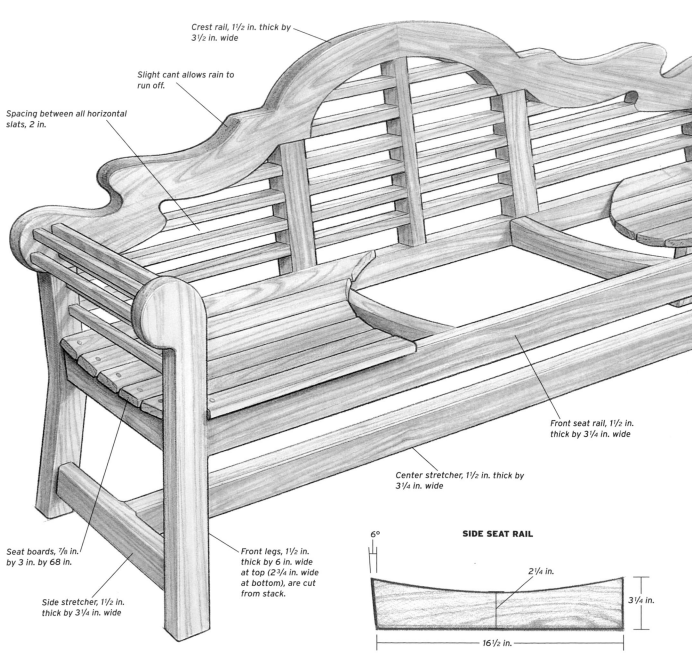

Crest rail, 1½ in. thick by 3½ in. wide

Slight cant allows rain to run off.

Spacing between all horizontal slats, 2 in.

Front seat rail, 1½ in. thick by 3¼ in. wide

Center stretcher, 1½ in. thick by 3¼ in. wide

Seat boards, ⅞ in. by 3 in. by 68 in.

Front legs, 1½ in. thick by 6 in. wide at top (2¾ in. wide at bottom), are cut from stack.

Side stretcher, 1½ in. thick by 3¼ in. wide

SIDE SEAT RAIL

6°

2¼ in.

3¼ in.

16½ in.

BACK ASSEMBLY

1 square = 1 in.

The upper, center horizontals are half-lapped to fit the vertical stile. Shaped ends are butt-jointed and screwed from underneath.

Crest rail is made of two identical pieces tenoned at center.

Holes accept dowels to secure arm supports.

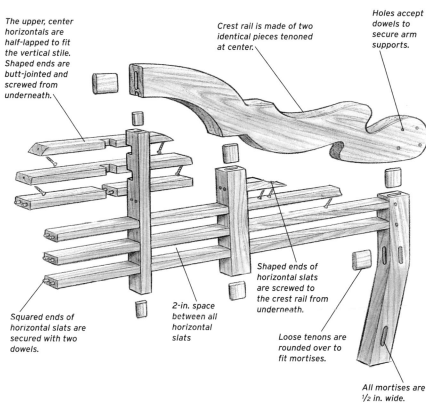

Arm slats are doweled into front and rear legs.

Squared ends of horizontal slats are secured with two dowels.

2-in. space between all horizontal slats

Shaped ends of horizontal slats are screwed to the crest rail from underneath.

Loose tenons are rounded over to fit mortises.

All mortises are 1/2 in. wide.

ROLLED ARMS

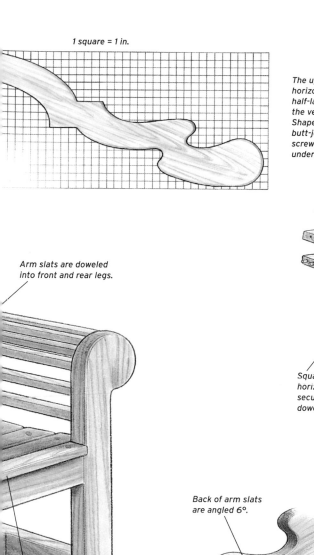

Front seat board, 2 1/2 in. wide, sits flat on the front rail.

Back of arm slats are angled 6°.

Dowels, 3/8 in. dia.

Arm slats, 1 in. by 1 in.

Seat boards are attached with screws, then plugged.

2 in. — 2 in.

1 1/4 in.

2 1/2 in.

3 1/2 in.

2 3/4 in.

3 in.

3/4 in.

19 1/2 in. to floor line

A GARDEN BENCH FOR ALL SEASONS

by David Snediker

When I got to the planning stage, I decided my garden bench—our garden bench—wouldn't have any vertical mortises to catch and hold rainwater, and I'd use copper rivets to fasten any mechanical connections. The bench would have a coved seat and a comfortable cant to the back. I wanted the seat height to be lower than the conventional 18 in.; my thought was that a 16-in. seat height would allow people to sit on the bench in a relaxed position. The bench would be held together with marine epoxy (see the box on pp. 190–191) and made from a maintenance-free wood that would weather to a salty gray in our seacoast town of Mystic, Conn.

Teak and mahogany are without a doubt very good marine woods, but I wanted to find something less expensive for the garden bench. Spanish cedar was the answer. It's about half the cost of mahogany, it's a quarter the price of teak, and its weather resistance is superb. Spanish cedar grows in Mexico and Central America, and it is more closely related to mahogany than it is to regular cedar. It has a color similar to mahogany and working properties similar to pine, although it's not nearly as soft as pine. It holds a crisp edge and glues up well.

All the wood I ordered was 6/4, which required that I laminate some of the bench's parts. Aside from allowing me to buy thinner, less expensive stock, laminating the back legs that cant at 9 degrees to form the bench's back allowed me to use two pieces of wood with opposing grains to ensure ultimate strength.

The slats for the seats are $^{15}/_{16}$ in. thick and $2^{1}/_{2}$ in. wide. They span almost 4 ft. Taken individually, the boards won't hold much weight, but five of them together, with a $^{3}/_{8}$-in. space between each board, comfortably support two people on the bench. In fact, the slight springiness of the narrow boards gives a cushioning effect when you sit on the bench.

In the garden catalogs my wife left (not so subtly) lying about, many of the benches had vertical mortises in the back rails. Vertical mortises can become water traps—something I wanted to avoid in my bench. I applied the slats to the back of the rails, which did several things. It let me avoid having any vertical mortises that could hold rainwater, and it gave the bench back a little depth, not unlike a fielded panel in a door. Also, I could assemble the rest of the bench and then experiment with different slat sizes and spacing until I found something that pleased my eye.

I used a hot-glue gun to tack different slats with different spaces between them before I found a pleasing configuration: 10 slats $1^{3}/_{4}$ in. wide. Of course, you could try different combinations of slats and spaces if you find my layout not to your liking. The space between the back slats is about equal to the width of the boards that make up the seat slats, with a half-width space between the back legs and the first back slat at each end.

The back slats and the seat slats are fastened with copper rivets (see the box on p. 190), a technique foreign to many woodworkers but as common to boatbuilders as nails are to carpenters.

David Snediker and his understanding wife, Roberta, live in Mystic, Connecticut.

Back leg template *serves dual purpose. A medium-density fiberboard (MDF) template, scaled from the plans, is traced on laminated stock for the back legs. Mortise locations for both front and back legs are also marked on the template. Once the template is laid out, measuring is kept to a minimum.*

Getting Set Up for Epoxy

With one big exception, a wooden boat is like a large piece of furniture. If you imagine your dining room table used as a surfboard, you'll get an idea of the stresses and strains a boat goes through.

We use a lot of marine epoxy when we build boats. If you've used epoxy before, you probably remember squeezing goo out of messy little tubes of hardener and resin and then being unsure if you got the proportions just right.

Well, forget the uncertain proportions of resin to hardener. A company called Gougeon Brothers makes an almost-foolproof, totally waterproof epoxy called West System.

Gougeon makes epoxies with different working times, and it makes a slew of different additives with weird names like microballoons and microlight. Some additives fill gaps, and some turn the epoxy into a structural component.

The second-best thing about West System® epoxies is the technical support offered by the company. It has a whole library of manuals that explains the different epoxies, the different additives, and their uses. And when you call the company (866-937-8797), you're not on hold listening to Mantovani for 10 minutes; there are patient technicians on the other end who know their stuff.

The first best thing about West System epoxies

Copper Rivets

Rivets are often used to fasten wood too thin to accept a screw and a bung, such as the back slats on the garden bench, but they can be used to face join all types of wood. In the simplest terms, riveting is a matter of through-nailing two pieces of wood, slipping a washer over the pointed end of a nail and then pounding on the end of the nail until it mushrooms over. In the age of self-drilling, galvanized drywall screws and biscuit joiners, rivets may seem low-tech, but it's somehow reassuring that their brute strength doesn't rely on high-torque spinning or the glue-activated expansion of compressed wood fibers.

Copper is wonderful for riveting wood. It is malleable enough to peen easily around a copper washer. All rivets are made of two parts: nails and burrs, sometimes called roves. Burrs look like washers. Nails look like carpenter's common nails, and in fact, they are sized in similar penny weights. Eight penny is referred to as 8d, 10 penny as 10d and so on. Like all nail wire gauges, the higher the number, the smaller the diameter.

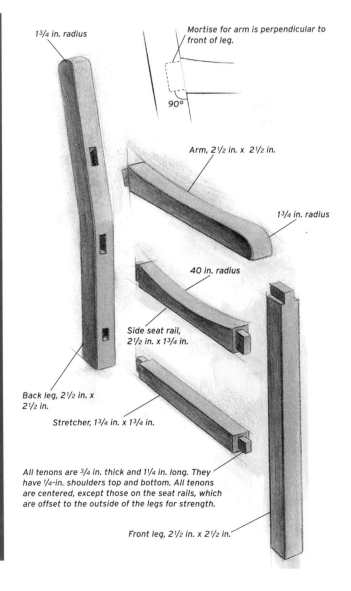

1³/₄ in. radius

Mortise for arm is perpendicular to front of leg.

90°

Arm, 2¹/₂ in. x 2¹/₂ in.

1³/₄ in. radius

40 in. radius

Side seat rail, 2¹/₂ in. x 1³/₄ in.

Back leg, 2¹/₂ in. x 2¹/₂ in.

Stretcher, 1³/₄ in. x 1³/₄ in.

All tenons are ³/₄ in. thick and 1¹/₄ in. long. They have ¹/₄-in. shoulders top and bottom. All tenons are centered, except those on the seat rails, which are offset to the outside of the legs for strength.

Front leg, 2¹/₂ in. x 2¹/₂ in.

is the calibrated pumps that screw onto the top of the containers of resin and hardeners (available in sizes from 1/2 pint to 5 gal.). No guessing, no messing—one push of the resin pump, one push of the hardener pump, and you have a perfectly proportioned batch.

There are a few things to keep in mind when using epoxy. When you think you've stirred the ingredients together for long enough, stir a little more.

And never spread epoxy with your stirring stick. Throw it away, and use a clean spreader. We use disposable flux brushes. Epoxy is good glue because of its tenacious adhesion to almost everything. During a glue-up, we lay down waxed paper on any surface we want to keep epoxy-free. White vinegar is pretty good at dissolving uncured epoxy; alcohol is better. We always wear gloves when working with epoxy, and if we have

a major glue-up to do, we don Tyvek® suits because if epoxy gets on your clothes, forget about it.

Epoxy cures by an exothermic chemical reaction; it gives off heat as it hardens. When the reaction starts, finish your clamping in a hurry, or pull everything apart and scrape off the still-viscous epoxy. What once was the consistency of maple syrup will quickly turn to heavy cream, then leather, and before you know it, your

tools will be stuck to the wood. The reaction is far from instantaneous, and as mentioned, different West System products go off at different speeds.

When we want something to stay glued forever, we use West System epoxies, available at most boatyards. They aren't inexpensive, but no good insurance is. –D.S.

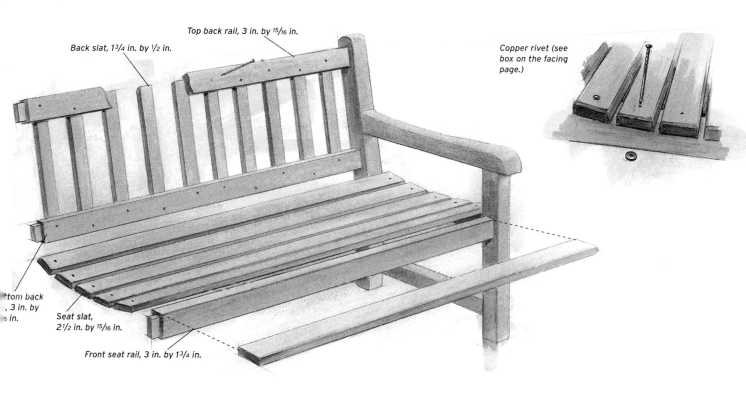

Top back rail, 3 in. by 15/16 in.

Back slat, 1 3/4 in. by 1/2 in.

Copper rivet (see box on the facing page.)

Bottom back ..., 3 in. by ... in.

Seat slat, 2 1/2 in. by 15/16 in.

Front seat rail, 3 in. by 1 3/4 in.

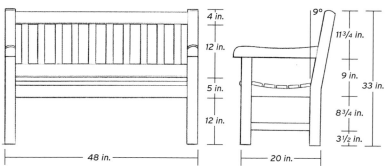

4 in.
12 in.
5 in.
12 in.
48 in.

9°
11 3/4 in.
9 in.
33 in.
8 3/4 in.
3 1/2 in.
20 in.

NO-MAINTENANCE OUTDOOR BENCH

The author's design, his construction techniques, even his choice of wood all kept in mind that the garden bench would stay outside year-round. The copper rivets will oxidize to a pleasant green color and won't stain the weather-resistant Spanish cedar wood. There are no vertical mortises in the bench's construction that will trap water, and the mortise-and-tenon joinery is held together with waterproof marine epoxy.

This Shaker-style wall clock is a beautiful adaptation of the original design. Its smaller size, about 7 in. shorter than the original, fits well in modern homes, and the shelves added behind the panel door provide storage in a space that was intended for a pendulum.

SHAKER-STYLE CLOCK

by Phil Lowe

The simple beauty of Shaker styling teamed with modern clockworks offers an attractive and accurate timepiece as well as room for storage.

However, when I had a commission for such a Shaker clock, I found a lot of pictures of clocks, but no dimensioned drawings. So I scaled my design from a photo.

Because of my clients' space limitations, my version is only about 80 percent as large as the original. The dimensions of this down-sized version fit very well in modern interiors. I proportioned the sides to the front, being careful to accommodate a modern quartz movement. That also left room for shelves in the lower compartment, which usually houses the pendulum.

The cherry and pine case is held together with typical Shaker construction: Mortises and wedged through-tenons join the carcase, and blind mortise-and-tenon joints connect the door frames.

Clock Design

A frequent admonition for any project is to buy your hardware before beginning to build. This is particularly true for a clock. You must accommodate hinges, latches, and clockworks, and don't forget to allow enough room between the clock's face and the glass in the door for the hands.

Although original Shaker clocks had wooden works, I substituted a quartz movement from Klockit^SM, Inc. Because the quartz movement I chose didn't have a pendulum, I added some shelves to the bottom compartment to make a convenient storage place for small items.

Phil Lowe designs, makes and restores fine furniture in Beverly, Massachusetts.

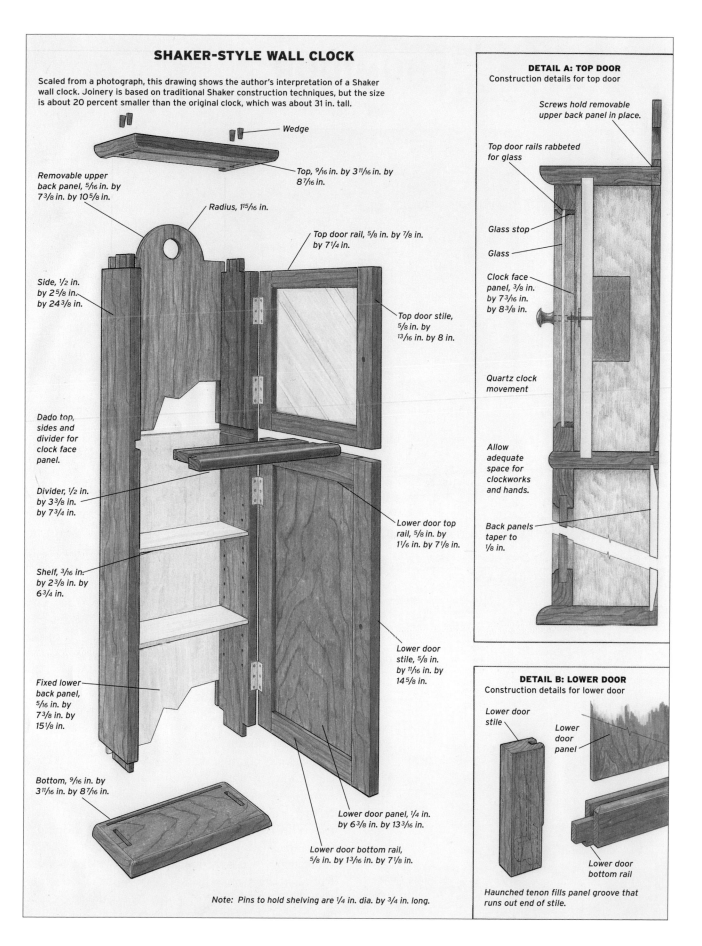

SHAKER-STYLE WALL CLOCK

Scaled from a photograph, this drawing shows the author's interpretation of a Shaker wall clock. Joinery is based on traditional Shaker construction techniques, but the size is about 20 percent smaller than the original clock, which was about 31 in. tall.

Wedge

Top, 9/16 in. by 3 11/16 in. by 8 7/16 in.

Removable upper back panel, 5/16 in. by 7 3/8 in. by 10 5/8 in.

Radius, 1 15/16 in.

Top door rail, 5/8 in. by 7/8 in. by 7 1/4 in.

Side, 1/2 in. by 2 5/8 in. by 24 3/8 in.

Top door stile, 5/8 in. by 13/16 in. by 8 in.

Dado top, sides and divider for clock face panel.

Divider, 1/2 in. by 3 3/8 in. by 7 3/4 in.

Lower door top rail, 5/8 in. by 1 1/16 in. by 7 1/8 in.

Shelf, 3/16 in. by 2 3/8 in. by 6 3/4 in.

Lower door stile, 5/8 in. by 11/16 in. by 14 5/8 in.

Fixed lower back panel, 5/16 in. by 7 3/8 in. by 15 1/8 in.

Bottom, 9/16 in. by 3 11/16 in. by 8 7/16 in.

Lower door panel, 1/4 in. by 6 3/8 in. by 13 3/16 in.

Lower door bottom rail, 5/8 in. by 1 3/16 in. by 7 1/8 in.

Note: Pins to hold shelving are 1/4 in. dia. by 3/4 in. long.

DETAIL A: TOP DOOR
Construction details for top door

Screws hold removable upper back panel in place.

Top door rails rabbeted for glass

Glass stop

Glass

Clock face panel, 3/8 in. by 7 3/16 in. by 8 3/8 in.

Quartz clock movement

Allow adequate space for clockworks and hands.

Back panels taper to 1/8 in.

DETAIL B: LOWER DOOR
Construction details for lower door

Lower door stile

Lower door panel

Lower door bottom rail

Haunched tenon fills panel groove that runs out end of stile.

HUMIDOR

by Rick Allyn

SIMPLE JOINERY MAKES A STURDY BOX

The front, back, and sides of the box are cut from one long piece of veneered Spanish cedar. The top is veneered MDF; the bottom is plywood. All the joints are rabbets and depend on precise fitting for strength.

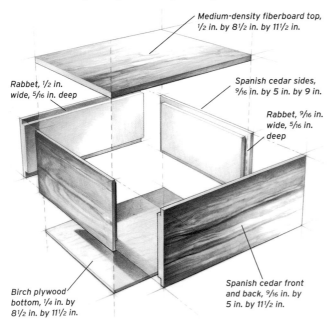

Medium-density fiberboard top, 1/2 in. by 8 1/2 in. by 11 1/2 in.

Rabbet, 1/2 in. wide, 5/16 in. deep

Spanish cedar sides, 9/16 in. by 5 in. by 9 in.

Rabbet, 9/16 in. wide, 5/16 in. deep

Birch plywood bottom, 1/4 in. by 8 1/2 in. by 11 1/2 in.

Spanish cedar front and back, 9/16 in. by 5 in. by 11 1/2 in.

You can smoke a dry cigar, but you won't enjoy it. It will burn too hot, making the smoke acrid and unpleasant. Most of the flavor and all the subtleties of the tobacco will be lost. Cigars are made in the tropics where the relative humidity is a constant 70 percent, and they should be kept at that level. The relative humidity in Southern Idaho, where I live, is about 30 percent in the summer, and lower in the winter—a really hostile environment for cigars. I have had cigars dry up, even unwrap, four hours after I bought them.

A properly functioning humidor is a necessity for enjoying good cigars anywhere outside of the tropics. With only monthly upkeep, a well-made humidor will preserve cigars indefinitely. Very fine cigars even improve when aged in a humidor.

Building a humidor that works is not as simple as making a nice box and fitting a humidification device in it. This is often how they're made, and the results are cigars ruined from too little or too much moisture. Maintaining 70 percent humidity is a balancing act that depends in large part on the wood you use and the tightness of the lid's seal. It's not rocket science, but making a good humidor takes some care in design and execution.

A BOX INSIDE OF A BOX

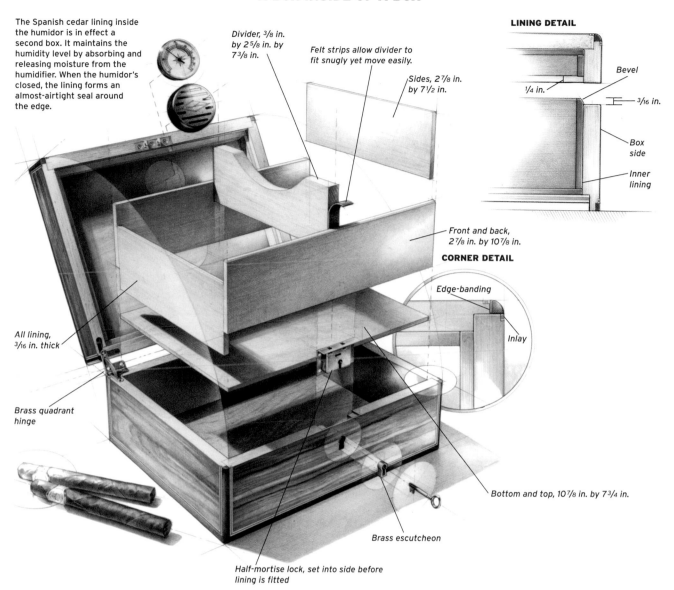

The Spanish cedar lining inside the humidor is in effect a second box. It maintains the humidity level by absorbing and releasing moisture from the humidifier. When the humidor's closed, the lining forms an almost-airtight seal around the edge.

Divider, 3/8 in. by 2 5/8 in. by 7 3/8 in.

Felt strips allow divider to fit snugly yet move easily.

Sides, 2 7/8 in. by 7 1/2 in.

LINING DETAIL

Bevel

1/4 in.

3/16 in.

Box side

Inner lining

Front and back, 2 7/8 in. by 10 7/8 in.

CORNER DETAIL

Edge-banding

Inlay

All lining, 3/16 in. thick

Brass quadrant hinge

Bottom and top, 10 7/8 in. by 7 3/4 in.

Brass escutcheon

Half-mortise lock, set into side before lining is fitted

The wood you choose to make and line the humidor is particularly important. It should not have an unpleasant smell or taste because the cigars will pick it up. The wood also should be porous so it will first absorb, then release moisture evenly, while remaining dimensionally stable. The wood will reach 70 percent moisture content on the inside, while the humidity on the outside could be as low as 20 percent. For many woods, this is a recipe for severe cupping.

Spanish cedar is the traditional and best choice for a humidor. When kiln dried, it is very stable and will not warp or grow much when it reaches 70 percent moisture content. Its oils inhibit the growth of molds and mildew that destroy cigars. Spanish cedar has a delicate aroma that is complementary, enhancing the cigar's taste.

Because I build humidors professionally, I make a variety of designs. But they're all simple and easy to build. The only joints are rabbets and grooves. I use Spanish cedar for the sides and the top, veneering only the outside. I glue up the whole box at once, and put a solid-wood edge-band along every side. Then I cut the box into top and bottom halves on a bandsaw. One of my favorite styles uses pau ferro (Machaerium spp.) veneer with wenge edge-banding and holly and mahogany inlay.

Rick Allyn used to make guitars, but now designs and builds studio furniture and humidors. He attended the College of the Redwoods. He lives in Twin Falls, Idaho.

More Than One Way to Store a Stogie

Though there are thousands of plain, manufactured boxes on sale everywhere, a few woodworkers have been making humidors that display the finest craftsmanship and imagination. A few that we've found are shown on these two pages.

1

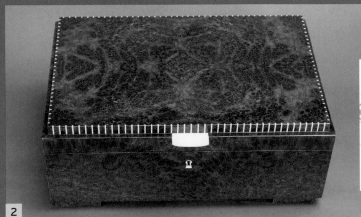

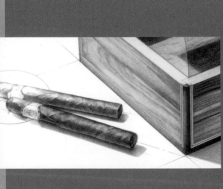

2

3

1. Humidor table by James Gray–Eastern walnut, wenge, tagua nut, red gum eucalyptus, and Spanish cedar; 36 in. high by 20 in. wide by 44 in. long.

2. Ruhlmann-style humidor by Frank Pollaro–Amboyna burl, ivory and Spanish cedar; 6³/8 in. high by 10 in. wide by 15 in. long.

3 & 4. Forbidden by Wendell Castle –Jelutong, lacewood and Spanish cedar; 58 in. high by 72 in. wide by 20 in. deep.

5. Humidor by Ken Frye–Pearwood, madrone burl and Spanish cedar; 6 in. high by 9 in. wide by 12 in. long.

6. Newporter by John Goff–Cuban mahogany and Spanish cedar; 5³/4 in. high by 9³/4 in. wide by 17 in. long.

4

5

6

PEAR MANTEL CLOCK

by Mario Rodriguez

My daughter Isabel's seventh birthday was fast approaching, and I wanted to build her something special. She had recently learned to tell time, so a clock seemed like the perfect way to mark the occasion. I designed the clock in the Arts and Crafts style; it looks somewhat contemporary but still has a traditional feel (see the photo at left). The joinery is simple, just stub tenons and dadoes, most of which can be cut quickly on a router table and tablesaw.

The clock consists of eight parts: the top, bottom, and two sides, the middle shelf assembly, veneered panels for the face and back of the clock, and a door below the middle shelf. The clock is just a bit taller than 16 in. As a result, not a lot of wood is required to build it, and the planing, sanding, and finishing don't take very long.

This clock is made of pear, which has a very mild grain that lets the clock's design dominate. A coarsely grained or heavily figured wood could overpower a clock of this size.

Mario Rodriguez teaches woodworking at the Fashion Institute of Technology in New York City and at Warwick Country Workshops in Warwick, New York. He is a contributing editor to Fine Woodworking *magazine.*

BACK VIEW OF DOOR

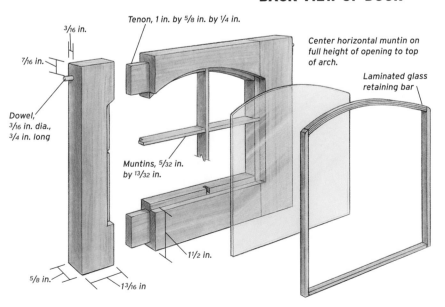

3/16 in.

7/16 in.

Dowel, 3/16 in. dia., 3/4 in. long

Tenon, 1 in. by 5/8 in. by 1/4 in.

Center horizontal muntin on full height of opening to top of arch.

Laminated glass retaining bar

Muntins, 5/32 in. by 13/32 in.

1 1/2 in.

5/8 in.

13/16 in

CROSS SECTION OF RAIL AT MUNTIN INTERSECTION

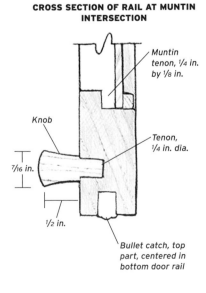

Muntin tenon, 1/4 in. by 1/8 in.

Knob

Tenon, 1/4 in. dia.

7/16 in.

1/2 in.

Bullet catch, top part, centered in bottom door rail

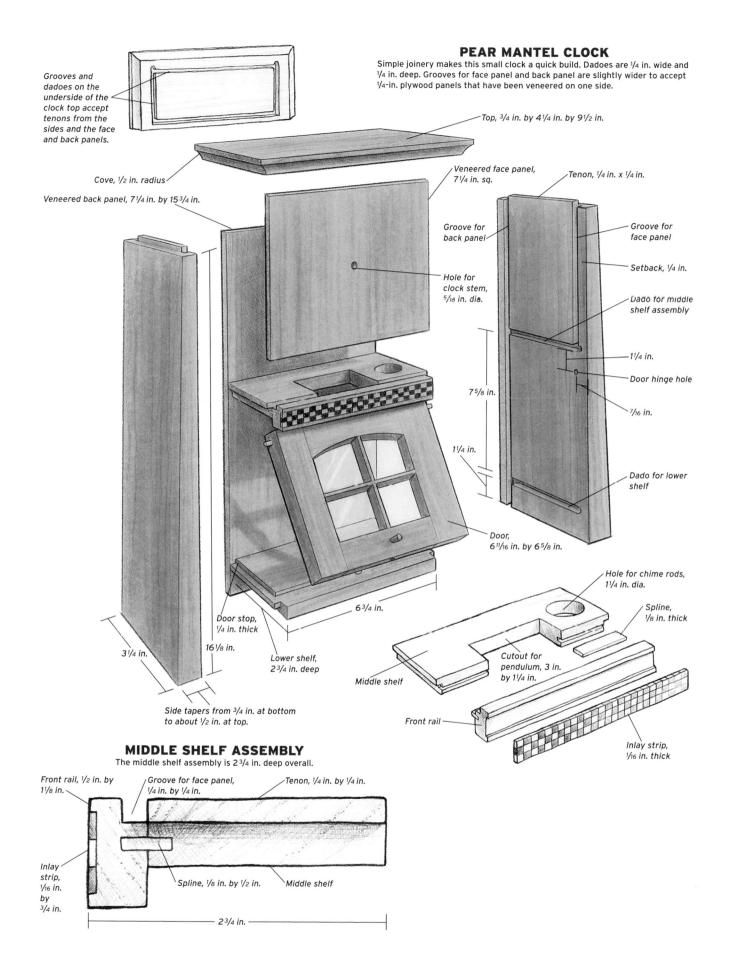

PEAR MANTEL CLOCK

Simple joinery makes this small clock a quick build. Dadoes are 1/4 in. wide and 1/4 in. deep. Grooves for face panel and back panel are slightly wider to accept 1/4-in. plywood panels that have been veneered on one side.

Grooves and dadoes on the underside of the clock top accept tenons from the sides and the face and back panels.

Top, 3/4 in. by 4 1/4 in. by 9 1/2 in.

Cove, 1/2 in. radius

Veneered back panel, 7 1/4 in. by 15 3/4 in.

Veneered face panel, 7 1/4 in. sq.

Groove for back panel

Hole for clock stem, 5/16 in. dia.

Tenon, 1/4 in. x 1/4 in.

Groove for face panel

Setback, 1/4 in.

Dado for middle shelf assembly

1 1/4 in.

Door hinge hole

7/16 in.

7 5/8 in.

1 1/4 in.

Dado for lower shelf

Door, 6 11/16 in. by 6 5/8 in.

3 1/4 in.

16 1/8 in.

Door stop, 1/4 in. thick

Lower shelf, 2 3/4 in. deep

6 3/4 in.

Hole for chime rods, 1 1/4 in. dia.

Spline, 1/8 in. thick

Middle shelf

Cutout for pendulum, 3 in. by 1 1/4 in.

Front rail

Inlay strip, 1/16 in. thick

Side tapers from 3/4 in. at bottom to about 1/2 in. at top.

MIDDLE SHELF ASSEMBLY
The middle shelf assembly is 2 3/4 in. deep overall.

Front rail, 1/2 in. by 1 1/8 in.

Groove for face panel, 1/4 in. by 1/4 in.

Tenon, 1/4 in. by 1/4 in.

Inlay strip, 1/16 in. by 3/4 in.

Spline, 1/8 in. by 1/2 in.

Middle shelf

2 3/4 in.

PENNSYLVANIA TALL CLOCK

by Lonnie Bird

With its decorated hood towering above the floor, a tall clock commands attention. Tall clocks, often referred to as grandfather clocks, are among the most elegant forms of 18th-century furniture. You can dress up a tall clock with embellishments, such as a gooseneck pediment complete with carved rosettes and finials, or you can choose to build a more subtle flat-top clock like the one shown here. This tall clock incorporates details found on several clocks fashioned in Pennsylvania during the late 1700s.

Despite its complex appearance, building a tall clock isn't difficult: It's really just three stacked boxes—the hood, waist, and base—and most of the joinery is not complicated. The waist and the base are the simplest to construct. In fact,

the waist is just two sides joined to a face frame; it has no top or bottom. The base of the clock has a bottom that is dovetailed to the sides, but it has no top.

Without a doubt, the hood is the most complicated part of the clock. It has an open frame at the bottom that allows the weights and the pendulum to hang into the waist below. The sides of the hood are joined to the bottom frame with through mortise-and-tenon joints, and the top of the hood is joined to the sides with dovetails. The rest of the hood—moldings, pediment board, and columns—are embellishments added on after assembling the hood.

Lonnie Bird teaches woodworking at his shop in Dandridge, Tennessee.

AN 18TH-CENTURY TIMEPIECE

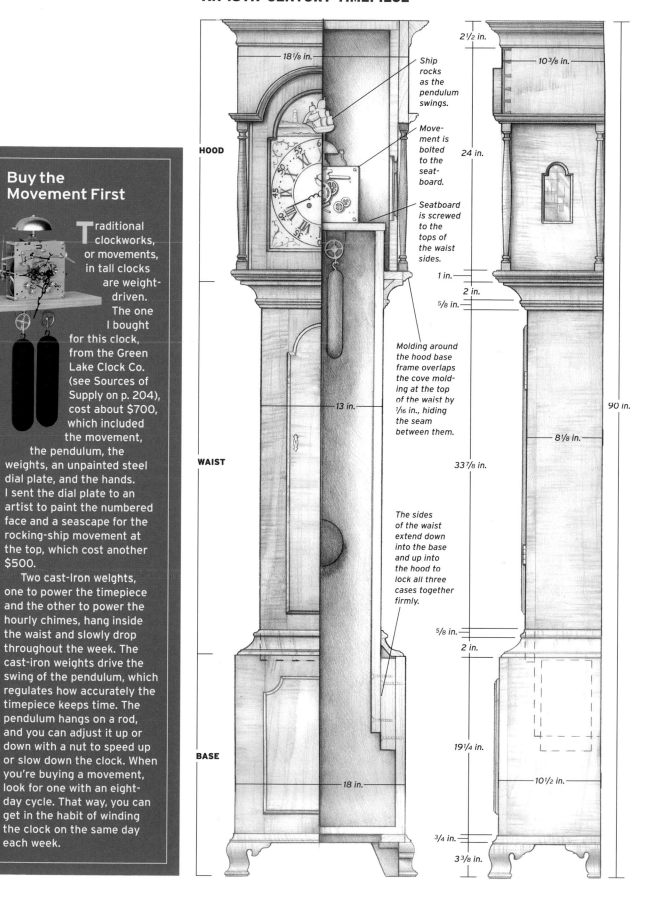

Buy the Movement First

Traditional clockworks, or movements, in tall clocks are weight-driven. The one I bought for this clock, from the Green Lake Clock Co. (see Sources of Supply on p. 204), cost about $700, which included the movement, the pendulum, the weights, an unpainted steel dial plate, and the hands. I sent the dial plate to an artist to paint the numbered face and a seascape for the rocking-ship movement at the top, which cost another $500.

Two cast-iron weights, one to power the timepiece and the other to power the hourly chimes, hang inside the waist and slowly drop throughout the week. The cast-iron weights drive the swing of the pendulum, which regulates how accurately the timepiece keeps time. The pendulum hangs on a rod, and you can adjust it up or down with a nut to speed up or slow down the clock. When you're buying a movement, look for one with an eight-day cycle. That way, you can get in the habit of winding the clock on the same day each week.

HOOD

18 1/8 in.

Ship rocks as the pendulum swings.

Movement is bolted to the seatboard.

Seatboard is screwed to the tops of the waist sides.

Molding around the hood base frame overlaps the cove molding at the top of the waist by 1/16 in., hiding the seam between them.

WAIST

13 in.

The sides of the waist extend down into the base and up into the hood to lock all three cases together firmly.

BASE

18 in.

2 1/2 in.

10 3/8 in.

24 in.

1 in.

2 in.

5/8 in.

33 7/8 in.

90 in.

8 1/8 in.

5/8 in.

2 in.

19 1/4 in.

10 1/2 in.

3/4 in.

3 3/8 in.

Screw the pediment to the hood. *Because of the cross-grain construction, do not glue the pediment assembly to the hood. Instead, use screws through large pilot holes, which will allow some seasonal wood movement.*

Dial-frame joinery. The stiles and rails of the dial frame fit together as glued half-lap joints. The dial frame, which is hidden from view most of the time by the arched door, slips into the hood from above in grooves that were cut into the sides of the hood.

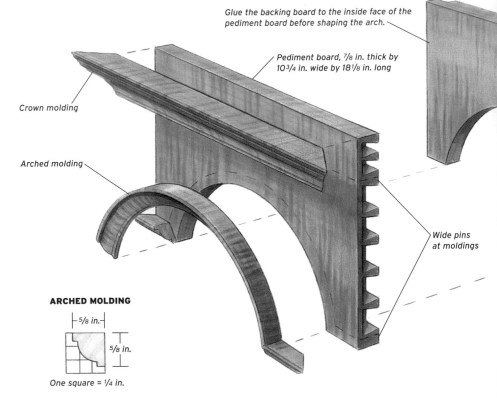

Glue the backing board to the inside face of the pediment board before shaping the arch.

Pediment board, 7/8 in. thick by 10 3/4 in. wide by 18 1/8 in. long

Crown molding

Arched molding

Wide pins at moldings

ARCHED MOLDING

— 5/8 in. —

5/8 in.

One square = 1/4 in.

DETAILS OF THE CLOCK'S HOOD

The hood is the most complex part of any tall clock, so it makes sense to build it first. After you have the movement in hand, verify the measurements that locate the center of the dial face and the swing of the pendulum. The molding around the bottom of the hood is thicker than the base frame, so when the hood is installed over the waist, the slight overlap hides the seam between the two cases.

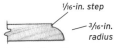

1/16-in. step

3/16-in. radius

Thumbnail profile

BASE-FRAME MOLDING

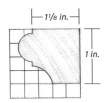

— 1 1/8 in. —

1 in.

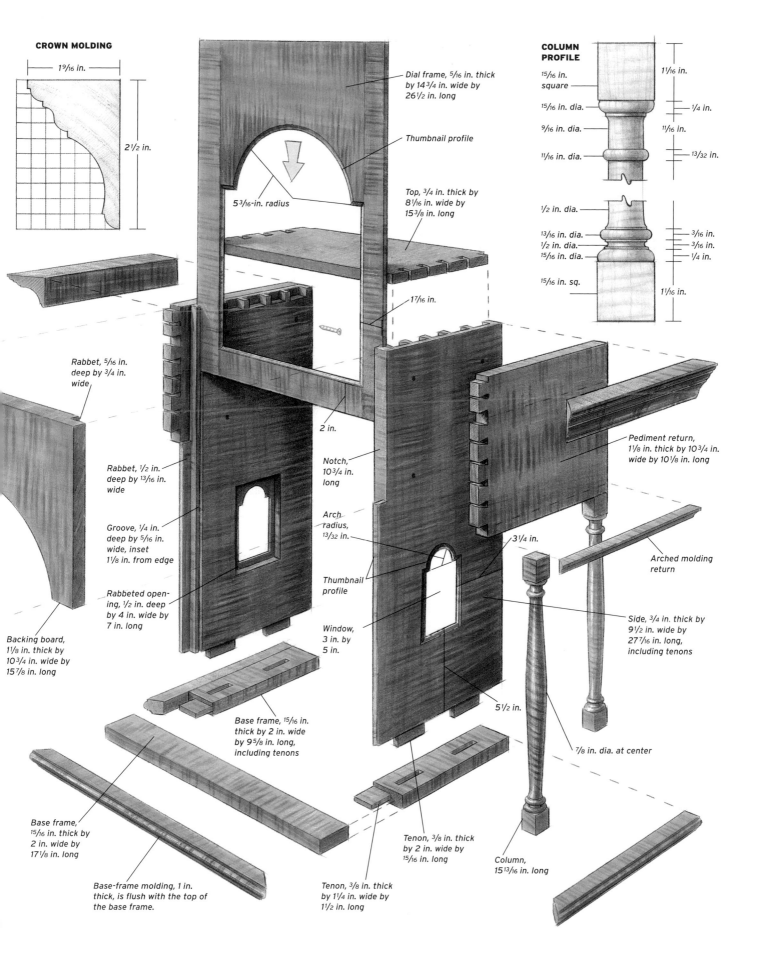

CROWN MOLDING

1 9/16 in.

2 1/2 in.

COLUMN PROFILE

15/16 in. square

15/16 in. dia.

9/16 in. dia.

11/16 in. dia.

1 1/16 in.

1/4 in.

11/16 in.

13/32 in.

1/2 in. dia.

13/16 in. dia.
1/2 in. dia.
15/16 in. dia.

15/16 in. sq.

3/16 in.
3/16 in.
1/4 in.

1 1/16 in.

Dial frame, 5/16 in. thick by 14 3/4 in. wide by 26 1/2 in. long

Thumbnail profile

5 3/16-in. radius

Top, 3/4 in. thick by 8 1/16 in. wide by 15 3/8 in. long

1 7/16 in.

Rabbet, 5/16 in. deep by 3/4 in. wide

Rabbet, 1/2 in. deep by 13/16 in. wide

Groove, 1/4 in. deep by 5/16 in. wide, inset 1 1/8 in. from edge

Rabbeted opening, 1/2 in. deep by 4 in. wide by 7 in. long

Backing board, 1 1/8 in. thick by 10 3/4 in. wide by 15 7/8 in. long

2 in.

Notch, 10 3/4 in. long

Arch radius, 13/32 in.

Thumbnail profile

Window, 3 in. by 5 in.

Pediment return, 1 1/8 in. thick by 10 3/4 in. wide by 10 1/8 in. long

Arched molding return

3 1/4 in.

Side, 3/4 in. thick by 9 1/2 in. wide by 27 7/16 in. long, including tenons

5 1/2 in.

7/8 in. dia. at center

Base frame, 15/16 in. thick by 2 in. wide by 9 5/8 in. long, including tenons

Base frame, 15/16 in. thick by 2 in. wide by 17 1/8 in. long

Base-frame molding, 1 in. thick, is flush with the top of the base frame.

Tenon, 3/8 in. thick by 1 1/4 in. wide by 1 1/2 in. long

Tenon, 3/8 in. thick by 2 in. wide by 15/16 in. long

Column, 15 13/16 in. long

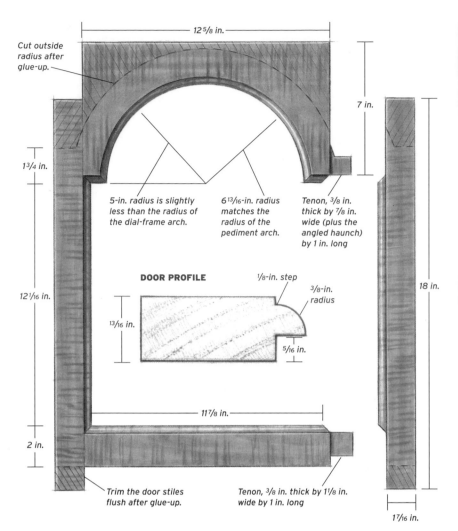

Cut outside radius after glue-up.

12 5/8 in.

7 in.

1 3/4 in.

5-in. radius is slightly less than the radius of the dial-frame arch.

6 13/16-in. radius matches the radius of the pediment arch.

Tenon, 3/8 in. thick by 7/8 in. wide (plus the angled haunch) by 1 in. long

18 in.

DOOR PROFILE

1/8-in. step

3/8-in. radius

13/16 in.

5/16 in.

12 1/16 in.

11 7/8 in.

2 in.

Trim the door stiles flush after glue-up.

Tenon, 3/8 in. thick by 1 1/8 in. wide by 1 in. long

1 7/16 in.

Fine-tune the fit. Wedge the door against the pediment. Mark the high spots, which should be planed and scraped for an even fit. After that, lay the door in place horizontally, and then use a shim to mark the front face for a consistent gap around the arch.

Use a gouge on the inside of the rabbeted corner. Chisel this corner round to prevent a stress crack in the glass panel that will be cut to shape and installed later.

Wide-throw pivot hinges for the glass door. Because the door is set in from the face of the hood and the columns, special offset hinges are required to throw it clear of the columns in the open position. The hinge plates are screwed to the door at top and bottom. Brass escutcheon pins nailed to the underside of the pediment board and to the base frame provide the pivoting action.

Sources of Supply

CLOCK MOVEMENTS AND PARTS
Green Lake Clock Co.
651-257-9166
www.greenlakeclock.com

Merritt's Clock and Watch Supplies
610-689-9541
www.merritts.com

CUSTOM PAINTING FOR CLOCK FACES
Angela Wendling Piacine
215-870-0791
a.wendling@juno.com

Kathi Edwards
770-943-5676
kedh2@aol.com

THREE BOXES AND A BACK

Building a tall clock may seem overwhelming to some woodworkers, but by breaking down the project into stages, you'll see that it's not very complicated.

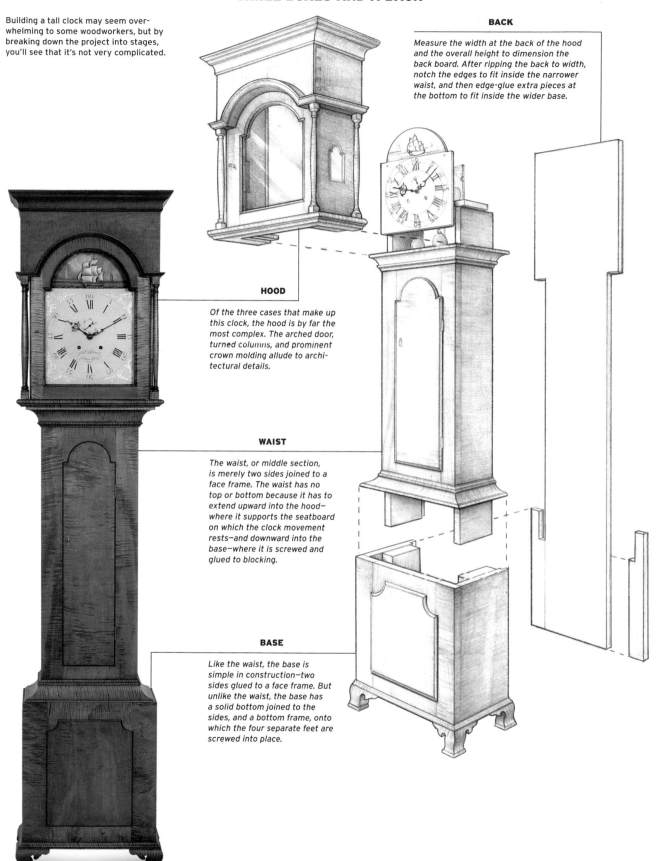

BACK

Measure the width at the back of the hood and the overall height to dimension the back board. After ripping the back to width, notch the edges to fit inside the narrower waist, and then edge-glue extra pieces at the bottom to fit inside the wider base.

HOOD

Of the three cases that make up this clock, the hood is by far the most complex. The arched door, turned columns, and prominent crown molding allude to architectural details.

WAIST

The waist, or middle section, is merely two sides joined to a face frame. The waist has no top or bottom because it has to extend upward into the hood—where it supports the seatboard on which the clock movement rests—and downward into the base—where it is screwed and glued to blocking.

BASE

Like the waist, the base is simple in construction—two sides glued to a face frame. But unlike the waist, the base has a solid bottom joined to the sides, and a bottom frame, onto which the four separate feet are screwed into place.

ALIGN THE BRACKET FEET TO THE BASE MOLDING

Dry-fit and clamp the base molding in place, mitering the two front corners, as a guide to follow when installing the feet. After that, you can nail the molding in place.

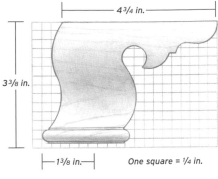

Join the sides to the bottom with dovetails. The first step in assembling the base is to join the sides to the bottom. Note that the bottom is made of poplar, a secondary and less-expensive wood for parts of the clock that aren't visible.

4³/₄ in.

3³/₈ in.

1³/₈ in.

One square = ¹/₄ in.

BASE-MOLDING PROFILE

³/₄ in.

⁵/₈ in.

One square = ¹/₄ in.

BASE-PANEL AND WAIST-DOOR PROFILE

³/₁₆-in. radius

¹/₈-in. step

⁷/₈ in.

⁹/₁₆ in.

¹/₄ in.

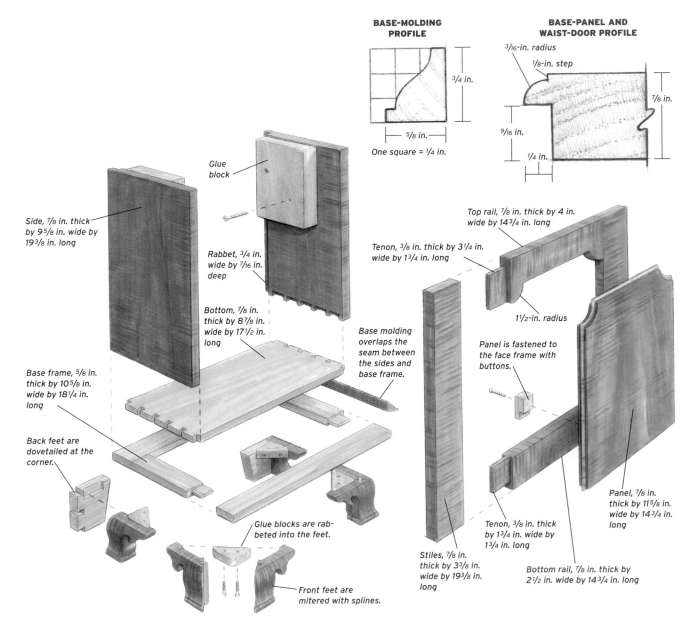

Glue block

Side, ⁷/₈ in. thick by 9⁵/₈ in. wide by 19³/₈ in. long

Rabbet, ³/₄ in. wide by ⁷/₁₆ in. deep

Bottom, ⁷/₈ in. thick by 8⁷/₈ in. wide by 17¹/₂ in. long

Base frame, ⁵/₈ in. thick by 10⁵/₈ in. wide by 18¹/₄ in. long

Back feet are dovetailed at the corner.

Base molding overlaps the seam between the sides and base frame.

Glue blocks are rabbeted into the feet.

Front feet are mitered with splines.

Top rail, ⁷/₈ in. thick by 4 in. wide by 14³/₄ in. long

Tenon, ³/₈ in. thick by 3¹/₄ in. wide by 1³/₄ in. long

1¹/₂-in. radius

Panel is fastened to the face frame with buttons.

Panel, ⁷/₈ in. thick by 11⁵/₈ in. wide by 14³/₄ in. long

Tenon, ³/₈ in. thick by 1³/₄ in. wide by 1³/₄ in. long

Stiles, ⁷/₈ in. thick by 3³/₈ in. wide by 19³/₈ in. long

Bottom rail, ⁷/₈ in. thick by 2¹/₂ in. wide by 14³/₄ in. long

WAIST ATTACHES TO THE BASE

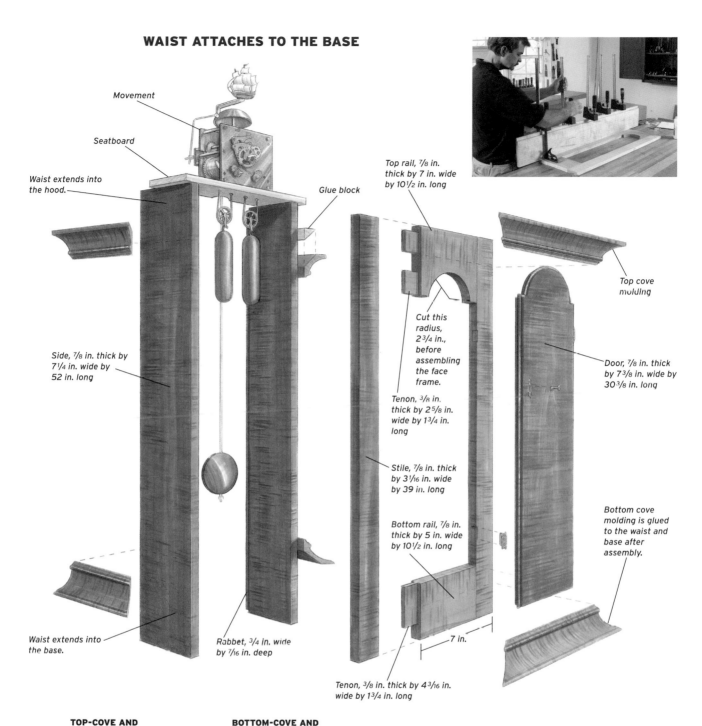

Movement

Seatboard

Waist extends into the hood.

Glue block

Top rail, 7/8 in. thick by 7 in. wide by 10 1/2 in. long

Cut this radius, 2 3/4 in., before assembling the face frame.

Tenon, 3/8 in. thick by 2 5/8 in. wide by 1 3/4 in. long

Side, 7/8 in. thick by 7 1/4 in. wide by 52 in. long

Stile, 7/8 in. thick by 3 1/16 in. wide by 39 in. long

Top cove molding

Door, 7/8 in. thick by 7 3/8 in. wide by 30 3/8 in. long

Bottom rail, 7/8 in. thick by 5 in. wide by 10 1/2 in. long

Bottom cove molding is glued to the waist and base after assembly.

Waist extends into the base.

Rabbet, 3/4 in. wide by 7/16 in. deep

7 in.

Tenon, 3/8 in. thick by 4 3/16 in. wide by 1 3/4 in. long

TOP-COVE AND BEAD-MOLDING PROFILES

2 in.

7/16 in.

2 1/16 in.

Glue block

1/8-in. radius

1/16-in. step

5/8 in.

1/2 in.

BOTTOM-COVE AND BEAD-MOLDING PROFILES

1/2 in.

5/8 in.

1/4-in. radius

1/8-in. step

2 in.

2 1/4 in.

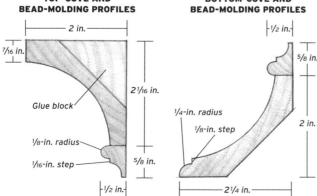

Glue the cove molding to the waist. Clamp scraps of 1/4-in.-thick plywood to define the baseline of the molding and to have an edge to push against. For the two side pieces, apply glue to the mitered corner joint and only partially to the bottom edge, near the front, which will allow for seasonal movement in the solid maple sides.

PENNSYLVANIA SPICE BOX

by D. Douglas Mooberry

When I started a woodworking business, my biggest obstacle was me. Though I was 22 years old, I looked 16. When making house calls, potential clients would eye me with an annoyed expression that seemed to say, "What, your father couldn't make it to our appointment?" To convince them that I was the craftsman and did indeed know something about woodworking, I started bringing a spice box that I had made. Once they saw the hand-cut joinery, pleasing design, and incredibly figured wood, they felt more comfortable.

Thanks to spice boxes, I am still woodworking 15 years later. Building one involves a variety of joinery, including hand-cut dovetails—lots of dovetails—machined joints and moldings, raised-panel construction, and precise drawer fitting. A spice box, or valuable chest, is a great way to learn, practice, or show off your woodworking skills (see the photo below).

Spice boxes have a heritage that goes back several centuries. The term *spice box* is really a misnomer. These small chests originally may have been used for storing rare spices, but they were usually filled with valuables such as jewelry and documents.

Because spice boxes don't demand a lot of wood, use the best you can find. The more figured the wood, the better. The box I designed for this article has bracket feet, a tombstone raised-panel door, and a typical interior drawer layout. The primary wood, meaning everything you see without pulling out the drawers, is walnut. The secondary wood is poplar. The hardware includes a pair of brass butt hinges, a lock, and nine drawer pulls.

I use round brass pulls on my drawers. They extend ³/₈ in. from the drawer fronts and are centered. You can vary your hardware to suit your tastes. I like the quality and style of hardware available from Ball and Ball (610-363-7639), Horton Brasses (860-635-4400), and Whitechapel, Ltd. (800-468-5534).

Finishing is the last opportunity to make a mess of the project. My rule is to use finishes that I am experienced with, so I use shellac and wax. When I have this much invested in a project, now is not the time to experiment.

D. Douglas Mooberry builds custom and reproduction furniture in Unionville, Pennsylvania.

A piece of furniture to show off. Spice boxes come in many styles (facing page) and deserve beautifully figured woods. The author (left) designs some boxes with decorative inlays.

SPICE BOX IS MADE WITH HAND AND MACHINE JOINERY

Although they're called spice boxes, these elegant small chests were used by Pennsylvania settlers to hold valuables. Hand-cut dovetails join the walnut case, and the molding and feet are glued and nailed on with traditional, square-cut nails. The chest contains nine drawers.

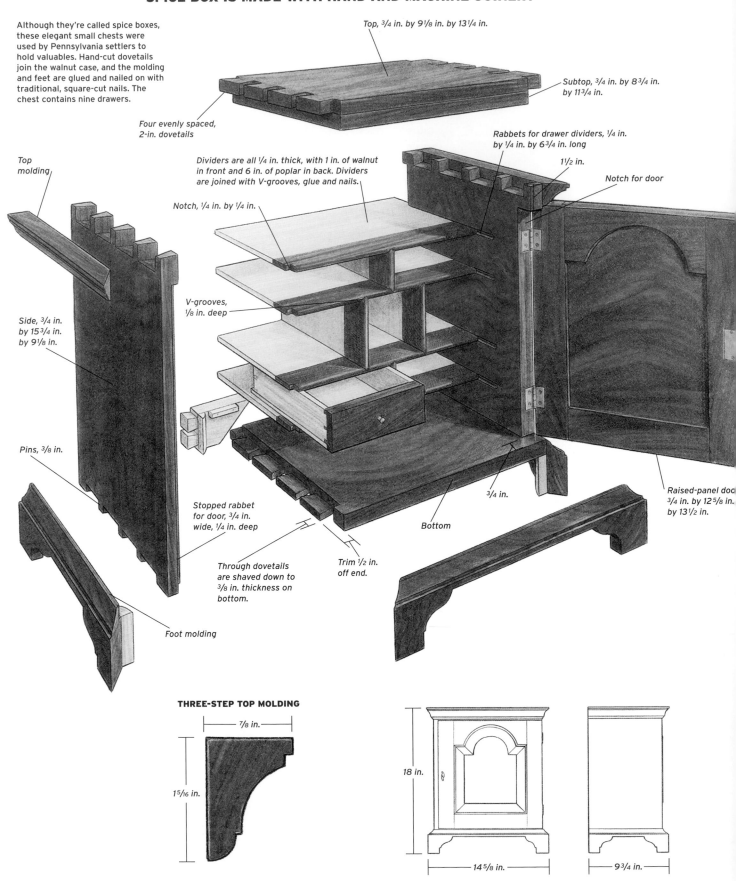

Top, ¾ in. by 9⅛ in. by 13¼ in.

Subtop, ¾ in. by 8¾ in. by 11¾ in.

Four evenly spaced, 2-in. dovetails

Rabbets for drawer dividers, ¼ in. by ¼ in. by 6¾ in. long

1½ in.

Notch for door

Top molding

Dividers are all ¼ in. thick, with 1 in. of walnut in front and 6 in. of poplar in back. Dividers are joined with V-grooves, glue and nails.

Notch, ¼ in. by ¼ in.

Side, ¾ in. by 15¾ in. by 9⅛ in.

V-grooves, ⅛ in. deep

Pins, ⅜ in.

Stopped rabbet for door, ¾ in. wide, ¼ in. deep

Through dovetails are shaved down to ⅜ in. thickness on bottom.

Trim ½ in. off end.

¾ in.

Bottom

Raised-panel door, ¾ in. by 12⅝ in. by 13½ in.

Foot molding

THREE-STEP TOP MOLDING

⅞ in.

1 5/16 in.

18 in.

14⅝ in.

9¾ in.

LAYING OUT A TOMBSTONE DOOR

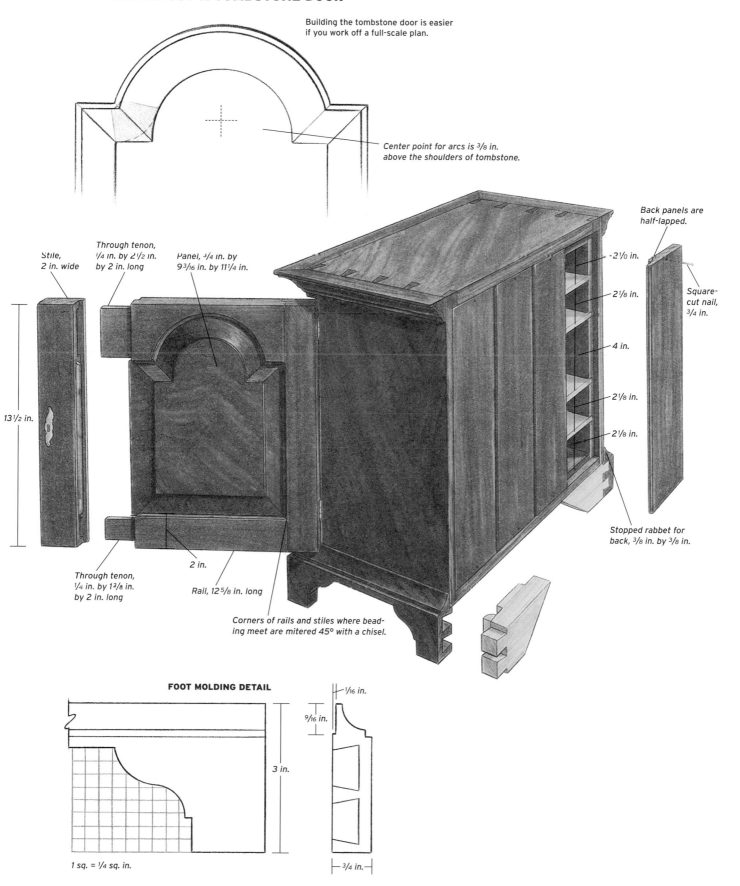

Building the tombstone door is easier if you work off a full-scale plan.

Center point for arcs is 3/8 in. above the shoulders of tombstone.

Back panels are half-lapped.

Square-cut nail, 3/4 in.

Stile, 2 in. wide

Through tenon, 1/4 in. by 2 1/2 in. by 2 in. long

Panel, 3/4 in. by 9 3/16 in. by 11 1/4 in.

2 1/0 in.

2 1/8 in.

4 in.

2 1/8 in.

2 1/8 in.

13 1/2 in.

Stopped rabbet for back, 3/8 in. by 3/8 in.

Through tenon, 1/4 in. by 1 3/8 in. by 2 in. long

2 in.

Rail, 12 5/8 in. long

Corners of rails and stiles where beading meet are mitered 45° with a chisel.

FOOT MOLDING DETAIL

1/16 in.

9/16 in.

3 in.

1 sq. = 1/4 sq. in.

3/4 in.

SHAKER WALL CLOCK

by Christian Becksvoort

Isaac Newton Youngs, a Shaker brother who lived in the Mount Lebanon, New York, community, built only 22 of these clocks, yet they still stand out as a hallmark of Shaker style. Some clocks were built with a glass door below, and a few were made with glass set into the side panels. My favorite is still housed at the Hancock, Massachusetts, Dwelling House and looks closer to the one I build. But you couldn't say that mine is an exact reproduction of the 1840 versions. *Furniture reproduction* is a slippery phrase. Though I'm known as a Shaker furniture maker, only twice in my career have I been asked to build historically accurate Shaker reproductions, meaning that all wood, hardware, dimensions, joinery techniques, tooling, and finishes must match the original.

I have no qualms with historical accuracy, except when it comes to techniques that may have worked in the past but are not suitable today. Wood movement is one of those areas. The Shakers did not have to deal with forced hot-air heat. We do. Shaker clock makers built their cases to fit their mechanisms. We must build our cases to fit mechanisms that are commercially available today. To me, that seems perfectly aligned with Shaker ideals.

For starters, the original clock was constructed predominantly of white pine. I chose cherry for its color, hardness, and grain. Because cherry moves more than white pine does, I had to make a few dimensional adjustments to allow for wood movement of the back panel. Second, I decided to use a top-of-the-line mechanical movement, which required a small amount of additional interior space. Consequently, my overall case is a little deeper, and the back is a bit thinner. So much for historical accuracy.

The construction of both the original and my version is as simple as the spare design. I will offer several options—in construction techniques, dimensional changes, and types of mechanisms—to suit the type of clock you want to build. Accurate dimensions for the original clocks (the glass door, not the panel-door version) can be found in John Kassay's *The Book of Shaker Furniture* (University of Massachusetts Press, 1980) or (for the clock with glass panels in the sides) in Enjer Handberg's *Shaker Furniture and Woodenware* (Berkshire Traveller Press, 1991). The version I built appears in my book, *The Shaker Legacy* (The Taunton Press, 1998).

Christian Becksvoort is a contributing editor to Fine Woodworking.

A SHAKER WALL CLOCK

A hand-painted face is a handsome touch, and a quality movement will keep the clock running smoothly for years to come.

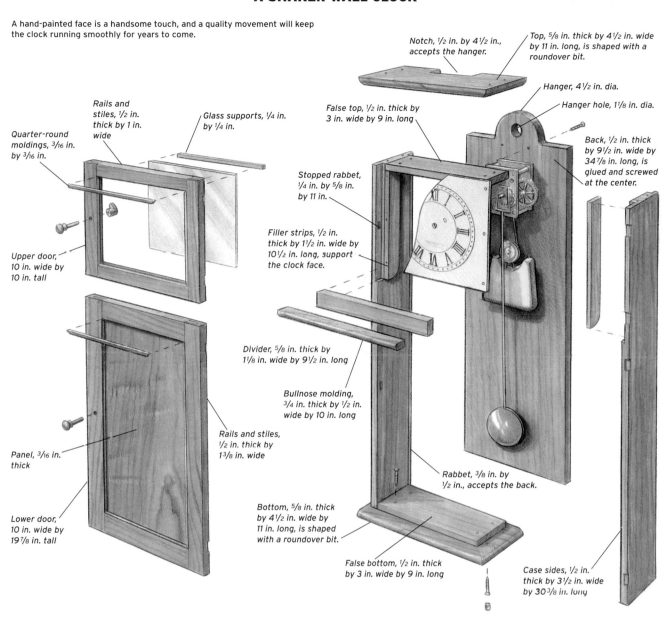

Quarter-round moldings, 3/16 in. by 3/16 in.

Rails and stiles, 1/2 in. thick by 1 in. wide

Glass supports, 1/4 in. by 1/4 in.

Upper door, 10 in. wide by 10 in. tall

Panel, 3/16 in. thick

Lower door, 10 in. wide by 19 7/8 in. tall

Rails and stiles, 1/2 in. thick by 1 3/8 in. wide

Notch, 1/2 in. by 4 1/2 in., accepts the hanger.

Top, 5/8 in. thick by 4 1/2 in. wide by 11 in. long, is shaped with a roundover bit.

False top, 1/2 in. thick by 3 in. wide by 9 in. long

Hanger, 4 1/2 in. dia.

Hanger hole, 1 1/8 in. dia.

Back, 1/2 in. thick by 9 1/2 in. wide by 34 7/8 in. long, is glued and screwed at the center.

Stopped rabbet, 1/4 in. by 5/8 in. by 11 in.

Filler strips, 1/2 in. thick by 1 1/2 in. wide by 10 1/2 in. long, support the clock face.

Divider, 5/8 in. thick by 1 1/8 in. wide by 9 1/2 in. long

Bullnose molding, 3/4 in. thick by 1/2 in. wide by 10 in. long

Rabbet, 3/8 in. by 1/2 in., accepts the back.

Bottom, 5/8 in. thick by 4 1/2 in. wide by 11 in. long, is shaped with a roundover bit.

False bottom, 1/2 in. thick by 3 in. wide by 9 in. long

Case sides, 1/2 in. thick by 3 1/2 in. wide by 30 3/8 in. long

DOOR-JOINERY DETAILS

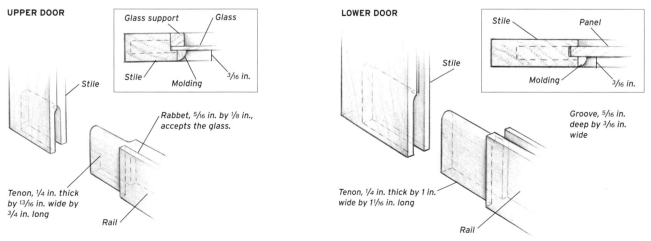

UPPER DOOR

Glass support

Glass

Stile

Molding

3/16 in.

Stile

Rabbet, 5/16 in. by 1/8 in., accepts the glass.

Tenon, 1/4 in. thick by 13/16 in. wide by 3/4 in. long

Rail

LOWER DOOR

Stile

Panel

Molding

3/16 in.

Stile

Groove, 5/16 in. deep by 3/16 in. wide

Tenon, 1/4 in. thick by 1 in. wide by 1 1/16 in. long

Rail

INDEX

CREDITS

The articles in this book appeared in the following issues of Fine Woodworking.

p. 4: A Classic Case by Gregory Paolini, issue 179. Photo by Andy Engel, © The Taunton Press, Inc. Drawings by Bob La Pointe, © The Taunton Press, Inc.

p. 6: Traditional Bookcase in the Craftsman Style by Gary Rogowski, issue 136. Photo by Marc Vassallo, © The Taunton Press, Inc. Drawings by Vince Babak, © The Taunton Press, Inc.

p. 8: Cherry and Fir Bookcase by Peter Zuerner, issue 161. Photo on p. 8 (left) by Kelly J. Dutton, © The Taunton Press, Inc.; p. 8 (right) by Scott Phillips, © The Taunton Press, Inc; p. 9 by Michael Pekovich, © The Taunton Press, Inc.; p. 10 by Tom Begnal, © The Taunton Press, Inc.

p. 12: A Blanket Chest With Legs by John McAlevey, issue 129. Photos by Dennis Griggs, © The Taunton Press, Inc.

p. 16: Frame-And-Panel Bed by David Fay, issue 134. Photos on p. 16 and 17 (top) by Ira Schrank, © The Taunton Press, Inc.; p. 17 (bottom) by Anatole Burkin, © The Taunton Press, Inc.

p. 20: Arts and Crafts Bed by Gary Rogowski, issue 156. Photos on p. 21 (top) by Asa Christiana, © The Taunton Press, Inc.; p. 21 (bottom) by Michael Pekovich, © The Taunton Press, Inc.; p. 22 (top) by Scott Phillips, © The Taunton Press, Inc.

p. 24: Bedstand by Roger Holmes, issue 152. Photos by Michael Farrell, © The Taunton Press, Inc. Drawings by Vince Babak, © The Taunton Press, Inc.

p. 26: Inspiration for a Bedside Cabinet by Michael Fortune, issue 171. Drawings by Vince Babak, © The Taunton Press, Inc.

p. 28: One-Drawer Lamp Stand by Mike Dunbar , issue 142. Photos by Michael Pekovich, © The Taunton Press, Inc.

p. 30: Sheraton Table by Steve Latta , issue 148. Photo by Anatole Burkin, © The Taunton Press, Inc.

p. 32: Cherry Chest of Drawers by Michael Pekovich, issue 170. Photos by Matt Berger, © The Taunton Press, Inc. Drawings by Bob La Pointe, © The Taunton Press, Inc.

p. 36: A Small Bureau Built To Last by Robert Treanor, issue 109. Photos by Jonathan Binzen, © The Taunton Press, Inc.

p. 38: A Little Masterpiece by Randall O'Donnell, issue 178. Photos by Randall O'Donnell, © The Taunton Press, Inc. Drawings by Bob La Pointe, © The Taunton Press, Inc.

p. 42: Component-Built Sideboard by Seth Janofsky, issue 137. Photos by Seth Janofsky, © The Taunton Press, Inc.

p. 46: A Stylish Credenza by Patrick Warner, issue 105. Photos by Kevin Halle, © The Taunton Press, Inc. Drawings by David Dann, © The Taunton Press, Inc.

p. 48: Veneered Sideboard by Paul Harrell, issue 107. Photos by Sloan Howard, © The Taunton Press, Inc. Drawings by Bob La Pointe, © The Taunton Press, Inc.

p. 50: Hall Table by Garrett Hack, issue 104. Photo on p. 50 by John Sheldon, © The Taunton Press, Inc.; on p. 51 by Vincent Laurence, © The Taunton Press, Inc.

p. 52: Contemporary Cabinet by Mark Edmundson, issue 155. Photos by Asa Christiana, © The Taunton Press, Inc. except top right photo on p. 52 by Michael Pekovich, © The Taunton Press, Inc.

p. 55: Pegged Post-and-Beam Armoire Knocks Down by Chris Gochnour, issue 132. Photos by Jonathan Binzen, © The Taunton Press, Inc. except photo on p. 55 (center) by Ron Stout, © The Taunton Press, Inc. Drawings by Bob La Pointe, © The Taunton Press, Inc.

p. 58: Entertainment Center in Quartersawn Male by Peter Turner, issue 139. Photos by Anatole Burkin, © The Taunton Press, Inc

p. 62: Colonial Cupboard by Mike Dunbar, issue 151. Photos by Asa Christiana, © The Taunton Press, Inc. except photo on p. 65 by Michael Pekovich, © The Taunton Press, Inc.

p. 66: Bow-Front Stand by Stephen Hammer, issue 163. Photos by Rodney Diaz, © The Taunton Press, Inc.

p. 69: Step-Back Cupboard by Mike Dunbar, issue 165. Photos by Matt Berger, © The Taunton Press, Inc. Drawings by Bob La Pointe, © The Taunton Press, Inc.

p. 72: An Everyday Cabinet by Scott Gibson, issue 152. Photo on p. 72 by Michael Pekovich, © The Taunton Press, Inc.; p. 73 by Tim Sams, © The Taunton Press, Inc.

p. 75: Corner Cupboard by Garrett Hack, issue 175. Photos by Mark Schofield, © The Taunton Press, Inc. Drawings by Bob La Pointe, © The Taunton Press, Inc.

p. 78: Craftsman Wall Cabinet by Ian Ingersol, issue 140. Photos by Michael Pekovich, © The Taunton Press, Inc. Drawings by Bob La Pointe, © The Taunton Press, Inc.

p. 80: Wineglass Cabinet by Scott Gibson, issue 158. Photos by Tim Sams, © The Taunton Press, Inc. Drawings by Bob La Pointe, © The Taunton Press, Inc.

p. 83: Hanging Cabinet by Chris Gochnour, issue 146. Photo on p. 83 by Michael Pekovich, © The Taunton Press, Inc. ; on p. 85 by Anatole Burkin, © The Taunton Press, Inc.

p. 86: Wall Cabinet in Cherry by Matthew Teague, issue 180. Photo by Kelly J. Dunton, © The Taunton Press, Inc. Drawing by John Hartman © The Taunton Press, Inc.

p. 88: Building an Open-Pedestal Table by John Burchett, issue 109. Drawing by Bob La Pointe, © The Taunton Press, Inc.

p. 90: Dining Table Has Tilt Top by Nigel Martin, issue 103. Photo by Tony Freeman-Cosh, © The Taunton Press, Inc. Drawing by Lee Hov, © The Taunton Press, Inc.

p. 92: Gate-Leg Table is Light but Sturdy by Gary Rogowski, issue 108. Photo by Jim Piper, © The Taunton Press, Inc.

p. 94: Harvest Table by Christian Becksvoort, issue 159. Photo by Dennis Griggs, © The Taunton Press, Inc. Drawings by Bob La Pointe, © The Taunton Press, Inc.

p. 96: Kitchen Classic by Thomas J. Calisto, issue 145. Photo by William Duckworth, © The Taunton Press, Inc.

p. 98 An Expandable Table by William Krase, issue 165. Photos by Tim Sams, © The Taunton Press, Inc. except for photos on p. 98 (top & bottom right) by William Krase, © The Taunton Press, Inc. Drawing by Heather Lambert, © The Taunton Press, Inc.